Practical Linux DevOps

Building a Linux Lab for Modern Software Development

John S. Tonello

Apress®

Practical Linux DevOps: Building a Linux Lab for Modern Software Development

John S. Tonello
Baldwinville, NY, USA

ISBN-13 (pbk): 978-1-4842-8317-2   ISBN-13 (electronic): 978-1-4842-8318-9
https://doi.org/10.1007/978-1-4842-8318-9

Managing Director, Apress Media LLC: Welmoed Spahr
Acquisitions Editor: James Robinson-Prior
Development Editor: James Markham
Coordinating Editor: Jessica Vakili

Distributed to the book trade worldwide by Springer Science+Business Media New York, 233 Spring Street, 6th Floor, New York, NY 10013. Phone 1-800-SPRINGER, fax (201) 348-4505, e-mail orders-ny@springer-sbm.com, or visit www.springeronline.com. Apress Media, LLC is a California LLC and the sole member (owner) is Springer Science + Business Media Finance Inc (SSBM Finance Inc). SSBM Finance Inc is a **Delaware** corporation.

For information on translations, please e-mail booktranslations@springernature.com; for reprint, paperback, or audio rights, please e-mail bookpermissions@springernature.com.

Apress titles may be purchased in bulk for academic, corporate, or promotional use. eBook versions and licenses are also available for most titles. For more information, reference our Print and eBook Bulk Sales web page at http://www.apress.com/bulk-sales.

Any source code or other supplementary material referenced by the author in this book is available to readers on the Github repository: https://github.com/Apress/Practical-Linux-DevOps. For more detailed information, please visit http://www.apress.com/source-code.

Printed on acid-free paper

Table of Contents

About the Author

John S. Tonello writes about technology, software, infrastructure as code, and DevOps and has spent more than 20 years working in and around the software industry for companies like Tenable, HashiCorp, SUSE, Chef, and Puppet. He's spent more than 25 years building Linux-based environments and regularly publishes a wide range of how-to guides and blogs about DevOps, Linux, and software-defined infrastructure.

About the Technical Reviewer

Nathan Haines is an instructor and a computer technician who has been using Linux since 1994. In addition to occasional programming projects and magazine articles, he is a member of Ubuntu, where he helps spread the word about Ubuntu and Free Software.

Introduction

The Power of Linux

When my mother gave me a cast-off x386 IBM-clone computer in the mid-1990s, I wasn't entirely sure what I was going to do with it, but I felt impelled to get it running. My biggest challenge in doing so was economic, not technical. I was too cheap to buy a licensed copy of Windows 3.1 and went hunting for an alternative. Fortunately, I came across a book titled *Linux Installation & Getting Started* by Matt Welsh, which showed me everything I needed to get started. I downloaded the Slackware Linux installation files over a 56k modem, wrote them to a stack of floppy disks, and literally gave an audible hoot when I got the system up and running.

The moment markedly changed my future, with Linux and open source software becoming a key part of my life, first as a hobby and ultimately as a career.

Other early Linux adopters have similar stories to tell, and like them, I was fascinated by the ability to freely download and install a complete operating system and do "real computing." In the ensuing years, I bought my share of thick Linux texts, installed hundreds (perhaps thousands) of Linux systems, and learned how to use and rely on open source software. That experience is encapsulated in this book.

A lot has changed in the technology world in the 30-plus years since Linus Torvalds first released Linux (and the hard-working kernel) in 1991, and much has been written about it. It's no accident that Linux and the Internet grew up together. Linux remains a critical component of the technical landscape, spawning whole industries and many well-paying jobs. It's at the core of modern life, though few recognize that fact. Today's software developers certainly have heard of it, but many have never had a chance to really explore it.

Practical Linux DevOps is written to be a go-to Linux book for IT practitioners—or those who want to be—who want to explore Linux and the technologies that make modern software happen. It provides real-world tutorials and examples centered around DevOps practices, the concept of continuously building, testing, and deploying software applications that bridge the development side (think software and security engineers) and operations (think hardware administrators). DevOps is how modern software is made, and Linux is in the midst of it all. This book seeks to teach you practical Linux concepts within the context of DevOps, giving you the knowledge you need to confidently continue your exploration.

Learning to Fish

The chapters in this book represent the culmination of my experience with Linux and open source software with new users in mind. I attempt to explain concepts in terms anyone can understand, and provide enough context to explain the *whys*, not just the *hows*. I want to leave you wanting more and with the ability to reason out how to keep learning. The adage goes, "If you give a man a fish, you feed him for a day. If you teach a man to fish, you feed him for a lifetime." The goal of *Practical Linux DevOps* is to teach you how to fish (and not fear the command line).

Where can Linux take you? With Linux running on NASA's Perseverance rover that's exploring Mars, the sky is no longer the limit. This book will help you become part of it all.

Tips for Setting Up Your Environment Your Workstation

This book presumes you'll use a Linux workstation for all the work you do, not just the virtual machines and containers you create. As you'll read in Chapter 1, you can make good use of older hardware for a Linux workstation. The examples in this book mostly use Ubuntu (based on Debian), and there are many flavors of Ubuntu and other Linux distributions that can run on older Windows and Macintosh computers. I recommend using an existing spare machine, but if money is no object, feel free to get a new or used Intel- or AMD-based machine and install Linux on it.

Environment Settings

After installing a fresh Linux desktop, there are a few steps I always take to make the workstation environment comfortable to my way of working. For example, when you run commands as a superuser (something you'll do all the time), sudo requires a password. When you're running dozens or hundreds of sudo commands a day, this can become tiring. I solve that problem by creating a file in /etc/sudoers.d/ that gives me superuser privileges without requiring a password.

To do this, create a new file in /etc/sudoers.d and add the following line, replacing <username> with the username you use on your Linux system:

```
$ sudo vi /etc/sudoers.d/<username>

<username> ALL=(ALL) NOPASSWD:ALL
```

After you save this file, you'll be able to run sudo commands without entering a password. Of course, this isn't exactly secure and shouldn't automatically be added to production systems, but when you're working on your Linux workstation, it saves a lot of time and hassle.

Terminal Look and Feel

You'll spend a lot of time in your Linux terminal, so take a moment to make it comfortable. There's no need to squint at tiny text or colors you don't like. Xterm and other modern Linux terminals allow you to easily adjust the font, font size, text colors, and background. I recommend editing the preferences to make your terminal suit your tastes.

Power Settings

It might seem like a little thing, but I hate when my workstation screen goes to sleep too often. By default, many Linux desktops go to sleep after just five minutes. You might look away for a few minutes to check headlines or focus on another machine, and you'll have to log back in. I recommend going into your system's **Power** settings to adjust the screen timeout to at least 30 minutes.

Multiple Computers, One Mouse and Keyboard

If you're running your Linux machine alongside another separate workstation, such as Windows or Macintosh, it can be quite cumbersome to have two different keyboards and mice. I resolve this by using a little tool called Barrier, a fork of Synergy, that allows you to share your mouse and keyboard with multiple systems on the same network. The machine with your physical keyboard and mouse attached becomes the Barrier server; every other machine becomes a Barrier client. You can set the geometry (left, right, up, or down) relative to your server machine and seamlessly control, copy, and paste (but not drag and drop) many different Linux, Windows, and Macintosh computers with a single keyboard and mouse.

SCP

There are times when you need to move files from one Linux machine to another. You can email them to yourself, but I've found the tool SCP to be the best way to move files. It uses SSH to copy files or folders from one system to another. There's no need to use FTP or other means:

```
$ scp /path/to/local_file username@remote_host:/path/to/
remote_file
```

You can copy whole directories using SCP by adding the -r (recursive) flag:

```
$ scp -r /path/to/local_folder username@remote_host:/path/to/
remote_folder
```

Set Up Passwordless SSH

When you're regularly SSHing or SCPing between machines, it can save a lot of time if you set up SSH keys between them. This enables you to use ssh and scp without having to always enter a password.

To set this up, start by creating an SSH key on your workstation:

```
$ ssh-keygen
```

Follow the prompts, but **do not** provide a password for the key. Then copy the newly generated key to one or more target systems:

```
$ ssh-copy-id username@remote_host
```

You'll be prompted to enter a password when you first use ssh-copy-id to copy the key, but never again after that. This simple setup makes for a more seamless integration between multiple Linux (and Macintosh) machines.

Enjoy the Ride

With that, you're ready to start digging in. Be sure to take advantage of the GitHub repo associated with this book for code examples. They'll get you moving quickly and help you avoid having to manually type out longer code snippets.

CHAPTER 1

Gather Your Hardware

To start building your Linux lab for DevOps, you first need to assemble some hardware. The idea is to be able to experiment without messing up your workstation with applications and packages that could leave it unstable or even unusable. In this chapter, you'll deploy everything for your lab on a separate machine, or machines, where you can install what you need without worrying about wrecking your daily driver.

Today, public cloud providers are a big part of DevOps, making it relatively simple to spin up instances and get to work. Unfortunately, services like AWS and Azure obscure some important aspects of the environment itself and, of course, cost money. By building your own local Linux lab, you'll get the benefits of speed and ease without having to worry about costs. Along the way, you'll also learn a lot about the full environment your servers and applications are living in, giving you a greater insight—and greater abilities—to manage it all.

This book presumes you have access to the following:

- At least one separate physical computer system

- At least one basic network switch

- Perhaps a spare monitor, keyboard, and mouse

- Ethernet and peripheral cables to put it all together

If you're like most tech-curious pack rats, you probably have some older equipment lying around that will do the job. If not, the goal is to get you up and running without spending a lot of cash.

© John S. Tonello 2022
J. S. Tonello, *Practical Linux DevOps*, https://doi.org/10.1007/978-1-4842-8318-9_1

The Basics: What You'll Need to Build Your Linux Lab

The principles of building your lab environment are simple. Create a beefy virtual machine (VM) host with as much memory and CPU resources as possible so you can create as many VMs and Linux containers (LXCs) as possible.

Here are the basics for each physical lab node, which will run the Proxmox Virtualization Environment:

- A 64-bit-capable CPU, such as an Intel i3, i5, or i7 or AMD Ryzen 3, 5, or 7

- At least 8GB of RAM

- A spinning disk or solid-state drive (SSD) that's at least 256GB

- An Ethernet port

- One VGA or HDMI video port

- One free USB port

For a more robust lab that will provide more speed, performance, and flexibility, each physical node should have

- At least 32GB of RAM

- Multiple hard drives or SSDs

- Two Ethernet ports

When you're building your lab, it's important to spend a little time thinking about your ultimate goal. Will you be running dozens of virtual machines or just a couple? How important is performance? Will you have an intricate network layout or something simple? Even if you don't know the answers to these questions now, keep them in mind as you plan to add capabilities. For example, when using Proxmox as your virtualization environment (described in detail in Chapter 2), you can't easily add machines to a cluster if you've already added VMs to the running environment. That means you need to set up two or more Linux lab hosts *before* you start deploying any virtual machines.

Using New Equipment for Your Lab

Part of the fun of building a Linux lab is finding new ways to put older gear to use, and you can certainly do that to accomplish most of the projects in this book. Sometimes, however, old hardware can be more trouble than it's worth, and starting with clean, modern systems can get you up and running quickly and with less frustration.

It wasn't so very long ago that if you wanted a computer with an eight-core CPU, 32GB of RAM, and a 1TB drive, you needed to buy a big, expensive blade server. Today, such systems are commonplace, much smaller, and far cheaper than ever before. Some good candidates for home-based Linux labs on a budget include products made by Intel, Gigabyte, ASRock, Asus, and Kingdel.

For the most part, you'll want mini PCs or tower systems for your Linux lab host servers. The former are small and compact and don't consume much power. The latter give you the most flexibility for CPU, RAM, and storage. Laptops are effective also, but the price point is probably more than you want to spend, although a laptop rig can mean fewer cables and peripherals. No need to drag out a monitor, keyboard, and mouse when you want to do initial configurations.

Something to keep in mind is that you'll access your Proxmox server remotely via a browser-based dashboard and, occasionally, a remote shell. Once it's initially configured, you'll manage the environment from your workstation. The host machine will run headless.

CPU Core Considerations

All the mini PCs built by the vendors mentioned previously come in various sizes and capabilities, including bare-bones systems without memory or hard drives preinstalled. Shop for devices that have the fastest x86_64 (Intel or AMD) CPUs and the most cores you can afford. The more cores the underlying system has, the more virtual CPUs you'll have available for your virtual machines. That's particularly important as you deploy solutions like Kubernetes or OpenStack, which require you to have several machines running simultaneously. Without enough CPUs, performance will suffer, which, in some cases, renders your Linux lab too slow to use.

You can use ARM-based CPUs as well, but recognize that the architecture still is not as robust a development environment as x86_64. Yes, many applications will run fine on ARM-based processors, but some bleeding-edge or legacy applications may not be available.

Another thing to keep in mind if you're planning to use a mini PC is its limited expandability. Some of these small boxes come with the CPU soldered to the motherboard, meaning you can't remove it or replace it. If you'd rather not go the mini PC route and prefer a tower-sized system that can, say, accommodate a removable CPU or many internal hard drives, opt instead for those systems. Just keep in mind that these systems are generally noisier and consume more power.

Of course, be sure that any system you choose supports Linux, even if it initially comes with a flavor of Windows installed. Traditional BIOS or UEFI booting frameworks are fine. With Proxmox you can deploy systems with SeaBIOS and OVMF, an open source UFI implementation.

A CPU with multiple cores—typically four—is critical for running multiple virtual machines at the same time. In the next chapter, you'll learn about the virtualization platform, but for now, be aware that the faster the CPU and the more cores each of your Linux lab machines has, the better.

Each virtual machine you create on top of your Proxmox system will consume both CPU and RAM from the host system, so you can never have too much of either. Some applications are CPU-intensive; others are RAM-intensive. The host environment will share everything among the VMs, so the more memory you have, the more systems you can create, and the more robust they'll be.

At the same time, the virtualization environment will commit only the necessary CPU and RAM to your running VMs, so even though you might assign, say, an openSUSE system 8GB of RAM, it might require only 2GB most of the time it's running. The rest of the Proxmox host's RAM is free to be used by other running systems.

Memory Considerations

As I mentioned earlier, the more memory you can afford, the better when it comes to deploying a versatile Linux lab. Generally speaking, mini computers like those listed previously may have a hard limit of 32GB. That's nothing to sneeze at, but an affordable tower machine will likely give you the ability to easily double or triple that amount.

If you come across a good deal on a mini computer with just 4GB of RAM, don't buy it with such little memory. Plan to add more. Since most motherboards—large or mini—want memory chips installed in pairs, you might be limited to adding just another 4GB chip, which would give you only 8GB total in most mini PCs, which typically have only two RAM slots. It's better to order the device with at least one 8GB RAM chip so you can expand it later.

Remember, it can be tricky to buy the correct memory for a computer, and some computers require RAM chips that are far more expensive than others. Check the technical specs before buying.

Storage Considerations

The price of most storage devices continues to drop, and you shouldn't have any trouble finding a 500GB SSD for about the price of this book. SSDs and the newer NVMe solid-state drives are fast and come in many different sizes. Plan on at least half a terabyte, but if you can afford more, buy it. Proxmox itself doesn't require much disk space at all. The disks you use will be filled by your virtual machines.

If you're planning to mix and match new drives with old ones, that'll work fine. Just be sure to have a physical machine that can fit them all and has enough motherboard connectors to accommodate them. One scenario is to install Proxmox itself (the server runs a version of Debian Linux) on a smaller drive and reserve additional drives for your VMs.

Some mini devices come with NVMe connectors and no SATA connectors. You can get PCIe adapters that plug into a device's USB 3.0 port to add external storage, which can be an inexpensive option. Without SATA interfaces, you won't be able to add an SSD as a secondary internal drive, and in those situations, you'll want to install the biggest single drive you can afford. Most towers, on the other hand, have motherboards with six or more SATA drive connectors, ideal for your older spinning SATA drives and most SSDs. NVMe drives are a different matter. They require a special slot. Do your homework before shelling out.

You can make do with spinning hard disks, but recognize that they'll be slower than SSDs when it comes to reading and writing data. For example, an operating system running on a spinning disk will take longer to boot than one booting from an SSD. Depending on your use cases, an SSD's higher input/output (I/O) speed can make a big difference and make life less tedious, but they're not critical for your lab hosts.

If you have several older drives available and your lab host nodes have the room, install as many as you can. You'll be able to take advantage of those drives, even if they're relatively small. I've built nodes with a laughably small 60GB drive that enabled me to run several VMs without any trouble. That's because the virtual machines you create all use *thin provisioning*, which means they don't consume any disk space until they need it. If you install Ubuntu on a 32GB virtual disk, it initially uses only 5GB, but the virtual machine won't touch the other 27GB you committed until it needs it.

A Linux lab based on a virtualization platform like Proxmox or VMware gives you the ability to overcommit all the physical system's resources without requiring you to do any tricky math to make everything work.

Using Old PCs and Laptops for Your Linux Lab

Although it's true that new computers and networking gear can save you some time and frustration, there's a lot to be said for older hardware you might already have.

The first Linux lab I built was on an older tower desktop machine with an Intel i3 quad-core processor with 8GB of RAM and a 1TB spinning drive. It had two Ethernet ports and served my needs for years. In fact, I still have it and fire it up from time to time. You may have similar older desktops or laptops like mine gathering dust that can serve as nodes for your lab cluster.

The most important consideration for using older gear is the system's underlying architecture. Though you can still install Linux distributions on 32-bit systems, they don't make good Linux lab hosts because virtualization is limited or unavailable. For virtualization, you need the multi-threading capabilities of 64-bit systems. How can you tell the difference? Check the vendor's website for the original technical specs on the machines you have. That'll give you a good start.

An old laptop might be another good choice, particularly if portability is important to you. You can take your lab on the road if necessary (or at least to work).

If the system you're planning to use is running Windows, open the file manager (or any folder) and right-click the *This PC* icon and choose *Properties*. You'll see the system configuration there. If you have an Intel-based Mac, you can click the apple in the top-left corner and choose *System Properties* to see what it has under the hood. If there's no OS installed on the system, you can boot a live Linux USB and follow the instructions in Chapter 2 to check the system.

It's tempting to want to build a Linux lab environment right on your main workstation or perhaps set up a dual-boot configuration so you can switch back and forth. That's a workable option, particularly if you're digging into containerized environments with Docker and the like. However, I don't recommend it as the single resource for your DevOps lab. Later chapters will take you through container basics so you'll get a chance to work with microservices, but the idea here is to have a fully independent environment to work on *and* access from your regular workstation. Even if you're someone who always keeps their workstation up and running, this isn't quite enough for a good lab. Instead, find at least one separate machine to use.

Raspberry Pis and IoT Devices

Internet of Things (IoT) devices are becoming an important part of the hardware landscape, and you can definitely incorporate such devices into your lab environment. One of the best and easiest ways to do that is to get a few Raspberry Pis.

Though there are many, many single-board devices from which to choose, including the Pine64 and Orange Pi, Raspberry Pi devices are a good choice because they support a wide variety of Linux OSes (including the Debian-based Raspbian default), they're inexpensive, and they have a vast community of developers. This last point is important when it comes time to deploy applications and services because chances are good that someone else has tried what you want to do, and the Internet is full of guides and information. No other single-board device has as much readily available content for you to take advantage of when you're stuck.

When buying Raspberry Pis for your Linux lab, be sure to get a model that's at least version 3. RPi4 models are even better. These have faster CPUs, more RAM, and onboard WiFi and Bluetooth. Check with the vendor for the best storage options, armed with the knowledge that not all SD cards are suitable (durable and fast enough) to run a Raspberry Pi.

If you buy your Raspberry Pis as standalone devices, and not as part of a kit, be sure you get enough mini-USB and USB-C cables to power them. The Raspberry Pi 4 uses USB-C for power and has micro HDMI ports, so you'll need an adapter to connect to monitors with full-size HDMI ports. Most of the time, you'll run your Raspberry Pis headless—with no monitor or keyboard—but initial configuration often requires these interfaces.

Something else that's handy with RPis is a USB power hub. These enable you to plug five or more mini-USB cables into a single device that uses just one wall outlet. This is a much better option than adding power strips to accommodate half a dozen wall warts.

Raspberry Pis are small, so you can fit a lot of them in very little space. I like to buy inexpensive racks to hold four or more in a neat stack.

Once considered a mere plaything, the Raspberry Pi is now anything but. They can power 4k monitors, and with the additional USB storage, you can use them as media streaming devices. In your lab environment, they are a great choice for deploying applications and containers, giving you the option to expand your lab for very little money.

In my own lab, I've deployed a four-RPi cluster to host containerized applications and even a full-fledged Ceph storage cluster. Of course, the performance for storage isn't something you'd use in production, but for applications that require multiple devices, they provide an excellent, inexpensive learning platform.

The capabilities of modern RPis make them even more useful for lab environments, and it's possible to build an entire Linux environment using just them and your workstation. I won't go into a lot of detail of how to accomplish this, but it's something to keep in mind if you're limited on resources and cash. For the purposes of this book, consider them excellent supplements, but not primary resources.

Building Your Network

In order for your Linux lab to be truly valuable for all the DevOps work you want to do, it must connect to a network so you can install packages, remotely access it via the shell, and have it serve up resources like web pages and DNS information. That requires at least a single Ethernet interface on the host machine itself.

Fortunately, you have a lot of choices and can get great performance without having to spend much money. Well-known vendors, such as NETGEAR, Dell, D-Link, Linksys, and TP-Link, make suitable 1GB networking devices for your lab hosts, if they're not built in already.

If you plan to use an older system, you can make do with a 100MB Ethernet port, but a 1GB connection is better. Everything in your lab environment will perform better with faster networking, and network installations can really fly with the additional bandwidth. Of course, to take advantage of a 1GB network interface on any Linux lab host, you'll need a network switch capable of handling 1GB speeds. Many low-cost options are available.

Running two separate networks is ideal for your lab environment, and for lab purposes that requires two separate network interfaces on your physical systems, including your separate workstation. Ideally, these should be physical Ethernet ports or USB 3 dongles, but one physical port and WiFi capability can be better than just a single port. Two separate network interfaces enable you to isolate your network traffic and help keep your lab secure. If you're relying solely on your home network that everyone in your house uses for Netflix, having a separate lab network allows you—and your family—to avoid slowdowns.

The principle here is to create one network for all your lab traffic and one network for accessing the Internet. In a home environment, you typically accomplish the latter via the router provided by your ISP. The former would be a private network using a small gigabit Ethernet switch or router.

WiFi is robust enough to support most of the applications and deployments described in this book, but getting it to work can be tricky, and it's not always as robust as a wired network interface. If you're okay with spending a little more time and having a few more hiccups, try it.

Managed vs. Unmanaged Switches

If you're just starting out, unmanaged switches are easy to use and cheap to buy. They provide everything you need to get a simple network up and running. Just plug in some Ethernet cables, connect them to your workstation and lab hosts, and you're off and running. They move network traffic well and are pretty foolproof.

11

If you're planning a more robust environment, get yourself a managed switch. These enable you to add a number of network configurations that can greatly extend the capabilities of your Linux lab. For example, a managed switch with 802.1Q capabilities enables you to create virtual LANs, or VLANs you can use to segregate network traffic and improve performance for certain deployments. If one of your end goals is to become more adept at networking, plan to get a managed switch.

If you're buying new networking gear, it's certainly possible to get decent performance out of a basic eight-port switch, but you may find that you quickly run out of ports and throughput. Although even a four-node lab cluster plus your workstation will use up only five ports on an eight-port switch, what happens when you want to plug in a spare laptop, another switch, and a couple Raspberry Pis? Suddenly, what seemed like a wealth of riches isn't so great.

Consider getting a device with 16 or 24 ports so you never run out. Also think about what else you might someday want to plug in to your switch. Do you have designs on some cool power-over-Ethernet (PoE) cameras? These and other devices get their power from the Ethernet switch, which can be handy in all sorts of real-world applications.

If you don't want to buy anything to get started and all you have is a four-port 100MB switch (or old router), use it. You can always upgrade later without too much fuss.

Finally, give some thought to Ethernet cables. You'll need Cat 5 or Cat 6 (for less cross talk), and you'll likely need cables of different lengths. If you're super neat and tidy, a bag of 3-foot cables will do. Most of us aren't so fastidious, so get yourself a mix of 12-inch, 3-foot, 6-foot, and even longer cables. There always seems to be a time when I need to stretch a cable across my desk to reach a system I want to attach for some reason or another. Avoid frustration by getting different cables of different lengths and ones that come in different colors to help you keep things straight.

Using Your ISP Router

If you're building your Linux lab at home, you can take advantage of the router provided by your ISP. Newer routers now typically offer 1GB wired network speeds and dual-band wireless. If the router is physically located near your lab, you can plug your workstation and Proxmox virtualization hosts into it, and you're off and running.

However, there are a few caveats. All your home-based network traffic uses this router, which can mean bottlenecks. Everything in your house will have access to your Linux lab and vice versa, which can create security concerns. ISP-provided routers usually have only four ports, which is barely enough for a versatile lab environment. If you're going down this path, consider connecting another switch to one of the LAN ports to get more usable ports.

If your ISP router isn't located in the same place as your Linux lab, you can bring good network speeds to another location in your home by using Ethernet-over-power devices. These plug in to any standard three-prong power outlet and provide one or more Ethernet ports. Plug one in to a power outlet near your ISP-provided router and use an Ethernet cable to connect it to one of the router's LAN ports. Plug a second Ethernet-over-power device into a power outlet where your lab is located, and connect it to your network switch. You now have wired Ethernet without having to string cables. Keep in mind that these devices aren't completely perfect, but they offer a good way to extend your home network physically.

If you're just starting out, using your ISP router is a solid option, but ultimately, it's better to invest in a second router or switch to isolate your lab network traffic.

When I first started building Linux lab environments, I used old wireless routers for all my networking needs. These were 100MB four- and eight-port devices that worked great for linking together a bunch of machines and Raspberry Pis. They performed well, and because they had built-in DHCP capabilities and WiFi, it was easy to add network addresses dynamically to everything that came online.

13

If you have an old router lying around, I recommend using it. Even if you decide later to add a full-blown modern switch to your environment, these old routers work great for DHCP and are easy to expand by adding a multi-port switch to one of the existing LAN ports.

Most mini PCs come with a single Ethernet port, but what if you want two? Well, first see if the device you have in mind is sold in a dual-Ethernet configuration, such as the Kingdel models. If not, make sure the device has a fast USB 3.0 port you can use to attach a USB-to-Ethernet adapter. These adapters are inexpensive and work well for giving any system a second (or third or fourth) Ethernet port. Be sure any adapters you buy support Linux, and remember that USB 3.0 versions are much faster than USB 2.0.

Deploy Managed and Unmanaged Switches

In the next chapter, I'll discuss how to add two different networks to your workstation and lab servers, but here are a couple tips when adding a second router to your environment. The general idea is to create two entirely separate network *subnets* so all your traffic is isolated.

Nearly every consumer-grade router comes preconfigured to use a common private subnet like 192.168.0.0/24 or 192.168.1.0/24, which provides 254 usable addresses for your computers, phones, TVs, and what have you. In order to use a second router alongside the first, you need to reset the second device's subnet to something different from the first. If your ISP router uses 192.168.1.0/24, you can set your lab router to something like this:

- 10.128.1.0/24

- 172.16.1.0/24

- 192.168.2.0/24

Each of these options provides 254 usable addresses, which are plenty for a lab environment. The subnets listed below are part of the IPv4 private address space, which means they're not publicly routable on the Internet. The full range of private addresses you have available are as follows:

- *10.0.0.0/8 IP addresses*: 10.0.0.0 to 10.255.255.255

- *172.16.0.0/12 IP addresses*: 172.16.0.0 to 172.31.255.255

- *192.168.0.0/16 IP addresses*: 192.168.0.0 to 192.168.255.255

Since my home-based ISP router is set to `192.168.1.0/24`, I used the 10-net space for my lab (`10.128.1.0/24`).

To set up the lab router

- Reset it to its factory defaults.

- Connect it to an isolated workstation (not one already connected to another 192.168.1.0/24 address).

- Set the workstation to get its network configuration via DHCP.

- Log in to the router using the default IP address provided by the vendor.

- Edit the address range to what you want, setting the router's IP address to the first IP in the subnet range (i.e., 10.128.1.1).

- Apply the changes to the router.

- Disconnect and reconnect your workstation and access it via 10.128.1.1 (in this example).

These procedures vary a bit by device, but are straightforward. Once you're able to connect to your lab switch on its new private address, go in and edit the router's DHCP settings, as shown in Figure 1-1. Instead of having the router offer addresses between, say, `10.128.1.2` and `10.128.1.255` by default, change the lower number to something like `10.128.1.129`. This will allow you to use addresses 2–128 for static IP addresses later.

DHCP Settings for Network (Home/Office)				
Service				
IP Address Distribution:		DHCP Server ∨		
DHCP Server				
Start IP Address:		10	128	1	129
End IP Address:		10	128	1	254
Subnet Mask:		255	255	255	0
WINS Server:		0	0	0	0
Lease Time in Minutes:		1440			
☑ Provide Host Name If Not Specified by Client				

IP Address Distribution According to DHCP Option 60 (Vendor Class Identifier)

Vendor Class ID	IP Address	MAC Address	QoS

Apply   Cancel

Figure 1-1. *Setting DHCP range on the lab network router. The addresses 10.128.1.129 to 10.128.1.254 will be handed out automatically. The rest of the subnet can be used for static addresses*

If you want your private network to be able to reach the Internet, you'll need to use an Ethernet cable to connect any LAN port on your ISP router to the WAN port on the lab router. When I do this, I like to assign a static IP for the purpose, which means setting up a static IP address on the public router (something like `192.168.1.4`) and assigning that address to the WAN port on the private router. You also can do this via DHCP from your ISP router, but it's best to make the link between your lab router and your ISP router a static address to avoid connectivity issues and to keep things orderly.

In a /24 network (pronounced "slash 24"), you're setting the broadcast to 255.255.255.0, which is sort of the sweet spot for network overhead. Anything bigger than a /22 (identified as 255.255.252.0 with 1,024 usable addresses) starts to add network overhead that can slow traffic. That overhead can slow things down and start to make things tough to troubleshoot. Start small, and grow later if necessary.

Use Network Bridges and Bonds to Improve Connectivity

Adding network bridges to your workstation and your virtual machine hosts gives you significantly more flexibility, and you'll learn how to deploy them in Chapter 2. The key advantage is the ability to route virtual machine traffic, including virtual LANs (VLANs), across the network and not have network traffic isolated to a single machine.

For example, if you set up Kernel-based Virtual Machine (KVM) on your workstation to do some virtualization and you don't have a network bridge, each VM you create will only be accessible from a local Network Access Translation (NAT) address on that machine, not the subnet assigned to your network interface card (NIC).

Bridges solve that problem by creating a virtual network interface with your chosen subnet IP address range, and the physical network interface provides the actual connectivity as a pass-through. In this way, you can also effectively assign multiple routable IP addresses to a single physical interface.

Bonds are another network enhancement that allow you to join two or more physical Ethernet adapters into a single device, effectively doubling, tripling, or quadrupling the speed. For example, if you have two 1GB Ethernet adapters on a single physical machine, you can bond them together into a single 2GB interface. For network-intensive workloads, this can help improve performance.

Many modern applications, such as the OpenStack platform, take advantage of VLANs to separate network traffic and improve performance. VLANs work by assigning tags to each Ethernet packet and routing it accordingly. In this way, you can separate administrative and workload network traffic on a single physical or virtual network interface, reducing congestion, adding security, and speeding throughput.

In order to get VLANs working, you'll need a network switch capable of handling VLAN tagging. Switches with *802.1Q* capabilities support this capability.

Up to now, I've mentioned only IPv4 networking, which has been the standard for decades. However, with the rapid growth of Internet devices, those 3.7 trillion usable public IPv4 addresses—like `24.233.22.56` or `202.77.84.34`—are set to run out. That, in part, led to the development of a new IP address standard called IPv6, which provides 340 undecillion addresses (3.4×10^{38}). IPv4 addresses are 32-bit, whereas IPv6 addresses are 128-bit and look like *2001:db8::8a2e:370:7334*.

If you want to use IPv6 addresses in your Linux lab, you'll need a network switch that supports them. Many modern switches do, but the addressing itself can be quite confusing. And since IPv6 is not backward-compatible with IPv4, you'll need to create separate subnets to handle both. Nothing in this book directly requires you to set up IPv6, but nothing prevents you from using it, either.

Tips for Avoiding Common Hardware Headaches

The following tips are handy to think about as you assemble your Linux lab hardware and can help you decide on the best gear to use.

Reserve IP Address Pools *Now*, Not Later

Chances are good that everything you've ever connected to a router, either via a cable or WiFi, was given an address automatically via DHCP. With DHCP, the router assigns an available IP address to the device, the device connects to the router, and the router connects to the Internet. Everything just works.

In your lab environment, randomly assigned IP addresses handed out by a DHCP server can cause problems, not the least of which is having your devices get new addresses every few days or after they reboot. That means you'll need to guess at the IP addresses used by DNS, web, email, and every server you deploy.

You can solve this problem by giving each server a *static IP address* and, before that, setting aside addresses on each router that it will never assign automatically via DHCP. Editing the lower limit on the DHCP servers as mentioned previously takes care of this. That way, you have a pool of static addresses you can manually assign and a pool of auto-assigned addresses that can be initially handed out to your VMs and devices to get them online.

Test and Document Your Configurations

Before moving on to the next sections and chapters in this book, take some time to test your networking. This can be easily done by using the *ping* command on your workstation. If you can *ping* the private router's address (10.128.1.1 in this example), google.com, and 8.8.8.8, you're good to go. Success means you're able to access both public and private IP addresses. If not, double-check your network configurations before you start configuring your virtual machines.

This is also a good time to take a few moments to think about how you'll be using your Linux lab and the IP addresses you might use. For example, if you're planning to run a bunch of web servers, you may want to reserve addresses for them in a group, such as 10.128.1.20, 10.128.1.21, and 10.128.1.22. Assigning portions of your non-DHCP addresses this way will keep things orderly, so if you later want to add a bunch of database servers, you might make them 10.128.1.40, 10.128.1.41, 10.128.1.42, and so on. This little bit of organization can make your network layout more intuitive and make life much easier later, leaving room for additions.

It's easy to lose track of which IP addresses you assign to which servers, so it's good to come up with a way to keep track of them and map them out before you start to deploy equipment and VMs. You can use a simple spreadsheet or a Google Sheet, as shown in Figure 1-2, listing the IP address, machine name, and any other information you want. When it comes time to add a new virtual machine or server, you need only check the listing to ensure you're not reusing one of your static addresses. If your anticipated lab, on paper, includes lots of devices and VMs, you'll have a better idea of the speed and number of ports you'll need from a network switch—before you buy.

	A	B	C	D	E
1	IP	FQDN	System	DNS	Physical
2	10.128.1.1	Gateway	Netgear wireless router		x
3	10.128.1.2	dns01.tiny.lab	LXC on Proxmox	x	
4	10.128.1.3	dns02.tiny.lab	LXC on KVM	x	
5	10.128.1.4	D-Link DGS-1100-24	D-Link Managed Switch		x
6	10.128.1.5	mail.sandbox.lab	Ubuntu 18.04		
7	10.128.1.6	pve02.tiny.lab	ProxMox 6.1.2		x
8	10.128.1.7	docker.sandbox.lab	Ubuntu 18 LXC		
9	10.128.1.8	web.sandbox.lab	Ubuntu 18.04		x
10	10.128.1.9	progress.tiny.lab	Work machine		x
11	10.128.1.10	kingdel.tiny.lab	Kingdel Ubuntu 18.04		x
12	10.128.1.11	laptop.tiny.lab	Lenovo T61p laptop		x
13	10.128.1.12	pve03.tiny.lab	ProxMox 6.1.2		x
14	10.128.1.13	desktop.tiny.lab	Debian 10 VM		
15	10.128.1.14	win10.tiny.lab	Windows 10		x
16	10.128.1.15	pve01.tiny.lab	ProxMox		x
17	10.128.1.16	pizero.tiny.lab	Raspbian Stretch		x
18	10.128.1.17	elastic.tiny.lab	Turnkey LXC		
19	10.128.1.18	mail.tiny.lab	Ubuntu 18.04		

Figure 1-2. *You can use a simple spreadsheet to organize IP addresses, domain names, and system information*

Conclusion

With your hardware in place and some thought given to your environment and networking needs, you're ready to set up your Linux lab environment. In the next chapter, you'll learn how to deploy and configure Proxmox and KVM to run all the virtual machines you need to deploy servers and applications and really start to leverage the power of your Linux lab.

CHAPTER 2

Setting Up a Virtual Environment

In this chapter, you'll set up your base Linux lab environment by deploying one or more *virtualization* servers, which allow you to create virtual machines and containers that greatly extend the capabilities of one or more physical computers.

You'll use Proxmox, a powerful open-source virtualization platform that can handle very small or enterprise-grade clusters. This environment will enable you to transform one or more physical machines (which you gathered in Chapter 1) into hosts for DNS, web, database, email, and other servers that are at the heart of any modern DevOps environment. This virtualization, and the ability to deploy a variety of systems on demand, is at the core of your Linux lab.

Having a number of servers managed by Proxmox rather than just a single workstation running, say, Linux-native Kernel-based Virtual Machine (KVM), greatly expands what you can do because you'll be able to isolate your workloads. That isolation makes it easier to fix individual servers when things go wrong. You'll also be able to take advantage of the resources—RAM, CPU, and storage—of several computers, not just one.

© John S. Tonello 2022
J. S. Tonello, *Practical Linux DevOps*, https://doi.org/10.1007/978-1-4842-8318-9_2

System virtualization on your gathered hardware will give you plenty of oomph for virtual machines and containers, provide better resiliency, and, with Proxmox, enable you to move virtual machines around your physical cluster. That means you can migrate servers and do other tasks that closely replicate what you might find in an enterprise or cloud data center, where many machines of many types are running in harmony.

In this chapter, you'll deploy Proxmox; spin up some initial virtual machines and Linux containers (LXCs), which are essentially small VMs in this environment; and take a brief look at KVM running on a Linux workstation to supplement your Proxmox cluster VMs. When you're finished, you'll feel comfortable with the virtualization environment and be ready to start deploying real workloads.

About the Proxmox Virtualization Environment (PVE)

Proxmox VE is a robust open-source solution that's easy to deploy and use, which makes it ideal for a lab environment or something much bigger. Although it scales well, in its most basic form—namely, running on a single machine—Proxmox works well for everything you'll learn in the rest of this book. With a few tweaks, it can scale to manage a large cluster of machines.

Proxmox installs from a single USB thumb drive and becomes the base operating system on its physical host. It creates partitions and does some other things under the hood that don't make it ideal for a dual-boot environment. Any box you install it on will become a Proxmox Virtualization Environment (PVE) machine. If you're thinking of setting up Proxmox VE as part of a dual-boot configuration with, say, Ubuntu or Windows, that's possible, but recognize that switching to your non-Proxmox environment renders your Linux lab inert.

Under the covers, Proxmox is based on Debian and its latest long-term support (LTS) kernel, but when you log in via the shell, what you'll experience is a preinstalled, fully operational Linux environment. Don't worry if you don't know your way around Debian systems. You'll spend 99.9% of your time using Proxmox's web-based dashboard building pretty much any kind of Linux or Windows systems you can imagine, including managing a single- or multi-node lab cluster from any web browser, creating VMs and LXCs, adding or removing resources, setting network parameters, and more.

Finding your way around Proxmox will be largely intuitive and easy to master. If you're a more experienced systems administrator who's used to VMware, Proxmox will feel familiar. The dashboard allows you to create new VMs and LXCs, interact with each through built-in terminal console capabilities, create custom storage, configure your networks, and much more. The look and feel of Proxmox has been incredibly consistent over the years, but slight version enhancements may make your dashboard look a little different from the version I use throughout this book.

If you decide you want even more capabilities and support, you can buy a paid subscription to Proxmox, but that's not necessary for any of the activities in this book.

Set Up Proxmox

To get started with Proxmox, use your workstation to download the latest version of the Proxmox Virtualization Environment (PVE) installer *.iso* file from www.proxmox.com/en/downloads and write it to a USB thumb drive. The version used in this book is just 778MB, so even an older 2GB thumb drive should suffice. Keep in mind that everything on the drive will be wiped and destroyed.

When it comes to burning an *.iso* file to a USB drive, you can find any number of graphical tools to do the job on Linux, Windows, and Mac platforms. Since we're working in a Linux environment here, let's use the built-in dd tool.

First, insert the USB, open a terminal, and list your system's drives, also known as block devices, using the lsblk command, as shown in Listing 2-1. This helps ensure you're targeting the correct drive for writing your Proxmox boot disk and helps you avoid accidentally deleting everything on one of your workstation's system disks.

Listing 2-1. Use lsblk to view your system's storage

```
$ lsblk
NAME    MAJ:MIN RM    SIZE RO TYPE MOUNTPOINT
sda       8:0    0 119.2G  0 disk
├─sda1    8:1    0   500M  0 part /boot/efi
├─sda2    8:2    0 114.8G  0 part /.snapshots
└─sda3    8:3    0     4G  0 part [SWAP]
sdb      8:16    0 465.8G  0 disk
├─sdb2   8:18    0 463.8G  0 part /storage1
└─sdb3   8:19    0     2G  0 part
sdc      8:80    1  28.9G  0 disk
```

In this example, the device sdc is a 32GB thumb drive, and it has no partitions. If it did, executing dd would delete them. The preceding output also shows the other physical disks on my system: sda and sdb. Each of those already has partitions, and they're bigger than the USB, so I know not to target either of them during the dd process.

Now, execute the dd command, as shown in Listing 2-2. Set the .iso file as the value of if, the USB device as the value of the output of, and the block size as the value of bs. These tell dd to use the Proxmox .iso as its input and to expand it onto the device located at /dev/sdc. The bs setting tells dd to write 4096 bytes at a time, which speeds up the writing process.

Listing 2-2. Using the dd command to burn an .iso image to a
USB device

```
$ sudo dd \
> if=/home/$USER/Downloads/Proxmox-ve_6.0.1.iso \
> of=/dev/sdc \
> bs=4M \
> status=progress \
> done;
```

The optional last bit, status=progress, provides feedback about the
write process, which is useful because dd won't otherwise display anything
while it's doing its work. If you omit it, burning the .iso to the USB will work
fine, but you won't see any output until the disk-writing is done.

When the write is complete, you'll probably see the newly created
partitions (named *PVE*) show up in your workstation's folder list. Safely
eject the USB drive from your workstation and plug it in to your Linux lab
machine. If you're using multiple systems, you'll repeat the following steps
on each.

Note   Make sure the BIOS settings on your PVE lab host are set
to boot from the USB drive. Most systems recognize F12 or F8 to
post the boot drive selection menu. Alternatively, press F2 or the Del
key (common ways to access the BIOS menu) during system boot
to select the thumb drive temporarily. Most modern machines are
smart enough to detect the USB and boot from it, but not always. If
you don't do this, your target system will try to boot from the main
internal disk, skipping the installation.

When you first boot your Linux lab Proxmox machine, you'll see the Proxmox splash page. Select the default "Install Proxmox VE" and agree to the end user license agreement to continue.

By default, Proxmox uses the entire target disk on your lab host and sets up Logical Volume Management (LVM) partitions that will generally consume the entire internal disk on which you install Proxmox. It will leave other separate disks alone.

LVM partitions are logical, rather than physical, so they can span multiple disks and provide other benefits. For example, they can be resized more easily and make point-in-time snapshots simpler. However, they're not as transparent as traditional ext3 or ext4 Linux partitions, and they can be complicated to set up or modify. As the main disk type on your Proxmox nodes, LVM is fine because each virtual disk created for each virtual machine will appear as any format you want, merely storing the files for any virtual disks in the Proxmox LVM volume. For simplicity, keep this default setting.

If you want to do something more advanced, such as splitting the internal disk into multiple partitions, click the Options button and change the *hdsize* entry. The number you enter will become the Proxmox primary LVM disk; later, you can set up any remaining free space as a separate storage partition.

Next, select your country, time zone, and keyboard layout. Enter a password, confirm it, and provide an email address. The password you enter here will become the *root* password for the system, so make note of it.

Take your time when configuring the network management interface and other details, shown in the installation summary in Figure 2-1, particularly if you have a Linux lab host with multiple network interfaces. If your server is connected to a network during installation, Proxmox may autofill the network values with the wrong network for your purposes. Be sure to check this information carefully before proceeding.

Summary

Please **verify** the displayed informations. Once you press the **Install** button, the installer will begin to partition your drive(s) and extract the required files.

Option	Value
Filesystem:	ext4
Disk(s):	/dev/sda
Country:	United States
Timezone:	America/New_York
Keymap:	en-us
E-Mail:	user@gmail.com
Management Interface:	ens3
Hostname:	pve
IP:	10.128.1.10
Netmask:	255.255.255.0
Gateway:	10.128.1.1
DNS:	10.128.1.2

Abort   Previous   Install

Figure 2-1. *Look over the Proxmox configuration summary information carefully before clicking the **Install** button. Take care to enter network settings that match your desired environment*

Later, when creating your network and DNS server, you'll want to make sure you're using your private Linux lab network for your Proxmox traffic. In this example, the network is 10.128.1.0/24, so I've given the Proxmox host network values that make sense for that subnet. If your Linux lab host is connected to an active network during installation, Proxmox will typically detect the first network interface and autofill values via DHCP. Be careful **not** to select the defaults blindly.

Note, too, that in the preceding example, *ext4* is configured for the *Filesystem*, not *LVM*, a customization I made on the previous *Harddisk* screen. Confirm the values that suit your needs before installing.

If you notice an error on the summary screen, click the **Previous** button to make changes. Carefully review the network settings; they can't be easily changed later. Otherwise, click **Install** and wait for the system to deploy. When prompted, reboot the Linux lab host.

After the installation and reboot, you'll see the boot screen, as shown in Figure 2-2. There's no need to press Enter to boot. The system will self-select the first line—Proxmox Virtual Environment—and after a few seconds it will start up. The Proxmox Virtual Environment shouldn't need to be changed, but this menu provides advanced options and tests in case you run into trouble.

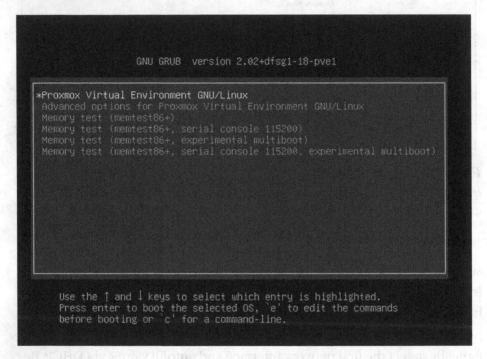

Figure 2-2.   *The initial system Proxmox boot screen defaults*

Post-install Configurations

Once the system reboots, you'll be prompted with a Debian-style boot menu, and after a few moments, the system will initialize and come online.

Once the Proxmox system boots and you see the login prompt, you no longer need to interact with this server directly. You can disconnect its keyboard, mouse, and monitor. From here on, you'll use the web-based Proxmox dashboard, and if necessary, you'll use SSH from your workstation to manage the PVE host itself.

Switch back to your workstation computer to continue the rest of this chapter's work setting up VMs and applications to run on them. Recall the IP address of the PVE Linux lab host you entered during setup. The Proxmox login banner will show that IP address and the proper URL (with the port) to connect to. In my example, it's **https://10.128.1.10:8006**.

Notice that the URL begins with *https*, not *http*. When you first attempt to access the dashboard, you'll likely get a warning screen saying the connection is not secure. If that happens, click the **Advanced** option and choose **Accept the risk and continue** (or similar). It's safe to proceed.

At the login screen, enter your credentials—**root** and the password you created earlier—and log in with the *Realm* set to the default, *Linux PAM standard authentication*. This Realm allows you to log in with the existing root user, but you can configure your system to use other system users with encrypted credentials. For the purposes of this lab, you can always use the root credentials.

After logging in, you'll be taken to the main Proxmox dashboard, as shown in Figure 2-3.

Figure 2-3. *The Proxmox dashboard, ready to use*

Whenever you log in to the Proxmox dashboard, you'll see a warning pop up about your system being unlicensed. You can safely ignore the warning. Everything you'll do in this book does not require a Proxmox license, but if you use it a lot, it might be worth paying for a license.

The default view of the PVE node includes the *local* and *local-lvm* storage Proxmox created during installation. Note the green check mark showing the system is indeed up and running and healthy.

Take a few minutes to poke around, and be sure to click the *Datacenter*, *pve*, and *local* and *local-lvm* links in the left-hand Server View column. Each will open a wider view into the details of your PVE system. If you click **Datacenter** and choose **Summary**, you'll see CPU load, server load, memory usage, and network traffic. If you click the name of this node (pve in this example) and then **Summary**, you'll see similar information. Later, when you add systems to your cluster, the *Datacenter* view will show a summary for all the resources on all the machines, not just one host. This is a handy way to see how you might move VMs around your cluster to take best advantage of your compute resources.

If you click the **Documentation** button at the top of the screen, you'll have access to extensive Proxmox documentation. The *Tasks* and *Cluster* log tabs at the bottom of the screen provide real-time views of any actions you take, such as deploying, stopping, or shutting down a VM or LXC.

Prepare a Single-NIC Network Setup: VLAN-Aware

When you first set up your Linux lab host, Proxmox automatically configured a physical network connection, which the underlying Debian system sees as *ens3* in this example. Proxmox automatically created a network bridge named *vmbr0* for the physical interface it discovered and configured on the machine. Regardless of the name the Proxmox host assigns to the network Ethernet adapter and the Linux bridge, your VMs running on this Proxmox system will all get their own interface names, like *eth0*. The network bridge provides the connectivity for everything, meaning your VMs can get and use network addresses on your private lab network, not a network limited to just the Proxmox box itself.

If you're planning to use VLAN tagging with your system so you can take advantage of more sophisticated network setups with a smart switch, you'll need to edit your Proxmox host's network settings to make that happen. VLAN tagging is useful when you have a single network interface that you want to add multiple addresses to. VLANs also can be helpful if you're planning to deploy complicated software like OpenStack and want to be able to access OpenStack services across your Linux lab environment.

By default, VLAN tagging isn't enabled when Proxmox sets up the networking and bridged connection, but it's simple to add it and a useful feature to have. You can do this from the browser-based dashboard by clicking the Proxmox node name in the left-hand column (pve) and then System ➤ Network. Double-click the name of the Linux bridge interface you want, vmbr0 in this example, and tick the *VLAN aware* box. That's it.

Note   According to the IEEE 802.1Q standard, the maximum number of VLANs on a given Ethernet network is 4,094, which is 4,096 values provided by the 12-bit VID field minus reserved values at each end of the range, 0 and 4,095.

Prepare a Dual-NIC Network Setup: VLAN-Aware

A dual-NIC machine has two network interfaces: one used for your Linux lab traffic and one for Internet traffic. If your Proxmox Linux lab host has two physical network connections, you'll need to set up the second interface bridge from the Proxmox web dashboard. Proxmox doesn't do anything with this second interface automatically when you install the system.

In this example, I have two network interface cards (NICs) on the Linux lab host. One is attached to my private Linux lab network (10.128.1.0/24), and the other is attached to my home public network (192.168.1.0/24). Both are reachable from my workstation, which also has a dual-network interface. The public network is connected to the Internet. I use this setup for two primary reasons. My Linux lab network is capable of 1GB speeds, and I want all my VM traffic on that network to take advantage of the fast speed. My home network is connected to every computer, TV, cell phone, and other device in the house. I don't want those devices to access my Linux lab environment, and I don't want my Linux lab work to bog down the network my family uses.

Note It's a good idea to set aside some addresses on your home ISP router for static routes you can use in your lab. You can do this by changing the DHCP server settings on the router. Instead of handing out addresses between, say, 192.168.1.3 and 192.168.1.254, you can change the lower end to 192.168.1.50. That'll give you and your family plenty of addresses on the public network and a nice pool of static IP addresses you can use in your lab. You won't need to worry about network conflicts with other devices in the house.

With this configuration, your Linux lab host will have a static address on your private network and a static address on your public network. So far, you've already set up the private network, which was 10.128.1.10 in my example. To set up the public address interface so it's usable in your Linux lab, create a new virtual bridge called vmbr1.

When you click the dashboard Linux lab hostname, *pve* in this case, and then click **System ➤ Network**, you'll see the unused network device in the right-side pane. In this example, it's named *ens7*, as shown in Figure 2-4.

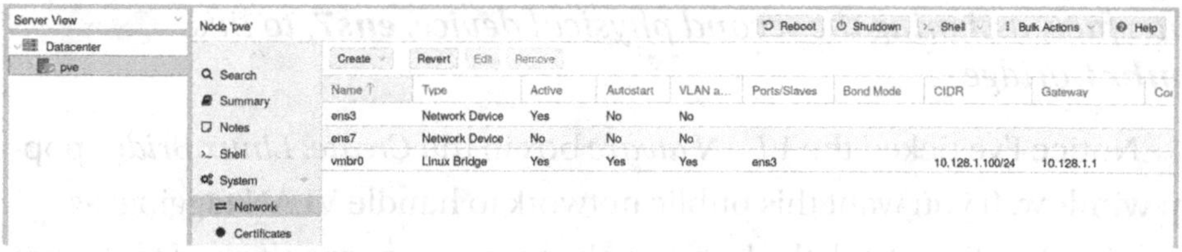

Figure 2-4. *The network view for the lab host, which shows the two physical interfaces, ens3 and ens7, and the vmbr0 bridge Proxmox created automatically when you installed the system*

In this network view, click the **Create** button and select **Linux Bridge** from the drop-down menu to assign the static IP address and gateway for the public network, and add the name of the network device for the bridge port. In this example, in the resulting pop-up, shown in Figure 2-5, the static address is 192.168.1.40/24, the gateway is 192.168.1.1, and the bridge port is ens7.

Note   If you set up a *gateway* on your vmbr0 bridge and prefer to use the gateway with the second bridge, you'll first need to remove the gateway address from vmbr0. The system can have only one gateway.

Create: Linux Bridge				⊗
Name:	vmbr1	Autostart:	☑	
IPv4/CIDR:	192.168.1.40/24	VLAN aware:	☑	
Gateway (IPv4):	192.168.1.1	Bridge ports:	ens7	
IPv6/CIDR:		Comment:		
Gateway (IPv6):				
				Create

Figure 2-5. *Set up the Linux bridge for your second network interface, assigning the second physical device, **ens7**, to this **vmbr1** bridge*

Notice I've ticked the *VLAN aware* box in the *Create: Linux Bridge* pop-up window. If you want this public network to handle VLAN tagging, as explained earlier, check the box, but chances are you won't need to do that if you're segregating network traffic and confining lab work to your private network. Remember, assign a gateway address to one bridge or the other, not both.

When you click **Create**, the new *vmbr1* bridge is set up and ready to use by all your VMs and LXCs, as shown in Figure 2-6.

Node 'pve'										Reboot Shutdown Shell ∨ Bulk Actions ∨ Help
Q Search	Create ∨	Revert	Edit	Remove						
Summary	Name ↑	Type	Active	Autostart	VLAN a...	Ports/Slaves	Bond Mode	CIDR	Gateway	Cor
Notes	ens3	Network Device	Yes	No	No					
Shell	ens7	Network Device	No	No	No					
System	vmbr0	Linux Bridge	Yes	Yes	Yes	ens3		10.128.1.100/24	10.128.1.1	
Network	vmbr1	Linux Bridge	No	Yes	Yes	ens7		192.168.1.40/24		

Figure 2-6. *In this Proxmox dashboard view, both network bridges are now set up and available to use in any VM or LXC you deploy*

Any VM you create from here on out can use either of these networks or both. Your VMs also will be able to have multiple interfaces on one network, say, *eth0* and *eth1* on the 10.128.1.0/24 private subnet. That sort of configuration lets you experiment with a variety of different network configurations, including network bonding, a practice that allows you to improve network throughput by joining two or more physical interfaces. In Proxmox, each VM you create can have multiple network interfaces from either network.

Additional Storage Considerations

When you deployed Proxmox on your lab host, you set up basic storage by having it allocate what it needed to run the system on an LVM disk partition, and it automatically used what was left for storage that can be used by your VMs and LXCs. In reality, more storage is better, and you may want to take advantage of additional drives on your Proxmox host. The basic steps to increase storage are as follows:

1. Attach the additional drive(s) to your lab host.

2. Use that mounted device in Proxmox.

For best performance, attach a SATA or SSD drive to any open bay or slot you have on your Proxmox host. The faster the drive, the better, but don't worry if all you have is an older spinning disk. After all, this is a Linux lab environment, and disk performance won't bog down most of your deployments.

After you've installed the disk, start your lab host and navigate to the **pve ➤ Disks** entry, as shown in Figure 2-7. You should see your newly added drive, shown as /dev/sdb in this example.

Figure 2-7. *A newly added disk appears in the Proxmox lab host Disks menu after you've physically added it to the machine. Additional drives you add now or in the future will also appear here*

You can now add that new disk as an LVM, LVM-Thin, Directory, or ZFS device. For this example, use the Directory feature under **pve ➤ Disks ➤ Directory** to mount the disk and make it available in your cluster. When you create the new directory, follow these steps:

- Provide the raw device (/dev/sdb/ in this example).

- Choose a filesystem type (ext4 or xfs).

- Give your storage directory a name (*storage01* in this example).

- Tick the Add Storage box.

Proxmox will automatically mount the disk at /mnt/pve/storage01, format it, and make it available to your system. You should now see it in the main dashboard Server View on the left.

When you build VMs or LXCs, you can use this *storage01* just as you would the original disk. If you want all the Proxmox hosts in your cluster to share it, navigate to Datacenter ➤ Storage and double-click the name of the disk to edit it. Tick the Shared box to make the drive visible and usable on each host.

For even better performance, consider creating a ZFS disk. These volumes can span multiple disks and be shared among all your Proxmox hosts. Complete information is available on the Proxmox wiki, but the key is to create ZFS volumes on each machine, giving them all the same name. If the ZFS volume on your first host is called *my-zfs*, name the ZFS volumes on your other Proxmox hosts the same.

Thinking Ahead to Clustering

If you have more than one machine available for your Linux lab, put those machines to use and fortify your environment by creating a Proxmox cluster. Doing this will give you several advantages, including the ability to replicate your VMs and migrate them from one machine to another. It's especially useful if you're planning to deploy Kubernetes or OpenStack, which can gobble up lots of resources.

To enable a cluster, simply follow all the above steps to create a second (or third or fourth) Proxmox host, giving each its own *hostname* and static IP address. Add these to the spreadsheet you're using to keep track of all your IP addresses and hostnames to help you avoid headaches later. As I mentioned in Chapter 1, sketch out your Linux lab first, so you can build your environment without having to backtrack.

Note   If you're planning to use multiple Proxmox hosts, give them names like pve01, pve02, and pve03 rather than just "pve". This will help you stay organized.

Once your second Linux lab host is up and running, open a second browser window and log in to its own dashboard at its static IP address (and :8006). You'll now have two browser windows open, one for each Proxmox host dashboard. In what will be your primary Linux lab host (pve in this example), navigate to **Datacenter ➤ Cluster** and click the **Create Cluster** button.

If you now have two networks available, choose the private network (10.128.1.10/24 in this example) so all cluster traffic uses that. This will ensure any traffic going between your Proxmox hosts doesn't bog down your home network. If you have a 1GB switch for the private network and only a 100MB switch for your public/home network, your cluster can take advantage of the higher private network speed, which will improve your Linux lab performance and keep congestion off your other network.

Once complete, close the status window to return to the **Cluster** view, and click the **Join Information** button. It will provide everything you need for the other lab host (or hosts) to use to join the cluster managed by your primary Proxmox host.

Copying the configuration is as simple as clicking the **Copy Information** button and pasting the settings into the **Datacenter ➤ Cluster ➤ Join Cluster** pop-up window over on the new lab host (*pve2*), as shown in Figure 2-8. Be sure to add the root password for your primary *pve* host, and again select the private network from the *Link 0*: drop-down menu.

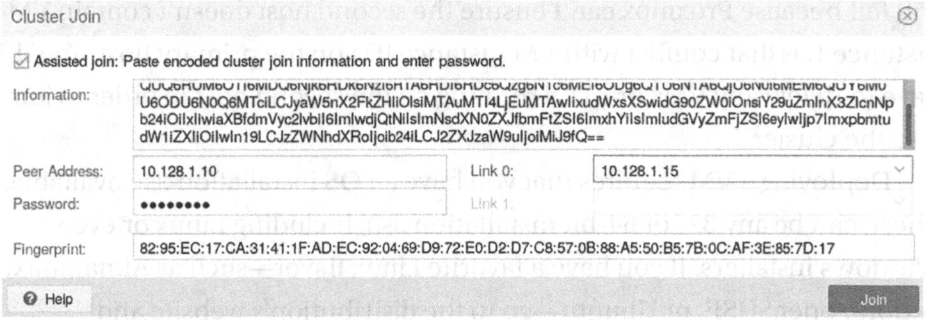

Figure 2-8. *Paste the cluster information into the second host configuration dialogue box and click **Join** to automatically connect the machine to your cluster*

When you click the **Join** button, this second Proxmox host will communicate with the primary lab host, *pve*, and it will appear in that host's dashboard menu. You can now close the second browser window and manage both machines from the single *pve* dashboard. Be sure to use the private network for better performance.

Deploy Your First VM

Up to now, you've given your Proxmox Linux lab host or hosts all the basic configurations you need to start deploying virtual machines. Proxmox has many more capabilities, but the base you've built is all you need for the rest of the projects in this book.

If your Proxmox Linux lab environment contains more than one physical host, follow the steps for joining them together into a cluster *before* you deploy your first virtual machine. Proxmox gives each VM or LXC (essentially tiny VMs) a unique instance ID that must be unique across all the systems in the cluster. If you add a VM to a second Proxmox host and decide later to add that separate host to the cluster, the action will fail because Proxmox can't ensure the second host doesn't contain VM instance IDs that conflict with VM instance IDs on the primary host. You'd have to delete any VMs or LXCs running on the second host in order to join it to the cluster.

Deploying a VM requires that you have an OS installation .iso available. These can be any 32- or 64-bit installation .iso, including Linux or even Windows installers. If you have a favorite Linux flavor—such as AlmaLinux, Fedora, openSUSE, or Ubuntu—go to the distribution's website and download the latest .iso. You can choose a live CD version, which enables you to test the OS without installing it, a server version without a graphical interface, or the standard installers that often include desktop environments. For this example, I'll use openSUSE.

Note   It's good practice to save your installer .iso files in the same place on your workstation so you can easily organize them. Once you copy them to the Proxmox host, they're no longer needed locally, but it's nice to have them handy. This will also help you avoid redownloading .iso files you already have.

In the main Proxmox dashboard under **Datacenter ➤ pve**, the last entries in the left-hand navigation include your disks (they have a stacked-disk icon). Select **local (pve).** The disk's navigation pane includes a menu with options to upload *ISO images* and *CT templates*. Click **ISO Images** and browse your workstation for the location of the Linux OS .iso you previously downloaded. After selecting it, Proxmox will begin the upload. When the upload progress completes, the .iso file will appear in your *local (pve)* content view.

You can upload as many different .iso files as you want; the storage capacity of the *local (pve)* disk is your only limitation. Once the images are uploaded, you can use them over and over again.

You're now ready to deploy a virtual machine based on the .iso you just uploaded by clicking the dashboard's **Create VM** button. In the pop-up dialog, you'll see the name of your Proxmox host (*pve*) and an auto-assigned VM ID, typically *101*. You can change the ID to anything you want. For example, if you're planning to run a group of VMs for, say, a Kubernetes cluster, you can give the first VM an ID of 1000, the next one 1001, and so on. This helps group the hosts in the main *pve* Server View.

Give the VM a name, and in the next OS view, shown in Figure 2-9, the default *Use CD/DVD disc image file (.iso)* will be selected and storage set to local, which is where you placed your uploaded .iso. Be sure the *Type:* and *Version:* match the system you're building. The defaults are usually fine. Finally, select your .iso image from the *ISO Image* drop-down. Ensure the *Guest OS Type* is set to *Linux*.

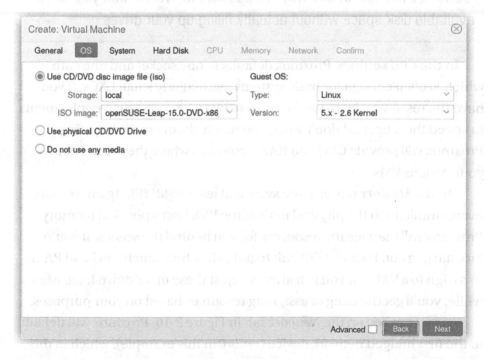

Figure 2-9. *When creating a virtual machine, select the **local** storage disk and then your .iso file*

Accept the defaults under the *System* tab setting *Graphic card to Default* and *BIOS* to *Default (SeaBIOS)*. You'll need to tick the Advanced box at the bottom of the window to see the BIOS option. This will use a GRUB-style bootloader. If you need UFI instead, select *OVMF (UEFI)* and create an EFI disk when prompted. The Hard Disk tab allows you to select the location where your VM's virtual disk will live. Accept the default *Storage*: *local-lvm*, and adjust the *Disk size* (GiB) to something smaller than *32* if you have limited storage space. Leave the rest of the default settings as they are.

Note   By default, Proxmox VM storage disks are thin-provisioned, meaning the system will reserve the space for the disk, but won't use it until it's needed. In this way, it's possible to overcommit your actual available disk space without actually filling up your drives.

In the *CPU* settings, Proxmox defaults to one socket and one core, which is often enough for basic systems, particularly small LXCs. If you have the resources, increase the cores to two for most system deployments to speed them up, and don't worry too much about overcommitting. Proxmox will provide CPU and RAM resources where they're needed to your various VMs.

On the *Memory* tab, give the system at least 2048MiB. Again, you can overcommit up to the physical limit of the PVE host's physical memory. Proxmox will manage the resources for you behind the scenes. If you're just starting out, it can be difficult to judge just how much CPU and RAM to assign to a VM, but you can always adjust these up or down later. After a while, you'll get the hang of assigning resources based on your purposes.

As you can see on the *Network* tab in Figure 2-10, Proxmox will default to the first bridged network device (*vmbr0* in this example), which in this case is fine, because that's the private 10.128.1.0/24 subnet you deployed earlier. Keep that choice and leave the rest of the defaults. Uncheck the

Firewall box so Proxmox doesn't apply any of its external firewall rules that might block traffic you need to get in and out of your VM. This firewall is separate from any firewall you might deploy inside your VM; and, for now, it's easiest to keep things open while you're experimenting. Remember, too, that your lab network is not publicly accessible, so the risk of an external hack is nearly nonexistent.

The *Confirm* tab allows you to review your system parameters, and if you like what you see, tick the *Start after created* box and click **Finish** to build and launch your VM.

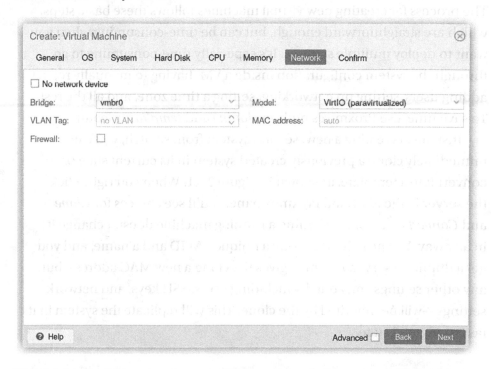

Figure 2-10. *When setting any VM's network, be sure to choose the bridge that matches your private lab network. You can always add more network interfaces later*

After a few moments, your VM will be created and start running. Select the system from your Proxmox *Server View* list and click **Console** in the right-hand pane to view the running system. At that point you can manually go through the on-screen steps to install the actual OS.

Server Replication with Cloning and Templates

The process for creating new virtual machines follows these basic steps, which are straightforward enough, but can be time-consuming when you want to deploy multiple systems. It's especially time-consuming to go through the system configuration inside a VM, having to manually repeat adding users, setting up networking, setting a time zone, and all the rest. To save time, use Proxmox's built-in *cloning* and *templating* feature.

Instead of creating a new, second system from scratch, you can immediately clone a previously created system in its current state or convert it to a template, as shown in Figure 2-11. When you right-click the server in the left-hand Proxmox pane, you'll see choices for *Clone* and *Convert to template*. Cloning a running machine doesn't change it in any way. You just give the clone a unique VM ID and a name, and you get a duplicate server. Proxmox gives the clone a new MAC address, but any other settings you added—including users, SSH keys, and network settings—will be inherited by the clone. This will replicate the system in its last configured state.

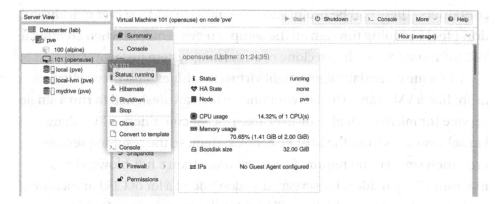

Figure 2-11. *You can clone any VM in your server list by right-clicking it and choosing Clone from the menu. Shut down the VM before trying to clone it*

Alternatively, you can convert an installed system to a template. This process changes the running server into a non-running template. That is, once turned into a template, you can no longer turn on and run the original server. However, you can right-click the template and clone it at any time as an exact replica (minus the new MAC address) of the originally configured server.

This process dramatically speeds up the creation of multiple servers of the same flavor, saving you all the time needed to step through a particular OS's installation steps. When cloning, it's handy to add all your customizations to the running VM system first, such as adding users and setting up system preferences. That way, those settings are in place in each new system you clone and boot.

Deploy an LXC Template Container

You'll primarily be building your own VMs throughout this book, but Proxmox also features pre-built LXC templates, which can come in handy by providing complete OS and software solutions in prepackaged containers. These can be useful when you need to add a server quickly and don't feel like going through all the setup screens required when creating a VM from scratch or when a clone of an existing system just won't do.

LXCs are essentially lightweight virtual machines, and they behave more like a VM than a Docker container, which are designed to run a single service (or microservice). However, like Docker containers, LXCs share kernel resources from the host Proxmox system, so the resulting servers are much smaller and require fewer resources than a full-blown virtual machine. They're ideal for servers that don't need a lot of CPU or memory, such as a DNS server, which you'll build in the next chapter. In that example, you'll see that a DNS server running in an LXC consumes about one-tenth the resources of a full virtual machine. That's especially useful in a Linux lab environment where resources are limited.

Let's use a simple LXC template to illustrate how to take advantage of this Proxmox capability.

First, download the source files to your cluster. Navigate to your disk *local* ➤ *CT Templates*. This is where Proxmox stores container templates. This is separate from the area that holds ISO images. Click the **Templates** button to open a window like the one shown in Figure 2-12 that reveals dozens of pre-built LXCs. These include everything from Linux distributions like CentOS, Fedora, openSUSE, and Ubuntu to pre-built solutions like Drupal 8, LAMP machines, GitLab servers, and more. These are pre-built containers featuring raw OS systems or full-fledged applications that are ready to use.

Templates			⊗
			Search

Type	Package ↑	Version	Description
lxc	fedora-31-default	20191029	LXC default image for fedora 31 (20191029)
lxc	gentoo-current-default	20190718	LXC default image for gentoo current (20190718)
lxc	opensuse-15.0-default	20180907	LXC default image for opensuse 15.0 (20180907)
lxc	opensuse-15.1-default	20190719	LXC default image for opensuse 15.1 (20190719)
lxc	ubuntu-16.04-standard	16.04.5-1	Ubuntu Xenial (standard)
lxc	ubuntu-18.04-standard	18.04.1-1	Ubuntu Bionic (standard)
lxc	ubuntu-19.04-standard	19.04-1	Ubuntu Disco (standard)
lxc	ubuntu-19.10-standard	19.10-1	Ubuntu Eoan (standard)
⊟ Section: turnkeylinux (101 items)			
lxc	turnkey-ansible	15.1-1	TurnKey Ansible
lxc	turnkey-asp-net-apache	15.1-1	TurnKey ASP .Net on Apache
lxc	turnkey-b2evolution	15.2-1	TurnKey b2evolution
lxc	turnkey-bugzilla	15.2-1	TurnKey Bugzilla
lxc	turnkey-cakephp	15.1-1	TurnKey CakePHP
lxc	turnkey-canvas	15.3-1	TurnKey Canvas LMS
lxc	turnkey-codeigniter	15.1-1	TurnKey CodeIgniter
lxc	turnkey-collabtive	15.2-1	TurnKey Collabtive
lxc	turnkey-concrete5	15.1-1	TurnKey Concrete5
lxc	turnkey-core	15.0-1	TurnKey Core

| | | | Download |

Figure 2-12. *LXC templates are available for download from the Proxmox dashboard*

To get started, select one of the *alpine* images and, with it highlighted, click the **Download** button. This will download the template's *tar.gz* file and store it in your Proxmox host's CT Templates storage library, much like the .iso file you manually uploaded previously. When the download is complete, you can click the blue **Create CT** button at the top of the dashboard to deploy the LXC.

The following steps on the *General* tab are much like creating a VM, but with fewer steps. Once the configuration window appears, enter a container ID (*CT ID*), which can be any number not currently in use by another LXC or VM, a *hostname* (*alpine* in this example), and a *password* (this will be used with *root* to log in to the new LXC). You can also upload a public SSH key from your workstation at this point, something like `~/.ssh/id_rsa.pub`, that will allow you to log in without a password.

On the *Template* tab, locate the downloaded *alpine* image. If you saved it in the *Storage* disk named *local*, the template will be available for you to choose from the *Template* menu. Next, select the *Root Disk* where you want to install the system's virtual disk. It will default to the *local-lvm* disk, but you can select any other available disk. The default disk size of 8GB is fine for this example.

On the next tabs, assign the number of cores to your LXC (one is fine) and the memory (512 is plenty), and assign a virtual bridge to your machine, as shown in Figure 2-13. If you have only one network bridge (*vmbr0*), you will have only one choice. If you have multiple network interfaces, be sure to select the private Linux lab network for this example. Assign a static IP address, including the CIDR (10.128.1.101/24 in this example). Also supply the gateway address for your private network, which is 10.128.1.1 in this case. Leave the default name *eth0* and uncheck the Firewall box.

Create: LXC Container

| General | Template | Root Disk | CPU | Memory | Network | DNS | Confirm |

Name:	eth0	IPv4: ⦿ Static ○ DHCP	
MAC address:	auto	IPv4/CIDR:	10.128.1.101/24
Bridge:	vmbr0 ⌄	Gateway (IPv4):	10.128.1.1
VLAN Tag:			○ SLAAC
Rate limit (MB/s):			
Firewall:			

Bridge ↑	Active	Comment
vmbr0	Yes	
vmbr1	Yes	

❓ Help   Advanced ☐   Back   Next

Figure 2-13. *Create an LXC from a turnkey image, choosing the template, root disk, CPU, memory, network, and DNS settings that meet your needs*

These basic settings will become familiar to you as you deploy more VMs and LXCs, and you can experiment later with different settings. Unchecking the Firewall box ensures that Proxmox itself is not blocking traffic to the LXC. Again, this is separate from any firewall settings you might later deploy inside the running virtual host. For now, using the defaults will help guarantee a successful deployment.

On the *DNS* tab, you can leave *Use host settings* for now. That way, the new LXC will just grab the DNS information you previously provided for your Proxmox host. If these addresses ever change, you won't need to reconfigure this system manually, but can do it at the *pve* level.

Finally, on the *Confirm* tab, review your entries and click **Finish**. If you want the alpine LXC to start automatically after it's created, tick the *Start after created* box.

When the LXC is ready, it will appear in the main Proxmox dashboard *Server View* menu under *pve*. Right-clicking it provides the options to start it, clone it, convert it to a template, or open a console to access it. If you start it and then click the *Console* tab in the right-hand pane, you'll see the system booting. You can log in to it using the credentials you provided earlier: **root** and your password.

As with Proxmox VMs, cloning will make an exact copy of the LXC you just created, including any changes you make to the system since building it. Proxmox will automatically assign a new, unique MAC address to the network interface so all the clones you make appear as separate machines from a network perspective.

Later in this book, I'll go into more detail about these actions and use them to create and clone both VMs and LXCs. For now, become comfortable with the process and use the dashboard to review the LXC's resources, network, DNS, and other features.

Set Up KVM

Though the majority of this book's projects are centered on Proxmox, it's worth touching on what I'm calling plain KVM, particularly if you're short on resources. KVM is virtualization that's part of the Linux kernel itself and is widely available and used across pretty much any flavor of Linux you can imagine. KVM also supports Windows workloads, which means you can use it to run Windows virtual machines on your Linux workstation. This comes in handy when you need to support mixed environments. KVM is also lightweight (it doesn't require a lot of resources from the host machine), and it's free. If you're familiar with VirtualBox, a virtualization application for Linux, Windows, and Mac, KVM works much the same way, but has much less overhead.

KVM is my go-to solution for running virtual machines or LXCs on any Linux workstation or server. It's even popular in public clouds like AWS, which cooked up its own specialized version of KVM. Graphical tools like *virt-manager* now make it easier to use KVM from a desktop environment, though virt-manager is not nearly as sophisticated as the Proxmox dashboard. Still, it has a number of capabilities, including simple network setups, that can make it a good option for a Linux lab environment, particularly if you're short on hardware.

Getting and installing KVM varies based on the Linux platform you're using, and some distributions provide multi-package patterns (preconfigured groups of packages) that will install all the software and package dependencies you need all at once. Later in this chapter, you'll see how to add KVM to an existing desktop or server.

With KVM, instead of running a completely separate Proxmox server or servers, you can deploy virtual machines and LXCs on the same Linux workstation where you do the rest of your work. This approach isn't as versatile, but if you're low on resources, it can be a viable Linux lab option. Again, the idea is to create separate virtual servers for your workloads rather than installing everything on your workstation.

Note   One thing to make sure you do is create at least one Linux network bridge on your workstation for your VMs to use. A bridge will enable you to add network addresses to your VMs that are reachable by other machines elsewhere on your private Linux lab network. If not, KVM running on your workstation will default to a NAT network that's accessible only from your workstation. That's far too limiting for your Linux lab purposes.

Check for Virtualization Support

Since we're all about Linux, we'll use a Linux workstation as your KVM host. The first step is to ensure that your system supports virtualization. Most modern Intel- and AMD-based 64-bit systems do, but you can run these checks to be certain.

On Debian and Ubuntu, install *cpu-checker* and run *kvm-ok*, as shown in Listing 2-3.

Listing 2-3. Check if your Ubuntu system supports virtualization

```
$ sudo apt install cpu-checker
$ sudo kvm-ok
INFO: /dev/kvm exists
KVM acceleration can be used
```

On AlmaLinux, Debian, Fedora, openSUSE, or Ubuntu, you can use *grep* to search the /proc/cpuinfo file and look for *vmx* or *svm* in the flags output, as shown in Listing 2-4.

Listing 2-4. Using egrep to identify your CPU capabilities for virtualization

```
$ egrep '(svm|vmx)' /proc/cpuinfo
flags        : fpu vme de pse tsc msr pae mce cx8 apic sep
mtrr pge mca cmov pat pse36 clflush dts acpi mmx fxsr sse
sse2 ss ht tm pbe syscall nx pdpe1gb rdtscp lm constant_tsc
arch_perfmon pebs bts rep_good nopl xtopology nonstop_tsc cpuid
aperfmperf pni pclmulqdq dtes64 monitor ds_cpl vmx smx est tm2
ssse3 sdbg fma cx16 xtpr pdcm pcid sse4_1 sse4_2 x2apic movbe
popcnt tsc_deadline_timer aes xsave avx f16c rdrand lahf_lm abm
3dnowprefetch cpuid_fault epb invpcid_single pti ssbd ibrs ibpb
```

```
stibp tpr_shadow vnmi flexpriority ept vpid fsgsbase tsc_adjust
bmi1 hle avx2 smep bmi2 erms invpcid rtm rdseed adx smap intel_
pt xsaveopt dtherm ida arat pln pts md_clear flush_l1d
```

Note that I've highlighted **vmx** in the output, which shows that this system has Intel-based virtualization available. On an AMD-based system, I'd see **svm** instead.

Install KVM and Related Utilities

Installing KVM on a workstation requires installing *qemu-kvm*, *libvirt-clients*, *libvirt-daemon-system*, *virt-manager*, and *bridge-utils*, if you didn't install them earlier. Together, these tools provide the virtualization layer and graphical tools to interact with KVM.

Depending on your system OS, run one of the commands shown in Listing 2-5.

Listing 2-5. Install KVM and supporting tooling on various Linux operating systems

Debian and Ubuntu:
sudo apt install qemu-kvm libvirt-clients libvirt-daemon-system virt-manager bridge-utils

AlmaLinux, CentOS and Fedora:
$ **sudo yum install qemu-kvm qemu-img virt-manager libvirt libvirt-python libvirt-client virt-install virt-viewer bridge-utils**

On openSUSE, install KVM with two patterns:
$ **sudo zypper install --type pattern kvm_server kvm_tools**

Once installed, add your local user (the same you used to log in to your desktop) to the *libvirt* group in /etc/group so you can run *virt-manager* without root privileges:

```
$ sudo usermod -aG libvirt $USER
```

Restart the terminal, and enable and start the *libvirtd* service:

```
$ sudo systemctl enable libvirtd.service
```

You may need to log out or reboot to ensure your local user can access the *virt-manager* connection without using root.

Set Up Bridged Networking on AlmaLinux, Fedora, and openSUSE

As mentioned earlier, network bridges enable VMs to appear on your lab network with unique IP addresses, enabling you to access them from any physical or virtual device in your environment.

To add a network bridge on Linux systems, you often can use graphical tools like *NetworkManager*, but it helps to see how to do it manually. On a Linux workstation, navigate to /etc/sysconfig/network and identify the file that represents your Linux lab network. In this example, it's *eth0*, so edit /etc/sysconfig/network/ifcfg-eth0. Remove any static or DHCP settings and give the interface a BOOTPROTO='none' setting, as shown in Listing 2-6, so you can assign the IP address to the bridge later.

Listing 2-6. Manually setting the network interface to create a bridge

```
BOOTPROTO='none'
BROADCAST=''
ETHTOOL_OPTIONS=''
```

```
IPADDR=''
MTU=''
NAME=''
NETMASK=''
NETWORK=''
REMOTE_IPADDR=''
STARTMODE='auto'
DHCLIENT_SET_DEFAULT_ROUTE='yes'
PREFIXLEN=''
```

The actual network information, namely, the IP address, will be added to a new ifcfg-br0 file. Create /etc/sysconfig/network/ifcfg-br0. Note that the *IPADDR* value is the base address for your workstation (10.128.1.9/24), with *BRIDGE_* entries set as shown in Listing 2-7.

Listing 2-7. Contents of a new ifcfg-br0 file that creates a bridge

```
BOOTPROTO='static'
BRIDGE='yes'
BRIDGE_FORWARDDELAY='0'
BRIDGE_PORTS='eth0'
BRIDGE_STP='off'
BROADCAST=''
ETHTOOL_OPTIONS=''
IPADDR='10.128.1.9/24'
MTU=''
NAME=''
NETWORK=''
REMOTE_IPADDR=''
STARTMODE='auto'
```

The file includes *BOOTPROTO*, which is set to *static* for a static IP address of the host machine; *BRIDGE*, set to *yes*; *BRIDGE_FORWARDDELAY* set to *0*; *BRIDGE_PORTS* set here to *eth0* because that's the physical device on the workstation; *BRIDGE_STP* set to *off* to avoid unintended network loops; and the *IPADDR* set to *10.128.1.9/24*, which is the IP and network mask of this example workstation.

Save the file and restart networking:

```
$ sudo systemctl restart networking
```

Test that your network is working by pinging your private Linux lab router and a public address:

```
$ ping 10.128.1.1
$ ping google.com
```

If pinging returns a time-out error, go back through these steps to double-check your configurations.

Set Up Bridged Networking on Debian and Ubuntu Desktops

It was once possible to manually configure networking on a variety of different Linux systems by editing an /etc/network/interfaces file, but there's been quite a divergence in recent years that makes the manual task hard to grasp. On the latest Ubuntu desktop systems, for example, you can set up a bridge network using *Netplan*. Netplan is a streamlined way to configure networking that uses YAML parameters. Instead of editing multiple network configuration files, Netplan takes care of the particulars in one place, making it easier to modify if necessary.

First-timers may find manually editing Netplan settings a little complicated—or discover that if they transition from Ubuntu to Debian, Netplan is no longer a thing. Fortunately, you can set up everything you need for bridged networking using *NetworkManager*, a graphical Linux tool for managing network connections. The following section explains how to do that.

Set Up a Linux Bridge Using NetworkManager

NetworkManager is a widely available Linux desktop utility that allows you to point and click your way to a stable, working network. It works with wired and wireless LAN connections and will be familiar to anyone who's worked with the Windows or macOS networking tools.

Many flavors of Linux support NetworkManager (or come with it by default, like Ubuntu and Debian), so it's a good option, particularly for newcomers. In most of these environments, clicking the *Network* icon in the *Preferences* or *Control Panel* launches the NetworkManager GUI. It can also be accessed by clicking or right-clicking the Network icon in many Linux desktop application panels.

When you use NetworkManager, you're making changes in a graphical interface, and those settings are stored in configuration files your Linux system understands (/etc/NetworkManager). By using the graphical tool, you don't need to manually edit those files.

Get started by opening the NetworkManager GUI from your system's main application window, from the panel, or by entering nm-connection-editor in a terminal. The window will look something like the example in Figure 2-14.

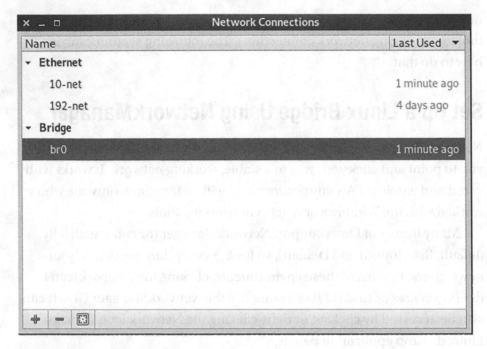

Figure 2-14. *The main NetworkManager utility view*

The preceding example includes two distinct network interfaces, one for each of the two subnets to which the Linux workstation is connected: 10.128.1.0/24 and 192.168.1.0/24. In the example, these connections are named 10-net and 192-net, respectively; by default, they might show something like "Wired connection 1" and "Wired connection 2."

Network bridges work by creating a new virtual network object that uses one or more physical devices. In the preceding example, the br0 bridge uses the 10-net as its physical interface to access the network.

To make this work, the easiest way to begin is to delete the Ethernet interface you plan to use for your bridge from the NetworkManager window. Do that by clicking it once and clicking the – icon at the bottom of the window. With that done, click the + icon and select **Bridge** under the **Virtual devices** list and **Create**. This will spawn a new window, like the one shown in Figure 2-15.

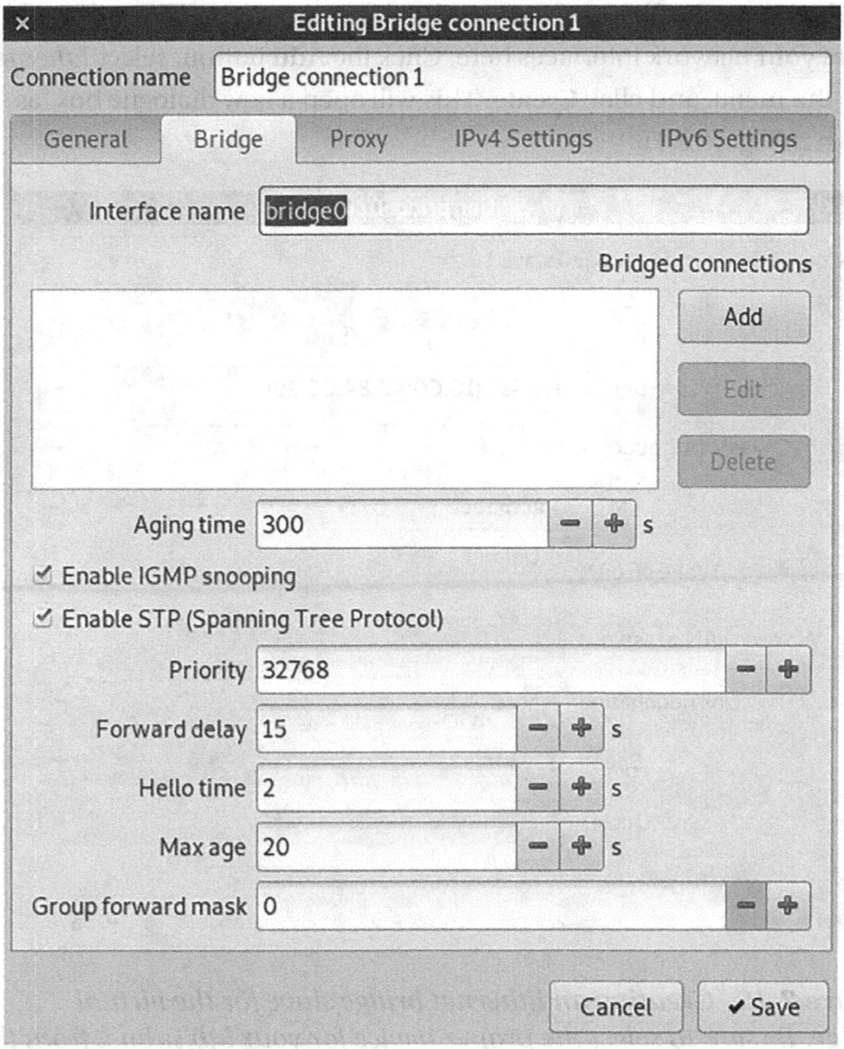

Figure 2-15. *The initial view of a newly created virtual network bridge using NetworkManager*

Notice that the window opens on the **Bridge** tab, with a default Connection name (*Bridge connection 1*) and a default Interface name (*bridge0*). You can rename these to whatever you want, but keep the names simple and memorable, such as bridge0 or br0.

The box under **Bridged connections** is empty, so you'll need to add one of your network interfaces here. Click the **Add** button, select *Ethernet* from the menu, and click **Create**. This will open a new dialogue box, as shown in Figure 2-16.

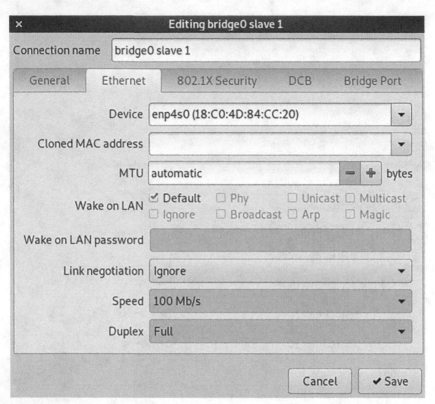

Figure 2-16.   *Creating an Ethernet bridge slave for the virtual bridge. Be sure to select the proper device for your lab subnet from the Devices menu*

Again, NetworkManager gave this new Ethernet interface a name (*bridge0 slave 1*), but you can change that to anything you want. In the preceding first example, this is set to *10-net* as a way to help me remember. The critical piece in this step is to select a **Device** from the drop-down menu. Be sure to select the proper interface for your DevOps lab network and not, say, the interface for your second 192.168.1.0/24 network. With that done, click **Save** and return to the main bridge configuration window.

When setting up network interfaces with NetworkManager, you have a number of options on how to set up IPv4 and IPv6 addresses. Most Linux systems default to *Automatic (DHCP)*. That's fine for everyday networking, but in your lab it's better to have static addresses associated with your workstation.

Click the **IPv4 Settings** tab in the main virtual bridge view and switch the **Method** to **Manual,** and click **Add**. In the **Addresses** box, enter a static *IP* on your DevOps lab subnet, a *Netmask* that matches your network (24), and the *Gateway*, as shown in Figure 2-17. Notice I've also added DNS servers for the two I have in my lab (10.128.1.2 and 10.128.1.3) and 8.8.8.8 for external name resolution. I also added devops.lab as my search domain, which will be appended to servers I try to ping and otherwise reach by their hostnames alone.

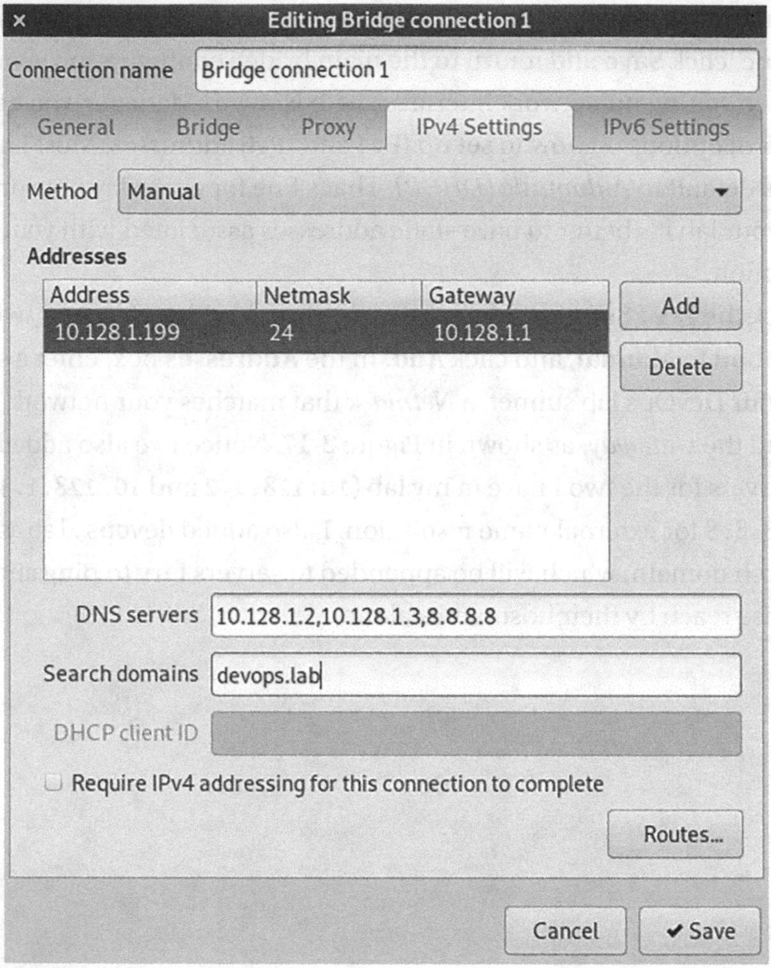

Figure 2-17. *Create a static IP address for your virtual bridge in NetworkManager, with an address from your lab subnet, DNS servers, and search domains*

You can optionally set up IPv6, but I generally leave it as-is or set it to **Ignore** to disable it. With everything double-checked, click the **Save** button.

To enable your new network configurations on your workstation, you can reboot (rather drastic if you have a lot of windows and applications open), or you can right-click the NetworkManager icon in your Linux workstation's panel and uncheck **Enable networking**. You can also run **sudo systemctl restart NetworkManager** from the CLI. Wait a few moments and then recheck it. Verify your network is configured by running a simple CLI command:

```
$ ip a

3: enp4s0: <BROADCAST,MULTICAST,UP,LOWER_UP> mtu 1500 qdisc
pfifo_fast master br0 state UP group default qlen 1000
    link/ether 18:c0:4d:84:cc:20 brd ff:ff:ff:ff:ff:ff
5: br0: <BROADCAST,MULTICAST,UP,LOWER_UP> mtu 1500 qdisc
noqueue state UP group default qlen 1000
    link/ether de:64:d1:c4:02:a3 brd ff:ff:ff:ff:ff:ff
    inet 10.128.1.10/24 brd 10.128.1.255 scope global
noprefixroute br0
      valid_lft forever preferred_lft forever
    inet6 fe80::dc64:d1ff:fec4:2a3/64 scope link
      valid_lft forever preferred_lft forever
```

Notice that the physical interface—enp4s0 in the preceding example—is shown as UP, but has no IP address. That's because it's now linked to the bridge—named br0 previously—and the bridge has the address assigned to it.

Having a bridge shouldn't impact your everyday networking in any way. The virtual bridge is largely invisible. Its value lies in its ability to give virtual machines and containers running on your system direct access to your *10.128.1.0/24* lab network. That allows you to assign lab-visible addresses to those machines and access them from anywhere on your subnet, not just your workstation machine.

Set Up a Bridge Network with Netplan (Ubuntu)

It's worth taking a closer look at how to configure networking on an Ubuntu workstation using Netplan because it highlights how it handles bridges. If you use this method on Ubuntu, it will take precedence over anything you set using NetworkManager.

The default Netplan configuration file is /etc/netplan/50-cloud-init.yaml. Edit the file, commenting out or deleting the default network device and adding a code block to define the bridge. In the example shown in Listing 2-8, the domain name is *devops.lab*.

Listing 2-8. A sample Netplan configuration with original settings commented out

```
network:
  version: 2
  ethernets:
    enp4s0:
      dhcp4: false
      dhcp6: false
#     addresses:
#       - 10.128.1.10/24
#     gateway4: 10.128.1.1
#     nameservers:
#       addresses:
#         - 10.128.1.2
#         - 8.8.8.8
#       search:
#         - devops.lab

  bridges:
```

```
br0:
  interfaces: [eth0]
  addresses: [10.128.1.199/24]
  gateway4: 10.128.1.1
  mtu: 1500
  nameservers:
    addresses: [10.128.1.2,10.128.1.3,8.8.8.8]
    search: [devops.lab]
  parameters:
    stp: true
    forward-delay: 4
  dhcp4: no
  dhcp6: no
```

In the preceding code example, I've commented out the original network configurations to remove the *addresses* setting for the physical *eth0* device and added bridge information to create *br0*. The *interfaces* entry uses the name of the physical device, *eth0*; the *addresses* entry is the workstation IP address; the *gateway4* address is the Linux lab network's IPv4 gateway or router; the *nameservers* addresses are DNS IP addresses with your Linux lab domain name; and *dhcp4* and *dhcp6* are disabled because you're using a static address.

Like the bridge settings you applied on your Proxmox host, the bridge gets the IP address, gateway, and name server information, and it's bound to the physical device on the system, *enp4s0* in this example. You can update these settings at any time if your network topology changes.

Save the file and apply the configuration, which will apply your network settings, and start the *libvirtd* daemon:

```
$ sudo netplan apply
$ sudo systemctl start libvirtd.service
```

If you need to make network edits, just be sure to rerun the `netplan` `apply` command to ensure everything is up to date.

Run virt-manager and Create Your First KVM VM

With the ***libvirtd*** daemon running, you can now launch the graphical KVM management tool, ***virt-manager***, either from the command line or from your application manager. The main window will open and look something like Figure 2-18.

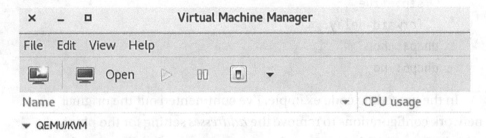

Figure 2-18. *The virt-manager window with no virtual machines running. Click the screen icon with the yellow burst to start creating a new VM*

A default connection should be visible as *QEMU/KVM*. Double-click that to connect to the locally running *libvirtd* daemon. Create a new VM with an existing .iso file by clicking **File ➤ New Virtual Machine** or by clicking the yellow burst icon. If you have trouble connecting, be sure your local system user has permissions to run ***libvirt*** in /etc/group. Also ensure that the ***libvirtd*** service is running:

```
$ sudo usermod -aG libvirt $USER
$ sudo systemctl status libvirtd.service
```

In the dialogue box, leave the default *Local install media* option checked, and then browse for a previously downloaded .iso file, such as Ubuntu, AlmaLinux, Fedora, or openSUSE.

For most common OSes, ***virt-manager*** will automatically detect the operating system type. If not, set it to *generic*. Now set the memory and CPU for the VM. If ***virt-manager*** auto-detected the medium and OS in the previous step, it will recommend minimal memory and CPU cores, but you can set them to suit your needs.

Next, create a disk, either in the default location, which is your primary system hard drive, or elsewhere on your system. If you don't have room on the default device or merely don't want to clutter up your primary drive with virtual machine disk images, choose *Select or Create custom storage*. This latter option will allow you to browse your filesystem for an alternate storage location, perhaps a second disk installed on your workstation. To keep things tidy, try to save all your disk images in the same place on your system.

Give the VM disk a name, *ubuntu01.qoow2*, for example, and set any size that suits your needs. As with Proxmox, the storage will be thin-provisioned, meaning that the virtual disk space you allocate won't be committed by KVM on your workstation until the VM actually needs it.

Finally, give your VM a name, and under *Network selection*, choose the network bridge you created earlier, in this example, *Bridge br0: Host device eth0*. This final screen offers a summary of your system and allows you to add more features, such as additional disks and network interfaces, USB interfaces, and the like. You can experiment with those by clicking *Customize configuration* before clicking **Finish**.

Return to the ***virt-manager*** console, right-click the VM name, and choose **Run**. Your new VM is up and running.

Command-Line Deployments

One of the great advantages of Proxmox and KVM is the ability to create and deploy virtual machines from the command line, which enables you to automate the deployment of systems without having to go through the sometimes tedious steps of clicking through the GUI. The GUI tools are great, but command-line tasks can greatly speed up and automate the process in a repeatable way.

The Proxmox qm Command

To create a virtual machine in Proxmox from the command line identical to the one you created earlier, log in to your Proxmox VE host and run the command shown in Listing 2-9.

Listing 2-9. The command to create a Proxmox virtual machine from the CLI

```
❶ $ qm create 101 \
❷ --cdrom local:iso/openSUSE-Leap-15.0-DVD-x86_64.iso \
❸ --name opensuse \
❹ --net0 virtio,bridge=vmbr0 \
❺ --bootdisk scsi0 \
❻ --ostype 26 \
❼ --memory 2048 \
❽ --onboot no \
❾ --sockets 1
```

Here, you're defining each aspect of the VM from nine parameters. Set the ID ❶ the disk path to the OS .iso ❷ the VM name ❸ the network ❹ the disk where the virtual image will be stored ❺ the type of OS (Linux) ❻ the amount of memory ❼ whether to start the VM automatically when your workstation host boots ❽ and the number of CPU sockets ❾.

The KVM virt-install Command

If you're using plain KVM on your workstation, the process is similar. To create a VM like the one you created earlier with ***virt-install*** from the command line, issue the following command shown in Listing 2-10.

Listing 2-10. The command to create a KVM virtual machine from the CLI

```
$ ❶ virt-install --name=ubuntu \
❷--vcpus=1 \
❸--memory=2048 \
❹--cdrom=/storage1/ubuntu-18.04.4-server-amd64.iso \
❺--network=bridge:br0 \
❻  disk size=32 \
❼--os-variant=ubuntu18.04
```

Again, you're defining each parameter of the VM. Set the name ❶, the number of CPUs ❷, the memory ❸, the .iso image ❹, the network ❺, the disk size ❻, and the type of OS (Ubuntu) ❼.

I'll go into more detail about these commands later in the book. For now, it's good to know these options exist and get a feel for how they work.

Conclusion

In this chapter, you deployed Proxmox and KVM on a workstation to establish the base of your Linux lab. These resources will be at the center of your work, so take some time to explore these options, spin up a few sample virtual machines, and test network connectivity. With these base systems in place, you're ready to start deploying services in your Linux lab environment.

In the next chapter, you'll deploy a DNS server to provide all your VMs and LXCs with hostnames that can be reached from anywhere on your private lab network. This will streamline how you connect to your systems and mirror the kind of deployments you'll find in the real world.

CHAPTER 3

Set Up a DNS Server

In this chapter, you'll use your newly deployed virtualization environment to create and launch your first meaningful workload: a domain name server (DNS), which can map IP addresses to easy-to-remember names and generally make life easier.

An important component of a DevOps Linux lab is DNS because domains are critical to the way different nodes communicate, including how they make secure connections. Once launched, your DNS server will give your Linux lab a true resolvable domain, like *example.com* or *devops. lab*, you can use with all your virtual machines.

Why It Matters

Setting up a domain on your private network is just as valuable as public domains are on the Internet. It makes it easier to reach your various servers via SSH, HTTP, and myriad other service ports and it enables a variety of services that require domain resolution, not just IP addresses, such as certificate-based connections.

DNS is a core service. You'll keep it running all the time, and you'll regularly edit it as your Linux lab grows. In this chapter, you'll set up the base environment, create a domain name, and add some names and IP addresses, such as *router.devops.lab*, *dns01.devops.lab*, *web01.devops.lab*, or *workstation.devops.lab*.

J. S. Tonello, *Practical Linux DevOps*, https://doi.org/10.1007/978-1-4842-8318-9_3

Planning Your Network

Before sitting down to deploy your DNS server, take a moment to think about the layout of your Linux lab. This will make the process more intuitive, logical, and easier as you grow your environment.

Throughout this book, you'll create several specific servers, including a DNS server, an email server, and a web server. But that's just the beginning. Depending on what you're planning, you could ultimately deploy a dozen or more virtual machines for various workloads. Some of those might include

- A database server

- A Docker container host

- Several Kubernetes hosts

- A DNS slave

- A Chef Infra Server

- A Linux distribution mirror

- A GitLab server

- A WordPress host

- Other non-virtual machines, like Raspberry Pis, workstations, and laptops

As you can see, the number of host machines can add up quickly, so it's important to think about your network and domain layout carefully before diving in. Each of your hosts will have its own static IP address and a DNS name, so it's a good idea to consider logical ways to group everything. For example, you can assign the single-digit IP addresses (10.128.1.2 to 10.128.1.9) to DNS servers, Proxmox hosts, and your Linux mirrors; the 10.128.1.20-29 to web servers; the 10.128.1.30-39 to Raspberry Pis; the 10.128.1.40-49 to laptops, and so on.

Work with the Gear You Have

In Chapter 1, I described the kind of physical networking gear you should use for your Linux lab, and if you're just starting out, the private network might use a retired four-port router you have lying around. If that's the case, you'll initially be limited to only four wired hosts. Adding other hosts would require you to use the router's WiFi capability or add an additional switch.

With that in mind, your Proxmox hosts should definitely each get one of the wired network ports. So should your workstation. That will leave one free port for, say, a spare laptop or a Raspberry Pi. Remember that each physical Proxmox server you run will host many virtual machines, each with its own static IP address and routable hostname, such as *dns01.devops.lab*.

If each Proxmox host has enough CPU, RAM, and storage to host a half-dozen running virtual machines, you'll need six static IP addresses and six unique names for them, but none will require a physical hardware port on your network device. In this way, you can get started with quite a few VMs without much physical network port capacity. If you have two or more Proxmox hosts, you'll need that many more IP addresses and names, but just one physical port on your network switch for each Proxmox host.

Will You Have Multiple Networks (Dual-Homed)?

If you're planning to connect each Proxmox host to your private network and your public network, you'll need to assign static addresses on both networks. That means keeping track of the static IPs you use to keep everything straight and to avoid network conflicts. Assigning the same IP address to two different servers—physical or virtual—is a ticket to chaos. The address will alternately, and randomly, point to one or the other and make life miserable.

As with your private network, you won't need a lot of physical ports on your public network router, but you will need many IP addresses. I assign static IP addresses to the Proxmox hosts and my workstation, but use DHCP on the public network for any dual-homed virtual machines, which are any server with more than one NIC. That way, I don't have to go through the hassle of setting aside static IP addresses on my public network router or a switch for what may likely be short-lived machines.

If you're using a single network to start with, plan to connect your private router physically to your public router, so your private network devices can reach the Internet. This isn't as ideal (or as fast) as having dual-homed Proxmox hosts, but it will enable your machines to download and install packages and allow each host and its guest VMs to have full network connectivity. This helps you avoid needing to set up a web proxy or some other intermediate network configuration.

For now, think about the total number of physical and virtual machines you plan to connect and plan accordingly.

What Domain Name Will You Use?

When setting up your Linux lab, it might be tempting to create a domain like *yourlastname.com* or *mylab.net*. Avoid this temptation. The *.com* and *.net* suffixes conflict with the public Internet naming conventions. In fact, avoid any public domain suffix like *.com*, *.net*, and *.org*. Instead, use something that's not publicly routable, like *test* or *lab*.

Since you won't need a publicly routable domain for your Linux lab traffic (connections from one lab machine to another), it's possible to set up a domain without any traditional suffix at all. The domain might just be *test*, and each physical or virtual host would get a name like *web01.test* or *gitlab.test*. There's nothing wrong with that, but I prefer to create domains that have the same look and feel as public domains, assigning third-level domain names to each host, such as

- web01.devops.lab

- gitlab.devops.lab

- pve01.devops.lab

In this scenario, my domain name is *devops.lab*, which isn't publicly routable, but it is short and easy to key in and remember. The sky's the limit, but decide on a domain that's short and sweet, and stick with it. If you use something like *mycoolsdevopslab.test*, you'll quickly tire of having to type that whole thing every time you set up a fully qualified domain name (FQDN) on a new virtual machine.

Reserving Pools of Addresses for Static and DHCP IP Addresses

Once you decide on your domain name, use the spreadsheet and notes you created in earlier chapters to start mapping those names to IP addresses. You'll want static IP addresses on your private network for all your physical and virtual machines. Take a moment to jot them down now. It's much easier to have this reference later when you set up your DNS server.

For example, a spreadsheet might look like the example in Table 3-1.

Table 3-1. *This is a sample spreadsheet with your IPs and hostnames*

IP	FQDN	System	Physical
10.128.1.1	router.devops.lab	NETGEAR router	x
10.128.1.2	dns01.devops.lab	Ubuntu 22.04	
10.128.1.3	dns02.devops.lab	Ubuntu 22.04	
10.128.1.4	pve01.devops.lab	Proxmox 7.2	x
10.128.1.5	pve02.devops.lab	Proxmox 7.2	x
10.128.1.10	workstation.devops.lab	Linux Mint 20.3	x

In this example, I've reserved the first address in my private
10.128.1.0/24 subnet for the router itself, then two DNS servers, then
two Proxmox hosts, and my workstation. The *System* column helps me
remember the specific type of OS I've installed, and the *Physical* column
indicates whether the host is physical (x) or virtual (blank). Of course, you
can add as many columns of information as you like, but these four are a
good start.

Further down this same spreadsheet are additional addresses, domain
names, and gaps, as shown in Table 3-2 below.

Table 3-2. *A continuation of your IP address and hostname spreadsheet*

IP	FQDN	System	Physical
10.128.1.30	web01.devops.lab	Ubuntu 18.04	x
10.128.1.31	web02.devops.lab	Centos 8	
10.128.1.32			

The gaps show at a glance which addresses are used and which are free, so if you deploy a third web server, you know quickly that 10.128.1.32 is available.

Configure Your Routers and Switches

For your private Linux lab network, you should have a standalone router and a managed or unmanaged switch connected to it. The setup is described in Chapter 1. Refer to that if you need a refresher. The switch attached to your lab router provides additional physical network ports by passing through your private subnet. You can configure most unmanaged switches by merely connecting an empty port on the router to an empty port on the switch.

The same is true for adding a switch to your public network. Simply connect an unused LAN port on one to an unused LAN port on the other, and you'll now have lots more ports to work with.

Add Internet Access to Your Private Network Switch

Connecting two routers together is a little more complicated than adding a switch to a router. Figure 3-1 shows a simple layout, which includes a static IP address on the public (ISP router) to the WAN port on the private router.

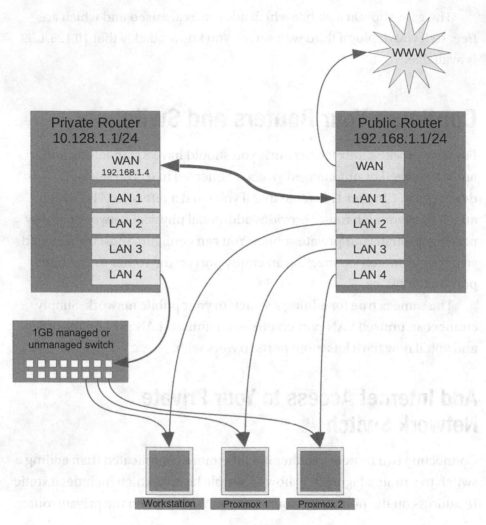

Figure 3-1. *Connecting two routers is fairly straightforward, with a LAN port from the public network router connected to the WAN (Internet) port on the private network router. The static address provides connectivity between the two networks*

Setting up a router's WAN port varies by device, but the premise is to assign a static address from one router to another. In Figure 3-2, you can see that I've given the private `10.128.1.0/24` router a WAN IP address of `192.168.1.4`. Network traffic will pass from the 10-net to the 192-net and on to the Internet through this connection.

Figure 3-2. *The view from a NETGEAR router, used as a switch and DHCP server to the 10.128.1.0/24 network. The WAN address (shown here as Internet IP address) is statically assigned to the 192.168.1.4 address from the public 192-net router*

Technically speaking, this is a double-NATted configuration. Network Address Translation (NAT) routes one network to another, like your home ISP router, which connects all your devices through a single public IP such as `74.22.110.23` via a `192.168.1.0/24` subnet. A double-NATted configuration uses one of those subnet addresses, such as `192.168.1.4`, to route all traffic via another attached subnet, like this `10.128.1.0/24` example. In this case, by assigning a 192.168.1.0/24 address to the 10-net router, you're adding another NAT layer. This can cause some congestion, but it's a solid configuration for your Linux lab, because it allows any assigned 10.128.1.0/24 address to resolve Internet addresses, negating the need to add two network interfaces to every virtual machine.

With any dual-homed physical or virtual machine, each must be set with only a single gateway address. The gateway provides external access to other networks, and for all your systems that need to get to the Internet, this will be the router address. When you set up VMs with a single interface attached to your Linux lab 10.128.1.0/24 subnet, the default gateway address will be 10.128.1.1, as in this example. That gateway moves network traffic from your 10-net to your 192-net, from the LAN to the WAN.

To DHCP or Not to DHCP

When you add a router to your Linux lab environment, it will give you a readily available DHCP server to use, which is handy when deploying new systems. You could instead deploy a DHCP server on a virtual machine in your environment, but the router option is built in, easy to configure, effective, and always on.

Deciding when to take advantage of DHCP on any particular VM is a question of how the system will be used. If you're spinning up something for brief testing, chances are a dynamically assigned IP address is fine, and it will provide connectivity to both your private and public networks. This is particularly useful during an OS installation, when the system looks to download the latest packages. You save a few steps by just letting DHCP do its thing. An available Linux lab network address is assigned on the fly, and the VM has all the network access it needs.

If, however, you're setting up a more permanent system to be a target for, say, DNS or a Linux mirror, you'll need a static IP address. Using your spreadsheet, you can locate the next available free IP address and assign it during the initial setup or use DHCP for initial configuration and then edit the network settings after the first boot.

When you use cloning in Proxmox, which replicates all the settings of an existing virtual machine to create a new machine, it's definitely easier to use DHCP initially. That way, each clone you launch will get its own unique IP address from DHCP when it boots. If you instead clone a VM with a static IP, the clone will have the same address as the original, which results in errors and often breaks networking on the new clone and the original if the source VM is still running. Using DHCP ensures each new clone can be up and running properly alongside the source VM. Otherwise, you'll need to shut off or pause the source machine, wait for the clone to boot, edit its network settings, apply them, and then restart the source machine. Needing to do all of that can really slow you down.

Before you start deploying your DNS server, it's always a good idea to do a sanity check to make sure your workstation and Proxmox hosts can reach the Internet. If basic connectivity doesn't work, you'll be left scratching your head when you go to test your private domain resolution later.

I like to perform four distinct *ping* tests, as shown in Listing 3-1, from my workstation and each Proxmox host.

Listing 3-1. Perform four pings to test your networking

❶ $ ping 10.128.1.1
❷ $ ping 192.168.1.1
❸ $ ping 8.8.8.8
❹ $ ping google.com

First, I ping the private network router ❶ to ensure I can reach the 10-net. Then I ping my public ISP router ❷ to make sure it's resolvable. Next, I ping a public Google name server ❸ and finally a public domain name ❹. Pinging a domain name ensures that each physical machine can resolve external addresses, which is critical for installing software packages. If the results of any of these pings are slow or time out, double-check your configurations. Failures are typically the result of gateway issues. Make sure each machine has a single gateway address and it's assigned to only one network interface.

Deploy a VM to Host Your DNS Server

With basic networking configured, you're now ready to deploy a virtual machine to host your private DNS server. You'll be using *bind* and *named* for the actual server, which are available on any modern Linux distribution. *Bind* is the full package you install for DNS services, and *named* is the daemon bind uses.

Here are the steps you'll follow:

- Create a virtual machine or LXC with one or two network interfaces.

- Install bind.

- Edit the configuration files.

- Configure the primary/master DNS file.

- Set up forward and reverse zones.

For the base OS, I'll use Ubuntu, but these steps apply to AlmaLinux, Debian, openSUSE, or your preferred Linux flavor. Note that if you use openSUSE, it has handy software patterns and the YaST configuration tool, which can make this process less manual.

Using a Proxmox LXC Template

DNS servers don't require much in the way of resources, so using an LXC (Linux container) is a good choice for the base OS. I've found that a running LXC DNS server will use about one-tenth the resources a full VM consumes, so it's ideal for this always-running service.

Start by logging in to your Proxmox dashboard and navigating to the content of your *local (pve)* storage and select Ubuntu from the available templates, as shown in Figure 3-3.

Type	Package	Version	Description
lxc	centos-7-default	20190926	LXC default image for centos 7 (20190926)
lxc	ubuntu-16.04-standard	16.04.5-1	Ubuntu Xenial (standard)
lxc	ubuntu-18.04-standard	18.04.1-1	Ubuntu Bionic (standard)
lxc	debian-11-standard	11.0-1	Debian 11 Bullseye (standard)
lxc	opensuse-15.3-default	20210925	LXC default image for opensuse 15.3 (20210925)
lxc	alpine-3.12-default	20200823	LXC default image for alpine 3.12 (20200823)
lxc	fedora-33-default	20201115	LXC default image for fedora 33 (20201115)
lxc	devuan-3.0-standard	3.0	Devuan 3.0 (standard)
lxc	fedora-34-default	20210427	LXC default image for fedora 34 (20210427)
lxc	rockylinux-8-default	20210929	LXC default image for rockylinux 8 (20210929)
lxc	archlinux-base	202104...	ArchLinux base image.
lxc	gentoo-current-default	20200310	LXC default image for gentoo current (20200310)
lxc	ubuntu-20.04-standard	20.04-1	Ubuntu Focal (standard)
lxc	alpine-3.13-default	20210419	LXC default image for alpine 3.13 (20210419)
lxc	debian-10-standard	10.7-1	Debian 10 Buster (standard)
lxc	ubuntu-21.04-standard	21.04-1	Ubuntu 21.04 Hirsute (standard)

Templates   Search

⊟ Section: turnkeylinux (112 Items)

lxc	turnkey-sitracker	15.1-1	TurnKey siTracker

Download

Figure 3-3. *Download the latest template version of Ubuntu to your local Proxmox machine. This will become the basis of your DNS server*

Install a Base Linux Template

Once the template is downloaded, click the blue **Create CT** button at the top of the Proxmox dashboard and create an LXC with the following parameters:

- *Hostname*: dns01.

- *Template*: The Ubuntu template file you just downloaded.

- *Root disk*: Your default storage location.

- *Cores*: 1.

- *Memory*: 512MB.

- *Network*: Use the default name eth0, your primary bridge vmbr0, IPv4 static IP 10.128.1.2/24, and gateway 10.128.1.1 and uncheck the Firewall box.

- *DNS*: Use host settings or add 10.128.1.2 and 10.128.1.3 so you resolve the server you're about to create and the DNS slave. Also ensure there's a public Internet DNS server, like 8.8.8.8.

Along with these basics, I like to add the existing *SSH public key* from my workstation in addition to a password. This step enables me to log in easily from a terminal without having to manually copy the SSH key later. If you don't already have an SSH key on your workstation, you can generate one with the following command:

```
$ ssh-keygen
```

Accept the defaults and don't set a password when prompted. The resulting keys—id_rsa and id_rsa.pub—are placed in /home/<user>/.ssh (~/.ssh/). From the Proxmox dashboard, browse to that location on your workstation and upload the id_rsa.pub file.

Enable a Second Network Interface

Before starting the LXC, optionally click **Network** and then the **Add** button to give the machine a second network interface on your public network. Name it *eth1* and set the IPv4 address to DHCP, as shown in Figure 3-4. Setting a dynamic IP address (DHCP) for the public network in this way is fine, but feel free to create a static address. Just be sure to add that static address to your ISP router, which is your public network.

Adding a second interface is really only necessary if you **have not** physically connected your Linux lab router to your public ISP router. If you have, you scan skip this step.

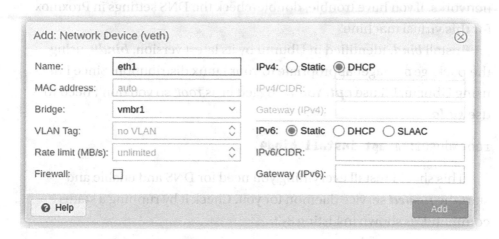

Figure 3-4. *Optionally add a second network interface to your DNS server*

Set Up Bind

Start the LXC and click **Console** to view a terminal via Proxmox. You'll notice that this host will boot up quickly because it's a container, not a full-blown VM. Log in with *root* and the password you entered when you created the LXC. Alternatively, you can use SSH to access your running LXC from a Linux terminal workstation:

```
$ ssh root@10.128.1.2
```

Before proceeding to install **bind**, the package that provides the DNS server, make sure this host can reach your private router and the Internet by issuing the **ping** commands shown previously. This will ensure that you can download packages and your DNS server can properly access your networks. If you have trouble, double-check the DNS settings in Proxmox for this virtual machine.

Install **bind**, identified in Ubuntu by its latest version, **bind9**, using the package manager appropriate to your Linux distribution. Since I'm using Ubuntu, I'll use **apt.** You're logged in as *root,* so you don't need to use **sudo**:

```
root@dns01:~# apt install bind9
```

This should install everything you need for DNS and enable and start the **named** service daemon for you. Check it by running a status command, as shown in Listing 3-2.

Listing 3-2. Run a simple systemctl command to check the status of the named service

```
root@dns01:~# systemctl status named
● named.service - Berkeley Internet Name Domain (DNS)
   Loaded: loaded (/usr/lib/systemd/system/named.service;
   enabled; vendor prese>
```

```
 Active: active (running) since Wed 2022-02-12 11:21:32 EST;
  4 days ago
Process: 3776 ExecStop=/usr/sbin/named.init stop
(code=exited, status=0/SUCCE>
Process: 3782 ExecStart=/usr/sbin/named.init start
(code=exited, status=0/SUC>
Main PID: 3823 (named)
   Tasks: 4 (limit: 4915)
  CGroup: /system.slice/named.service
          └─3823 /usr/sbin/named -t /var/lib/named -u named
--snip--
```

Depending on the operating system or shell settings you're using, some of this output will be in color. Look for *"active (running)"* and ensure there are no errors in the output.

Configure named.conf

You're now ready to start configuring your DNS server. This is most easily done on openSUSE systems using the YaST system configuration tool, but I'll cover the manual process to show you where everything is. In Ubuntu, it's /etc/bind/named.conf, but on openSUSE, the main options file is /etc/named.conf. If you're using a different distribution, the filename and location may be different.

Regardless of which system you're using, the named.conf file, as shown in Listings 3-3 and 3-4, will contain some default information. For example, adding Access Control List (ACL) entries limits access to your DNS server, and options set the directories for various files. To make things more modular, Ubuntu breaks out the options { ... } in a separate /etc/bind/named.conf.options file. Either way will work, but separating out the configurations is cleaner.

Listing 3-3. Working contents of the DNS (bind9) named.conf file on Ubuntu

```
acl trusted {
     10.128.1.0/24;
};
```

Listing 3-4. Working contents of the named.conf.options file on Ubuntu

```
options {
        directory "/var/cache/bind";
        # Allow the DNS server to search other servers
        recursion yes;
        # Allow hosts on 10.128.1.0/24 to use this DNS
        allow-query { trusted; };
        # dns01's private IP address
        listen-on { 10.128.1.2; };
        # Allow transfer to future secondary/slave zone
        allow-transfer { 10.128.1.3; };
        forwarders {
                # Forward requests not found on dns01
                8.8.8.8;
                8.8.4.4;
        };
};
```

Note   Be sure to add all the trailing semicolons (;), both inside and outside the brackets. Leaving any off will render your named.conf file's syntax incorrectly, and your DNS server won't be able to start.

As you can see in the preceding example, I've created an acl called trusted and added the Linux lab subnet 10.128.1.0/24. This *acl* entry ensures any server on the 10.128.1.0/24 subnet can query the DNS server and all other subnets are blocked. This is a good security measure that prevents servers you don't want from accessing your DNS server.

The options entries provide information to the **named** daemon, telling it how to handle and process DNS requests. Enabling *recursion* allows your DNS server to pass along DNS queries it can't resolve to the DNS servers defined in *forwarders*. The named.conf file also identifies the IP address of the server itself (10.128.1.2), which is the address on which it will listen for DNS queries.

The *forwarders* entries in this example are 8.8.8.8 and 8.8.4.4, Google's public DNS servers. Your server will use the Google DNS to resolve any domains outside yours, such as espn.com or launchpad. net. Since this is your DNS *master* or *primary* (as opposed to a *slave or secondary*), *allow-transfer* is set to the IP address of an as-yet-to-be-deployed secondary DNS server. Here, it means the primary server can transfer entries to the slave located at the provided IP address, allowing the slave to respond to DNS queries you define on the primary.

Note   Though *bind* still uses the master/slave naming convention, this is beginning to disappear. In this chapter and elsewhere, master and primary are synonymous when not shown in code examples, as are slave and secondary.

Notice that the *acl* entry of *trusted* is the same as the value in the *allow-query* option in the preceding example. If these don't match, your DNS server will reject query requests from your Linux lab servers.

In openSUSE, your *zone* configurations are included in the main /etc/ named.conf file, but on Ubuntu they're located separately in /etc/bind/ named.conf.local. Regardless of where they're located, these entries, as shown in Listing 3-5, define the domain names and files your DNS server uses to map IP addresses to server names.

Listing 3-5. Configuring zones allows your DNS server to accommodate one or more domains

```
zone "devops.lab" in {
        type master;
        # The path to your domain zone file
        file "/etc/bind/zones/devops.lab.zone";
        # The IP address of the future DNS slave
        allow-transfer { 10.128.1.3; };
};

zone "128.10.in-addr.arpa" {
        type master;
        # 10.128.1.0/24 subnet
        file "/etc/bind/zones/10.128.zone";
        # The IP address of the DNS slave
        allow-transfer { 10.128.1.3; };
};
```

The preceding example defines the *devops.lab* domain, sets this DNS server as type master, and allows transfers to a future DNS slave server at 10.128.1.3. The file entry is relative to the directory entry described earlier, but with the named.conf.options file pointing to /var/cache/ bind (and not /etc/bind), you'll need to provide the full path to your / etc/bind/zones/devops.lab.zone file. The second zone entry—128.10. in-addr.arpa—defines a *reverse* zone. That is, if you query the DNS server by IP address, it will return the *hostname* associated with it. By contrast, a *forward zone* looks up an IP address associated with a *hostname*. Enabling this is useful when you want to probe a network for hostnames that can be used as application variables and the like.

If you want to add other domain names later, you'll need to edit these zone entries to add them and create separate zone files in /etc/bind/ zones, described in the next step.

Check Your DNS Configurations

So far, so good. It's time to check that these basic **bind** configurations are correct before editing your DNS zone files. Execute the following command on your *dns01* host:

```
root@dns01:~# named-checkconf /etc/bind/named.conf
```

The result will be empty if you have no syntax errors in your named. conf file. Typical errors are related to leaving off necessary semicolons.

With a good result, restart **bind9**:

```
root@dns01:~# systemctl restart bind9
```

If you see no result, named restarted successfully, and you're ready for the next step.

Note   On other systems, like openSUSE, the command will be **systemctl restart named**.

Create a Forward Zone File

The forward zone file contains all the information about the hosts on your private network, including their static IP addresses and hostnames. Create your new zone file on Ubuntu by copying the existing db.local file to the directory /etc/bind/zones:

```
$ cd /etc/bind
$ cp db.local ./zones/devops.lab.zone
```

Notice the name of the file and its location match the entry you made in /etc/bind/named.conf earlier.

Edit the new devops.lab.zone file, changing the default local settings to entries that match your DNS layout. The finished file should look something like the sample shown in Listing 3-6.

Listing 3-6. A configured zone file containing your IP addresses and hostnames

```
$TTL    604800
@   IN   SOA   ❶dns01.devops.lab. ❷root.devops.lab. (
                          ❸7             ; Serial
                      604800             ; Refresh
                       86400             ; Retry
                     2419200             ; Expire
                      604800 )           ; Negative Cache TTL

; name servers - NS records  ❹
      IN   NS     dns01.devops.lab.
      IN   NS     dns02.devops.lab.

; 10.128.1.0/24 - A records  ❺
```

```
router.devops.lab.          IN    A       10.128.1.1
;
dns01.devops.lab.           IN    A       10.128.1.2
dns02.devops.lab.           IN    A       10.128.1.3
;
;
;
;
workstation.devops.lab.  IN    A       10.128.1.10
```

In this example, the SOA (Start of Authority) record designates your DNS master's fully qualified domain name ❶ and the same with the admin prefix for the admin email. This equates to "root@devops.lab" ❷. The Serial number ❸ should be incremented each time you add address (A) records. The NS records ❹ list both the master and future slave server names, and the A records ❺ are entered last. Add some sample A record entries, such as your private network router and your workstation. Note the dot (.) at the end of each hostname. It's required when adding fully qualified domain names to this zone file.

Create a Reverse Zone File

You'll follow similar steps to create the *reverse zone* file, starting by copying the db.127 file to 10.128.zone in the zones directory you created earlier. Note that the name matches the subnet of your private network:

```
$ cd /etc/bind
$ cp db.127 ./zones/10.128.zone
```

Edit the file to look something like the example in Listing 3-7.

Listing 3-7. Edit the reverse zone file. Notice it's very similar to the forward zone file

```
$TTL    604800
@   IN   SOA    ❶dns01.devops.lab. ❷root.devops.lab. (
                           ❸7            ; Serial
                       604800           ; Refresh
                        86400           ; Retry
                      2419200           ; Expire
                       604800 )         ; Negative Cache TTL

; name servers - NS records   ❹
      IN     NS     dns01.devops.lab.
      IN     NS     dns02.devops.lab.
; name server resolution
dns01.tiny.lab. IN A 10.128.1.2
dns02.tiny.lab. IN A 10.128.1.3

; PTR Records ❺
1.1   IN   PTR    router.devops.lab.        ; 10.128.1.1
;
3.1   IN   PTR    dns01.devops.lab.         ; 10.128.1.2
4.1   IN   PTR    dns02.devops.lab.         ; 10.128.1.3
;
;
;
10.1  IN   PTR    workstation.devops.lab. ; 10.128.1.10
```

The first part of this file looks much like the *forward zone* file, but instead of A records, this features pointer records (PTR), which identify IP hostnames associated with IP addresses.

The SOA record again designates your DNS master's fully qualified domain name ❶ and the domain with the root prefix for the admin email (root@devops.lab) ❷. The Serial number ❸ should, again, be incremented each time you add PTR records. The NS records ❹ entry lists both the master and future slave server names and A records for name resolution, and the PTR records ❺ are entered last. Add some sample PTR entries, such as your private network router and your workstation. Again, note the dot (.) at the end of each hostname entry. In this example, 3.1, 4.1, and the like indicate the IP address for the host, as in 10.128.1.3 and 10.128.1.4.

PTR records can be confusing. The first number is actually the last number of an IP address, and the number after the dot is the second-to-last number in your subnet, so 1.1 is the PTR entry for 10.128.1.1, and 1.2 is the PTR entry for 10.128.1.2, and so on.

Save and exit the file and run *named-checkconf* to ensure you have no syntax errors in either zone file. It's also best to check the actual zone files for problems by using the *named-checkzone* command:

Check the forward zones with the syntax named-checkzone zone-name zone-file-name:

```
root@dns01:~# named-checkzone devops.lab /etc/bind/zones/
devops.1%MCEPASTEBIN%ab.zone
```

Check reverse zones:

```
root@dns01:~# named-checkzone 128.10.in-addr.arpa /etc/bind/
zones/10.128.zone
```

If these commands return no errors, reload the configuration:

```
root@dns01:~# rndc reload
```

You should get a "Server reload successful" confirmation, and you can test the DNS server with *dig* and *dig -x* commands on the DNS server itself or by pinging one of your new hostname entries from the command line:

```
root@dns01:~# dig workstation.devops.lab
root@dns01:~# dig -x 10.128.1.10
root@dns01:~# ping workstation.devops.lab
```

In order to test your DNS server from your workstation, you'll need to edit your DNS server entries. This can be done using **NetworkManager** or by manually editing /etc/resolv.conf.

If you get a failure, ensure your workstation's /etc/resolv.conf has a nameserver entry for your new *dns01* server (10.128.1.2). The resolv.conf file maps network requests to your DNS servers, which are always written as IP addresses, not domain names, as shown in Listing 3-8. The search entry provides a domain suffix so you can ping *workstation,* and it will resolve to *workstation.devops.lab*:

Listing 3-8. Sample contents of an /etc/resolv.conf file on your Linux workstation

```
--snip--
nameserver 10.128.1.2
nameserver 10.128.1.3
nameserver 8.8.8.8
search devops.lab
--snip--
```

If you try pinging without the domain name and get a failure, add a search entry to /etc/resolv.conf, as shown previously.

On some Ubuntu systems, the /etc/resolv.conf file is really a link to another form of onboard DNS. To disable that, simply delete the original file and create a new one with the contents shown in Listing 3-7:

```
$ sudo rm /etc/resolv.conf
$ sudo vi /etc/resolv.conf
```

Set Up an Optional DNS Slave Server

Any good DevOps environment, whether it's a Linux lab or a full-blown enterprise, has redundancy, so it's a good idea to set up a *DNS slave* server to handle requests in case the master is unreachable. That means if your workstation and VMs can't reach *dns01* at 10.128.1.2, they'll fall back to using *dns02* at 10.128.1.3. Setting up a slave is similar to setting up a master, but much simpler because it gets all its A and PTR record entries from the master automatically.

The steps to create a DNS slave server are as follows:

- Create a second Proxmox template-based host.

- Install **bind9.**

- Edit the **named.conf** configuration files.

Create a Second Host

Follow the previous steps to create another Ubuntu LXC host from a Proxmox LXC template. Name the host *dns02* and give it an IP address of 10.128.1.3/24. Note that this is the same IP address you set up as the allow-transfer host during the master setup. Your master DNS server, at 10.128.1.2, has been pre-authorized to transfer its zone records to *dns02* at 10.128.1.3.

Once the LXC has booted, run updates, and upgrade the system if necessary:

root@dns02: # **apt update**

With the system up to date, install the packages necessary for *bind*:

root@dns02: # **apt install bind9**

As with the master, the configuration settings are located in /etc/ bind/named.conf and /etc/bind/named.conf.options, as shown in Listings 3-9 and 3-10, which you'll set up to look similar to the file on the master. In this case, however, allow-transfer is set to none: because you don't want the DNS slave to send any of its zone file information to another server.

Listing 3-9. The named.conf file on your DNS secondary/slave server

```
acl trusted {
        10.128.1.0/24;
};
```

Listing 3-10. The named.conf.options file on your DNS secondary/ slave server

```
options {
        directory "/var/cache/bind";
        recursion yes;
        allow-recursion { trusted; };
        allow-query { trusted; };
        allow-transfer { none; };

        forwarders {
                10.128.1.2;
                8.8.8.8;
        };
...
};
```

Notice that one of the forwarders is set to the DNS master (10.128.1.2), so it can check that server for entries it doesn't yet have before checking the public Google DNS server.

Set Up the DNS Slave Zone Entries

Next, set up the zone entries (on Ubuntu in /etc/bind/named.conf.
local), which look much like the zone entries on the DNS master.
However, the type is set to slave, and the master is explicitly identified by
IP address, as shown in Listing 3-11. There is no transfer stanza.

Listing 3-11. Zone entries for the dns02.devops.lab DNS
slave server

```
zone "devops.lab" {
    type slave;
    file "/etc/bind/zones/devops.lab.zone";
    masters { 10.128.1.2; };
},

zone "128.10.in-addr.arpa" {
    type slave;
    file "/etc/bind/zones/10.128.zone";
    masters { 10.128.1.2; };
};
```

Ensure you haven't made any syntax errors by using ***named-checkconf***
on each file:

root@dns02:~# **named-checkconf /etc/bind/named.conf**

If everything is good (no output), reload ***bind*** with ***rndc reload***. If you
get a "Server reload successful" response, you've successfully enabled
your DNS slave. There's no need to manually create zone files with A and
PTR records as you did on the master. The DNS slave will gather all that
information automatically from the master itself. That way, when you
make updates to your DNS master, the DNS slave will get all your new
entries.

101

Test Your DNS Slave

Test your new slave by using the **dig** command on one of the fully qualified domain hostnames you configured on the master, such as *workstation. devops.lab*:

root@dns02:~# **dig workstation.devops.lab @10.128.1.3**

Use the @10.128.1.3 to tell **dig** to use your slave server to resolve the host information. Remember, you don't have to create any zone files or zone entries. The slave server will get this information from the master. It's regularly updated to sync its information automatically.

The output should look something like the example in Listing 3-12.

Listing 3-12. The output of a dig command using the slave server

```
; <<>> DiG 9.11.3-1ubuntu1.11-Ubuntu <<>> workstation.devops.
lab @10.128.1.3
;; global options: +cmd
;; Got answer:
;; ->>HEADER<<- opcode: QUERY, status: NOERROR, id: 29780
;; flags: qr aa rd ra; QUERY: 1, ANSWER: 1, AUTHORITY: 2,
ADDITIONAL: 3

;; OPT PSEUDOSECTION:
; EDNS: version: 0, flags:; udp: 4096
; COOKIE:
53b221dd5d0b4bf1da78de985e124493841383d1f103aab4 (good)
;; QUESTION SECTION:
;workstation.devops.lab.        IN      A

;; ANSWER SECTION:
workstation.devops.lab. 604800 IN       A       10.128.1.10
```

```
;; AUTHORITY SECTION:
devops.lab.            604800  IN        NS       dns01.
devops.lab.
devops.lab.            604800  IN        NS       dns02.
devops.lab.

;; ADDITIONAL SECTION:
dns01.devops.lab.      604800  IN        A        10.128.1.3
dns02.devops.lab.      604800  IN        A        10.128.1.4

;; Query time: 0 msec
;; SERVER: 10.128.1.4#53(10.128.1.3)
;; WHEN: Sun Jan 05 20:18:26 UTC 2022
;; MSG SIZE  rcvd: 168
```

The ANSWER SECTION shows the *workstation.devops.lab* A record IP address of 10.128.1.10, and the ADDITIONAL SECTION shows your master and slave DNS servers.

Test the reverse by running the ***dig -x*** command:

root@dns02:~# **dig -x 10.128.1.10 @10.128.1.3**

This should return the name of the host at 10.128.1.10, which is *workstation.devops.lab*.

Be sure to add your master and slave DNS IP addresses (10.128.1.2 and 10.128.1.3) to your /etc/resolv.conf file (or network settings) on all future VMs and physical hosts you create (including your workstation). That will enable them to resolve your private domain addresses via your DNS servers.

Graphical DNS Deployments and Management

In addition to setting up DNS manually via the command line and editing the various named.conf files, you can instead use **Webmin**, or if you're using openSUSE, you can take advantage of the **YaST** configuration tool.

The Webmin DNS module, shown in Figure 3-5, enables you to deploy **bind** and configure your DNS master and slave servers quickly. It's also a good way to check your configurations. Details on how to install and use Webmin for your particular platform are explained later in this book and are available at www.webmin.com/deb.html.

Figure 3-5. *The Webmin dashboard view of the BIND DNS Server configuration. It allows you to manage all aspects of bind and named, including creating master and slave zones*

When installing DNS on openSUSE using the pattern *dhcp_dns_server*, it installs all the packages you need for **bind** and **named** and gives you what's known as a TUI (text-based user interface) YaST *dns-server* tool, as shown in Figure 3-6. This tool manages all the files and entries you created manually and is a good way to edit your configurations.

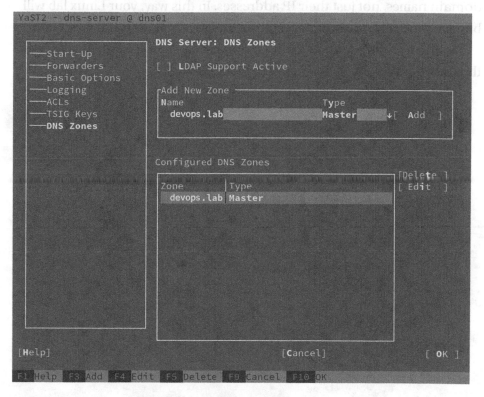

Figure 3-6. *The YaST DNS management tool in openSUSE. This tool can simplify DNS setup and adding hostnames*

Try these options to learn more about how DNS configurations can be tweaked and expanded to suit your needs. What you deployed in this chapter is fine for everything else in this book, but **bind** and **named** have many more features than discussed here.

Conclusion

You now have solid DNS master and redundant slave servers running in your Linux lab environment! This capability will dramatically simplify how you use your Linux lab by enabling you to reach all your servers by their domain names, not just their IP addresses. In this way, your Linux lab will behave much like the broader Internet and save you time and frustration.

In the next chapter, you'll put DNS to use by setting up an email server that takes advantage of hostname and MX records.

CHAPTER 4

Setting Up an Email Server

In the age of cloud-based services like Gmail, Office 365, and Yahoo, it's easy to forget that not long ago people ran and maintained their own email servers. Although the public cloud offerings are robust and widely used, having your own internal mail services is useful for sending and receiving log notifications, integrating with chat or software development tools, or just communicating in a lab environment.

In this chapter, you'll install two open source email tools: *Postfix* and *Dovecot*. Together they will enable you to send and receive email to and from any machine in your lab network. Postfix provides the sending mechanism used by the *Simple Mail Transfer Protocol (SMTP)*. Dovecot provides IMAP and POP3 capabilities for receiving email. IMAP allows a local email client to receive messages and also save them on a remote server. POP3 pulls email from the server so that messages are stored only on the local mail client machine. Of the two, IMAP has become the standard for email. Having copies of your email both locally and on a remote server means you can simultaneously access all your email from multiple devices, whether they're separate PCs, smartphones, or web-based email tools like RainLoop. In this chapter, you'll deploy IMAP, but feel free to experiment with POP3. If you want to be able to view email offline or if bandwidth is a concern, POP3 might be a good choice.

© John S. Tonello 2022
J. S. Tonello, *Practical Linux DevOps*, https://doi.org/10.1007/978-1-4842-8318-9_4

In addition to setting up an email server on a virtual machine in your lab, you'll create the same configuration in a containerized environment using Docker. This way, you'll gain a better understanding of how Postfix and Dovecot work and learn different ways to deploy and use those tools. You'll also set up a virtual machine to serve as a Docker host. The Docker setup will give you a taste of how modern applications are built and deployed, separating out individual services that can be updated and maintained on their own. This means faster deployments that are easy to scale because they are described in code, automating the steps.

Finally, you'll set up the Evolution open source email client to work with your new email server. And because you have a working domain name server (created in Chapter 3), you'll update your DNS entries to make everything function properly.

Set Up a DNS Server to Handle Email

DNS provides a specific MX record type for managing email, which serves as a domain-wide pointer for the mail server host. When sending mail, the remote *mail transfer agent (MTA)* queries the MX record for the domain and receives back the hostname (or hostnames) of your mail server and attempts to make an SMTP connection. If a successful connection is made, the remote email server sends the email, and you receive it in your inbox.

An email server can work without an MX record if you're just using IP addresses for everything, but since you're actively using DNS, adding this capability to your lab is useful. You're essentially setting up your lab in the way enterprises would, planning and locking in your configurations to provide stability and versatility.

Adding an MX record to your DNS configuration is straightforward, but like other DNS entries, it has a specific format. Before setting up your email server, edit your DNS configuration to add both an **MX** record and an **A** record for the virtual machine that will become the mail server. (You added this record in the previous chapter, but let's take a closer look at it.)

Log in to your *dns01.devops.lab* server and edit the forward address record, located at */etc/bind/zones/devops.lab.zone*. Below the `NS records` entry, you should add a line that looks like this:

```
devops.lab.     IN      MX      0 mail.devops.lab.
```

This line identifies the mail server's domain (`devops.lab`), record type (MX), priority (0), and hostname (`mail.devops.lab`), which is the server that will answer MX requests. Although it's counterintuitive, 0 represents the highest priority and tells the server to check *mail.devops.lab* before any other email server. With a single email host, this priority number can be any integer, typically less than 50. If you have two mail servers and give the first one a priority of 10 and the second a priority of 20, 10 would be the higher priority and respond first.

To set up email load-balancing, with two servers receiving mail, add a second MX record with the same priority as the first and point the second MX record to a different A record host, which would look like something like this:

```
devops.lab.  IN    MX    10    mail1.devops.lab.
devops.lab   IN    MX    10    mail2.devops.lab.
```

As with your other VM hosts, the mail server's hostname can be whatever you want, such as *email.devops.lab* or *orange.devops.lab*. Naming it *mail* is an easy-to-remember convention.

You may have noticed the MX record does not contain an IP address, which means network requests from other hosts on your network won't be able to find the mail server host just by designating it in an MX record, so you also need to add an A record in the same DNS forward zone file:

```
mail.devops.lab.        IN    A    10.128.1.5
```

The trailing dot after each domain name in these examples is necessary for proper name resolution. These additions designate mail. devops.lab as the definitive email server for your domain and forward any requests to the host at 10.128.1.5. If you set up two email servers, each needs its own A record.

Note   Having static IP addresses rather than random addresses handed out by a DHCP server is advantageous because DHCP addresses can (and do) change, which means you never really know where the server is on your network. With email, that means your email client configurations would change all the time, which simply isn't practical.

Before exiting the forward zone file, increment the serial entry by either adding +1 to the existing number or setting it to the current year, month, day, and hour (2022120100). This entry is typically at the top of your zone files:

```
$TTL 2d
@       IN SOA    dns01.devops.lab. jadams.devops.lab. (
                          2022040100        ; serial
                          3h                ; refresh
                          1h                ; retry
                          1w                ; expiry
                          1d )              ; minimum
--snip--
```

Save the file and edit the reverse zone file, which is */etc/bind/zones/10.128.zone*, in this example.

You won't add an MX record to the reverse zone file, but add a **PTR** record so the mail server host VM is configured the same way as all your other lab hosts, providing a reverse zone record for the email host:

```
5.1             IN    A       mail.devops.lab.
```

The 5.1 indicates the IP address for the host, which is *10.128.1.5*, the IP address you'll assign to your email server.

Increment the serial number at the top of the file, save it, and then run the following to apply your new DNS rules:

```
$ sudo rndc reload
```

Even though your mail server isn't set up or running, test DNS resolution first for the server itself:

```
$ ping -c 5 mail.devops.lab
PING mail.devops.lab (10.128.1.5) 56(84) bytes of data.
--snip--
```

The *ping* output should show that the DNS server is configured properly to direct requests to the server located at 10.128.1.5.

Checking for the MX record with *dig* should return something like the following:

```
$ dig devops.lab MX
--snip--
;; ANSWER SECTION:
mail.devops.lab.          172800 IN    MX    0 mail.devops.lab.

--snip--
```

The *dig* command should return the proper hostname and priority of your mail server. In fact, the ANSWER SECTION from the *dig* should look very much like the entry you made in your DNS zone file.

Install Postfix and Dovecot

Postfix and Dovecot are widely available on most flavors of Linux. For this example, you'll install both packages on an Ubuntu virtual machine that will become your email server. Postfix and Dovecot are lightweight enough to run alongside other applications on an existing server, but having a standalone email server helps with debugging and ensures that other application configurations don't present conflicts.

Create a new Ubuntu VM as described in Chapter 2. Provide it with a unique ID, a name (such as *mail.devops.lab*), 32GB of storage, at least one CPU, at least 1,024MB of RAM, and DNS servers set to 10.128.1.3 and 10.128.1.4 (your *devops.lab* name servers). When the VM finishes building, start it, and log in from the console.

Restart the VM to ensure the updated settings are applied, and then *ping* the mail server's IP address to test that its network settings are working.

Next, **ssh** in to the *mail.devops.lab* host:

```
$ ssh root@mail.devops.lab
```

Update your package repositories, upgrade the system to the latest, and reboot for good measure:

```
$ sudo apt update && sudo apt upgrade -y
```

You'll configure Postfix to use existing Linux system users for active email accounts so you don't have to maintain a list of authorized email users separately. Any user account on the machine will have permission to send and receive email. The username and password you set when creating the new system user will be the credentials you'll use later when setting up your Evolution (or other) email client.

To add additional users, enter the following command:

```
$ sudo adduser jadams
```

You'll be prompted to provide a password and other information. Under Ubuntu, the ***adduser*** command automatically creates a */home* directory for the user and sets the shell to *Bash*, the system default.

If you're using a different version of Linux, you may need to use the ***useradd -m <username>*** command to create the user and then set the password for that user with the ***passwd*** command:

```
$ sudo useradd -m <username>
$ sudo passwd <username>
```

System users need to have a home directory, which is the default location where Dovecot stores a user's mail. Double-check that the mail server system's */home* directory exists to ensure your user directory (or directories) has been created:

```
$ ls /home/
jadams
```

Since your user's */home* directory is where Dovecot will store email folders and mail, that directory should be owned (and writable) by that distinct user. Check that with the ls command:

```
$ ls -la /home
total 16
drwxr-xr-x  4 root     root     4096 Mar 23 21:11 .
drwxr-xr-x 24 root     root     4096 Mar 18 14:12 ..
drwxr-xr-x  2 jadams   jadams   4096 Mar 23 21:11 jadams
```

This output shows that the */home* folder itself—and the / above it—is owned by root, but */home/jadams* is owned by the *jadams* user, which is as it should be.

If the user's home directory is not owned by the username itself (*jadams* in the preceding example), correct it with the following command:

```
$ sudo chown jadams:jadams /home/jadams -R
```

The **chown** command with the **-R** flag makes this change on the directory recursive.

Dovecot is flexible, and you can configure it to use different email locations or other mail-related customizations. The steps described so far have followed the basic defaults. If you want to experiment with these settings, look at the configuration file: */etc/dovecot/dovecot.conf*.

Install Postfix

Postfix is a mail transfer agent (MTA) and works to send email, most commonly as SMTP. It's widely used both for standalone email servers and as a relay to move mail traffic from external servers. In this example, you'll set up a standalone server.

At its heart, Postfix sends email, but it has evolved to become a sophisticated and secure tool that can, for example, block unauthorized access that could turn your innocent mail server into a spam relay, or legitimately relay email to another server, including gmail.com or an Exchange server. Despite its powerful capabilities, it remains lightweight and doesn't need tons of CPU, RAM, or system resources, particularly for your lab environment using basic *Internet Site* functionality.

With your apt repos up to date, install Postfix:

```
$ sudo apt install postfix
```

If the latest **postfix** package is already installed, run the **dpkg-reconfigure** command to step through the default settings screens:

```
$ sudo dpkg-reconfigure postfix
```

During installation, you'll be asked a number of questions that hint at the underlying capabilities of Postfix, which you can explore in detail at `www.postfix.org/`. For our purposes, choose the following default settings when prompted:

- *General type of mail configuration*: Internet Site.

- *System mail name*: devops.lab.

- For the root mail recipient, set the username you added earlier.

- For other destinations to accept mail, leave the defaults (mail.localdomain, localhost.localdomain, and localhost).

- Force synchronous updates on mail queue? No.

- *Local networks*: In addition to the default localhost IP range, add an entry for your lab network, which is 10.128.1.0/24 in this example, to ensure that hosts on the lab network can reach the mail server and that it can answer. This also prevents other networks from accessing it.

- *Mailbox size limit*: 0 (no limit).

- *Local address extension character*: + (the default).

- *Internet protocols to use*: You can choose all, IPv6, or IPv4.

After you respond to the final question, Postfix stores its configuration information in */etc/postfix/main.cf*, which you can edit manually at any point. If you do edit it, be sure to reload Postfix with ***service reload postfix*** to ensure that the server picks up your changes.

Install Dovecot

You're now ready to install Dovecot to provide IMAP and POP3 email services, which are responsible for delivering email, either locally or to a remote email client like Evolution. Postfix is only the sending half of what you need for complete email services. Dovecot gives you the receiving half. In a production setting, you might separately install Postfix on some servers and reserve others for running Dovecot, where actual email is stored. The Postfix servers would handle all the responsibilities of sending email for your entire domain, and the Dovecot servers would receive and store all incoming, outgoing, draft, and trashed email messages for your users.

You need three packages to install Dovecot on Ubuntu with both IMAP and POP3 capability:

```
$ sudo apt install dovecot-core dovecot-imapd dovecot-pop3d
```

You shouldn't need to alter the configuration defaults for basic operation.

When the Dovecot installation completes, restart Postfix:

```
$ sudo systemctl restart postfix
```

Ensure that Postfix and Dovecot are running without errors:

```
$ systemctl status dovecot
$ systemctl status postfix
```

Each of these commands should output a screenful of information. Check that the services are running without errors.

Both halves of your email server are now configured and running. Postfix should be listening for connections on port 25 for outgoing email it should relay, and Dovecot should be listening on port 143 for incoming mail messages. To confirm, use the *lsof* command that checks for listening ports:

```
$ sudo lsof -i -P -n | grep LISTEN
sshd      1108    root   3u   IPv4   30818   0t0   TCP *:22 (LISTEN)
master    1426    root   4u   IPv4   30820   0t0   TCP *:25 (LISTEN)
dovecot   1922    root   4u   IPv4   56361   0t0   TCP *:143 (LISTEN)
--snip--
```

This output shows that the ***ssh***, ***master*** (Postfix), and ***imap*** (Dovecot) services are listening and lists their respective ports, **22**, **25**, and **143**. It also indicates that the system is ready to receive connections and is properly configured for email.

This configuration uses the default ports for non-encrypted SMTP and IMAP. If you're using a more secure setup, the ports would be different. For example, Transport Layer Security (TLS) uses port 587, and Secure Sockets Layer (SSL) uses port 465. Similarly, a secure, encrypted Dovecot setup would use port 993 instead of 143. I don't cover TLS and SSL configurations here, but consider exploring them on your own. On a LAN-only lab setup like this one, there's no need for encryption, but even private Internet-facing services should use encrypted ports. It can be tricky, so unencrypted ports are a good way to get started.

Mail Server Security Considerations

Whenever you set up an email server, you're opening yourself up to some serious security hazards, so it's important to keep a few things in mind as you go along. Remember, too, that you don't have to be too worried since your lab environment is isolated from the broader Internet, but it's important to think about these things.

First of all, you'll notice that Postfix and Dovecot were set up with their default email ports, 25 and 143, respectively. There's nothing wrong with these for a lab environment, but in a production setting, you'll likely use more secure ports as mentioned previously. During the base configuration, Dovecot actually defaults to using port 993 (SSL/TLS IMAP) and employs self-signed certificates to handle the secure connections. In a production environment, you'd use signed certificates attached to your public domain name.

When you created the virtual machine to host your `mail.devops.lab` server, you could optionally have disabled firewall filtering at the Proxmox level. You can also use a tool like `ufw`, the Uncomplicated Firewall, to set up firewall rules on the server itself. It's a good habit to get into. If your server's ports are wide open, it makes it easy to connect email clients in a lab environment. In production, the downside is that it makes it easy to connect email clients. The Web is full of bots and hackers hungry to exploit wide-open servers, so locking down ports with a software or hardware firewall is important along with setting up your servers to only allow traffic from certain domains or IP address ranges.

A final consideration is the power of the Sendmail tool described in the next section. It makes it really, really easy to send spoofed email messages. For example, adding a `From:` option to something like `jadams@foobar.com` will make the email appear to have come from a domain you don't control or own. If bad actors get access to your email server, they can do the same thing.

Remember, too, that your lab email server (configured as described so far) is not Internet *routable*. That means it can't send and receive email from outside your lab. If you try to use it to send email to, say, `someuser@gmail.com`, it will fail. The caveat, though, is that your mail server can be set up to relay email legitimately, so it's always best to deploy only the services you know you need and only where you need them. Some applications will deploy some form of mail server as part of their setups. Be conscious of those potential security holes and ensure you don't have "rogue" email servers in your cluster.

Initial Email Service Test

Before setting up a full-fledged email client in the next step, lets test the capabilities of your mail server with a simple command-line application called **Sendmail**.

Sendmail is a lightweight tool that allows you to send email from a terminal shell. In this case, you're using the shell of the email server itself, so log in to mail.devops.lab via SSH as one of your system users—such as jadams@mail.devops.lab—for these steps.

Install Sendmail

The Sendmail package is often installed automatically on many Linux systems, but run the which command to see if it exists on yours.

```
$ which sendmail
/usr/sbin/sendmail
```

The preceding is what's returned on an Ubuntu system, but it may differ on yours. The /usr/sbin directory may not be in your system path, so to invoke it, use the full path to send email in the following examples.

If Sendmail isn't already installed, install it:

```
$ sudo apt install sendmail
```

Since Sendmail is a command-line tool, it's not very intuitive. It doesn't offer obvious screen prompts, and to actually send your email, you have to type **CTRL + d** at the end of your message.

Install mailutils

While Sendmail takes care of actually sending email, you won't be able to see or read them without the command-line application *mailutils*. It provides an interface for system email and will even alert you when you have new messages.

Install it with the following:

```
$ sudo apt install mailutils
```

Unlike Sendmail, *mailutils* actually installs several components to keep track of mail on the system. Check out the documentation for all the features:

```
$ man mailutils
```

Whenever you send email on this system, *mailutils* will keep track of it. Even when you later use a graphical mail client, you can always see your email via the command-line interface.

Test Sending and Receiving Mail

With *Sendmail* and *mailutils* installed, you're ready to give your email server a try. Start by invoking /usr/sbin/sendmail followed by the target email address. In this case, you're sending it from jadams@devops.lab to jadams@devops.lab:

```
$ /usr/sbin/sendmail jadams@devops.lab
```

To give the email a subject line, start the email with Subject: followed by whatever you want it to be. You can then add the body of the email after that and type CTRL + d to send the email, as shown in Figure 4-1. There are other options you can include, such as To: to send to a different user or From: to make your email appear to be coming from a different user and domain altogether.

```
jadams@mail:~$ /usr/sbin/sendmail jadams@devops.lab
Subject: This is the email subject
This is the content of my email message.█
```

Figure 4-1. *A sample email message, with subject, using Sendmail*

Once the email is sent, check your user's email inbox by invoking the mail application from the command line:

```
$ mail
```

If everything worked correctly, you should see your email in the main mail list. To view an item, type the number next to it. To delete it, enter "*delete #*", as in "delete 1".

If you don't see your email, something went wrong, and you'll likely get a mail delivery error, which you can use to debug your server. Type exit to quit the application at any time, and be sure to check out the man page to see all the available options—including how to use mail to both send and receive local email:

```
$ man mail
```

Set Up an Email Client to Use the Email Server

Your mail.devops.lab server is up and running, so you can now start using it with Evolution, the freely available email client that's preinstalled on many Linux distributions. Evolution is a full-featured, modern, cross-platform email client that's easy and intuitive to use. Another popular Linux email application is Thunderbird. Both email clients provide email folder views, HTML email, signatures, and most functions you'd expect in a graphical email tool. Your email server is robust enough to use any number of email clients, so if you have a preferred application, feel free to try it, but we'll use Evolution here.

If Evolution isn't already on your Ubuntu workstation system, enter the following to install it:

```
$ sudo apt install evolution
```

When you start Evolution the first time, it prompts you to set up an email account and asks you for the proper credentials (Figure 4-2). If you're already using Thunderbird or another desktop mail client with a public email setup, just create a new account there with your lab mail credentials.

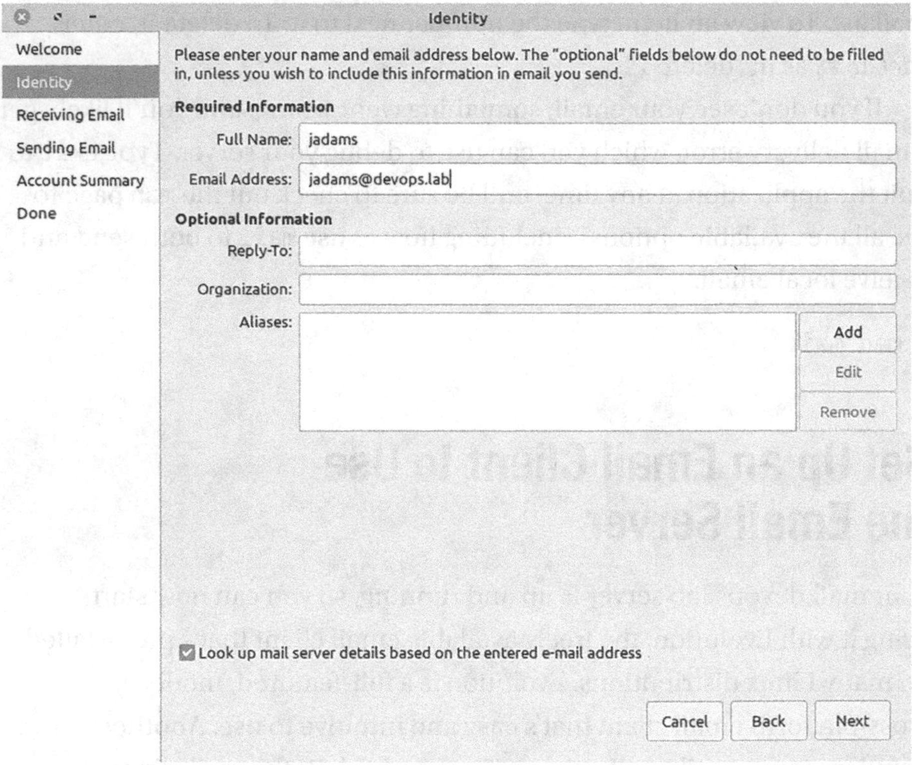

Figure 4-2. The email account setup screen in Evolution

The email address uses the username you entered when creating the Ubuntu VM and the MX record name of your email server. In this example, the email address for that user is jadams@devops.lab. DNS knows to forward mail requests to mail.devops.lab. Without the MX record, you'd need to use the full hostname, which is jadams@mail.devops.lab in this example.

When you add this basic information during account setup, Evolution locates and populates the email server settings automatically. It's using the MX record and automatically trying some common configurations so you don't have to set up everything manually, which is nice. By default, your email connection uses STARTTLS, which Evolution should automatically discover along with the ports you're using, 25 and 143 (and maybe 993). If Evolution doesn't find those settings by default, be sure to add them under *Receiving Email* and *Sending Email*.

When the account is added, try to get messages or send an email. You should be prompted to approve a certificate. When you installed Postfix and Dovecot, a self-signed certificate was created. Since it's self-signed, it provides only a minimum level of security; it's fine for your lab, but don't use it in production. If you have a signed certificate, you could replace the self-signed one to harden your email server. I won't go into that here, but the process is well documented by various certificate providers, including Let's Encrypt.

Save the certificates permanently and then try to get messages or send an email again. You should see a new email appear in your *Inbox* and *Sent* mail folders.

If you have difficulty, particularly when you're adding the SMTP and IMAP servers to your email account, double-check your DNS entry and make sure you're using the password you set for your Ubuntu user on the mail server itself. Remember, the username is just the account name— *jadams* in this example—not the email address.

Install Postfix and Dovecot in a Docker Container

As you can see, installing mail services is fairly straightforward. In the previous example of installing Postfix and Dovecot in a virtual machine, the installation steps configured everything necessary to run mail services, including adding SSL keys to handle encryption. Again, in a production environment, you would replace those self-signed certificate keys and make a number of other modifications to harden your setup.

For the purposes of your lab, though, let's deploy the same email services in a Docker container by creating a Docker host, installing *docker.io* and *docker-compose*, creating a *docker-compose.yml* and *Dockerfile*, and running the mail host from there.

By going through these containerization steps, you can see a side-by-side comparison of how traditional and modern applications are deployed. Today, software development often happens in containers, which are small, self-contained, highly portable services that are easy to replicate and scale up. For example, instead of creating a new VM for each new Postfix host you want, you can create new containers from a few files and guarantee the same configuration is deployed anywhere you need it. This flexibility, speed, and portability make containers very popular indeed.

The open source Docker container runtime package (not the enterprise version) is called *docker.io* or *docker-ce* in many Linux distros. It is the engine that allows you to build and run Docker containers, and *docker-compose* is a separate application that runs on top of Docker. It allows you to define your container services in simple *docker-compose.yml* files and extend their build-time specifications in associated *Dockerfiles*. With *docker-compose*, you can easily build Docker images, which can then be used to run containers that contain your services.

Before deploying a Docker version of your mail server, start by shutting down the *mail.devops.lab* VM server you just created so there aren't any conflicts with the Docker one you're about to create. Having conflicting mail servers can cause a lot of headaches, and this simple step helps you avoid them.

Since you're creating a second email server, you'll need to set up DNS to know about it. There are several ways to do that, including reusing your existing MX record as is (with *mail.devops.lab*), modifying that existing record, or adding a new MX record altogether. In this example, you'll modify the existing zone record, replacing the MX entry with one for your Docker host, which is *10.128.1.6* in this example. Remember, the MX record is a domain-wide setting.

Edit your forward and reverse zone files, replacing *mail.devops.lab* with *docker.devops.lab* in your MX record entry and adding an A record for the Docker host itself. In this example, that would look like this:

```
--snip--
devops.lab.          IN MX          0 docker.devops.lab.

--snip--

docker.devops.lab.  IN A          10.128.1.6
```

Be sure to increment the `serial` values and run ***rndc reload*** after you've made these changes to ensure your new DNS settings are applied. Test the updates by pinging *docker.devops.lab*. It should resolve to *10.128.1.6* in this example.

The ***dig*** command should show the hostname for the new server:

```
$ dig devops.lab MX
--snip--
;; ANSWER SECTION:
devops.lab.  2048   IN    MX      0 docker.devops.lab.

--snip--
```

In the next few steps, you'll be building and configuring two Docker containers, one for Postfix and one for Dovecot, but I won't go into a lot of detail about Docker itself. What you should know is that containers are much smaller than full virtual machines. They make use of the underlying operating system's kernel and other resources, which live outside the container, and provide only the services you need for an application running inside the container.

When creating a container, you generally build it to run just a single service. This makes each container easy to recreate, and it also makes it easy to manage application components separately. This will become more obvious as you work through the following example and the slightly more complex example in Chapter 5.

You'll be setting up a new Linux VM as your Docker host, but you can learn how to install Docker on other platforms by reading the documentation available at *https://docs.docker.com*. I like to use a separate VM for Docker—at least initially—because the installation adds networking and other configurations that can be confusing. It's also safer to run Docker on a separate machine if you fear messing up your workstation.

For the Docker host, create another Ubuntu clone (or VM created from scratch), giving it a unique IP address of *10.128.1.6* to match the DNS entry you made, and update the */etc/hosts* and */etc/hostname* files if you manually added the entry on your workstation. Update the system and reboot before proceeding.

While the system is rebooting, double-check the changes you made to your DNS server. The name and IP don't have to match my example, but they should match what you set up for your own lab's Docker server.

Docker provides a script for installing Docker and ***docker-compose***, but this example uses the packages available in Ubuntu itself. Feel free to experiment with the scripted version, available from the Docker website.

Enter the following to install the Docker runtime and ***docker-compose***:

```
$ sudo apt install docker.io docker-compose
```

Once this installation is complete, add your username to the *docker* group so you can run Docker commands as a regular user; be sure to use the username you assigned when creating the VM. This simple action means you don't need to type ***sudo*** before every Docker command:

```
$ sudo usermod -aG docker jadams
```

Log out and back in to ensure this configuration has been applied, and run a simple ***docker ps*** command to list running containers:

```
$ docker ps
```

Of course, you don't have any yet, so you won't see any results, but if it runs properly without errors, you know that you have permission as a regular user to run Docker commands.

Building a Docker container with ***docker-compose*** requires at least a *docker-compose.yml* file, but you'll also use *Dockerfiles*. These tell Docker exactly how to build a container image, including the Linux OS on which to build everything. For example, even though your Docker host is running Ubuntu, the container could run Alpine, Fedora, or any number of other base Linux OS images.

Since the container build process is entirely hands-off, you need to provide details about each component of the email server build, including things that were automatic when you built your email server in a virtual machine. This is the heart of containerized application deployments. You define what you want, and your application services are built the same way every time. I'll explain these as we go.

Log in to your Docker host, create a folder called *mailserver*, use cd to move into it, and create a file named *docker-compose.yml*. Add the following content to the file:

Note   This is written in YAML, so each indented line uses two spaces, not tabs, to make the proper spacing.

```
version: '2.1'
services:  ❶
  postfix:
    restart: always
    hostname: mail.devops.lab
    build: ./postfix  ❷
    container_name: postfix
    ports:
      - "25:25"  ❸
    volumes:  ❹
      - 'mail:/var/mail'
      - 'home:/home'
      - 'postfix-certs:/etc/ssl'
  dovecot:
    restart: always
    hostname: mail.devops.lab
    depends_on:
      - postfix
    build: ./dovecot  ❷
    container_name: dovecot
    ports:
      - "143:143"  ❸
    volumes:  x
      - "mail:/var/mail"
      - "home:/home"
      - "dovecot-certs:/etc/dovecot/private"
volumes:  ❹
```

```
mail:
home:
postfix-certs:
dovecot-certs:
```

The file begins with the services: entry and the services called postfix and dovecot ❶. All the indented parameters below postfix and dovecot pertain to each service. The build: ❷ commands tell **docker-compose** to build the container images based on the files in the **postfix** and **dovecot** subdirectories. The ports: ❸ entries tell the containers to expose ports 25 and 143, respectively, mapping the container's ports 25 and 143 to the host's ports 25 and 143. These are the incoming and outgoing ports needed for Postfix and Dovecot to be reachable by any system attempting to connect to your **docker.devops.lab** host. When you deployed these applications in your VM, these ports were automatically made available, but containers are truly isolated from the host system and don't inherit those settings. You must define them explicitly.

Finally, **docker-compose** is told to create four persistent volumes: ❹, which will retain data even after the container is stopped or restarted. Without persistent volumes, the user's mail and mail folders would disappear after each container stop, and the system certificates would change, requiring an email client like Evolution to request new authorization each time the container starts.

The final volumes: entry—given the same indentation as services:— provides names for the persistent volumes used in the postfix and dovecot services ❹. Without them, the container builds will fail. By adding the same volumes in each container, the containers share access to data in those directories, which simplifies how those two services work together.

Save the *docker-compose.yml* file, and create a new folder within your *mailserver* directory called *postfix*. In that folder, create a new file called *Dockerfile*, and add the following contents:

```
FROM ubuntu:20.04

# Create a system user, a trusted network and other variables
ENV MYUSER jadams ❶
ENV MYPASS mypassword ❷
ENV TRUSTED_NETWORK 10.128.1.0/24 ❸
ENV HOSTNAME devops.lab ❹
ENV DEBIAN_FRONTEND noninteractive

# Install the debconf utilities, and in copy the pre-
configured files
RUN apt update && apt install -y debconf-utils openssl ❺

RUN useradd -rm -d /home/${MYUSER} -s /bin/bash \
        -p "$(openssl passwd -1 ${MYPASS})" ${MYUSER}

WORKDIR /usr/src/app ❻
COPY postfix-debconf ./

RUN sed -i "s|TRUSTED_NETWORK|${TRUSTED_NETWORK}|g" postfix-
debconf ❼
RUN sed -i "s|HOSTNAME|${HOSTNAME}|g" postfix-debconf

RUN debconf-set-selections postfix-debconf ❽

# Install Postfix ❾
RUN apt install -y postfix

EXPOSE 25

CMD [ "/usr/sbin/postfix","start-fg"] ❿
```

130

The file begins with the base OS Docker image, which is likely the same version of Ubuntu you used for your *mail.devops.lab* virtual machine. The FROM tells **docker-compose** to download and use that specific image version of Ubuntu. Since you're using Ubuntu, all the commands that follow will be specific to that distribution, such as using **apt** to install packages. If you were using Fedora, for example, those package commands would use **yum**.

The *Dockerfile* then sets five environmental variables that hold values you can pass to the containerized application and scripts running inside it. The MYUSER ❶ and MYPASS ❷ variables create a user with that password inside the running container. Set those to anything that suits your needs. Note that this is **not** secure at all because your credentials are exposed. There are ways around this with Docker secrets, which would make for a good side project to do on your own. For now, this exposed way of doing things makes the process a little clearer and easier to follow.

The TRUSTED_NETWORK ❸ variable is defined here and will be later copied to the *postfix-debconf* configuration file, allowing any server on the *10.128.1.0/24* subnet to access your email server. This is a security measure that prevents any system not on your network from using your system to send and receive email. If you leave it off, machines on your lab network won't be able to connect.

The HOSTNAME ❹ variable sets the name of the mail server, again allowing remote connections to work properly. In this example, reuse the same *hostname* you used in the VM example, *docker.devops.lab*. It will properly resolve to the Docker host because of the previous DNS edits you made.

The first RUN ❺ command tells **docker-compose** to update the Ubuntu repository information on the system and install **debconf-utils** and **openssl**. The first is a utility that allows you to import configuration data for Postfix (instead of entering that information interactively like you did with your VM example), and **openssl** will be used in the next RUN statement to create an encrypted password for your user. The next RUN statements create an *Inbox* folder a *Sent* folder, and set the proper permissions on a newly created user *mail* directory.

The WORKDIR ❻ directive sets an optional directory inside the container to store your configuration files. When the *postfix-debconf* file is copied into the container, it is copied from the *postfix* directory on your workstation into the container's */user/src/app* directory. This is a handy way to have files you need populated inside the container, including test scripts, *.tar* files, and configuration files.

The next step runs two *sed* commands ❼ to replace plain-text placeholder terms in *postfix-debconf* (TRUSTED_NETWORK and HOSTNAME) with the environment variables 10.128.1.0/24 and devops.lab. Once that change is made, *debconf-set-selections* is run on *postfix-debconf* to import the values ❽. With all the preconfiguration done, the next RUN command installs Postfix and Dovecot, just as you did on your VM ❾.

The EXPOSE line is technically redundant since you already defined port 25 in your *docker-compose.yml* file, but it won't hurt to leave this line as a reminder of the port needed to access SMTP remotely. In this example, the Docker host is passing along requests on ports 25 and later 143 to the running containers listening on those ports.

Finally, the *Dockerfile* instructs *docker-compose* to execute the command to start Postfix in the foreground.

Now, create a new file in your *postfix* folder named *postfix-debconf*. This will import the necessary Postfix settings so you won't need to enter them manually (as you did in the VM installation) or edit configuration files inside the container. I created the following example with *debconf*, a utility that shows you the system configurations for various applications installed on your system. If you install *debconf* on your VM email server and run *debconf-get-selections > postfix-debconf*, the contents of the outputted file will include settings for various applications, including Postfix. You'll need to edit out everything not related to Postfix to use the information for your Postfix container, and feel free to experiment on your own, but my following example is all set to use.

Add the following to the *postfix-debconf* file:

```
debconf      postfix/destinations      string HOSTNAME,
mail, localhost.devops.lab, , localhost
debconf      postfix/newaliases    boolean    false
debconf      postfix/relayhost     string
# Install postfix despite an unsupported kernel?
debconf      postfix/kernel_version_warning    boolean
debconf      postfix/sqlite_warning     boolean
debconf      postfix/retry_upgrade_warning      boolean
# Set this variable to match your network
debconf      postfix/mynetworks     string    127.0.0.0/8
[::ffff:127.0.0.0]/104      [::1]/128 TRUSTED_NETWORK
debconf      postfix/lmtp retired warning      boolean    true
debconf      postfix/rfc1035_violation    boolean    false
debconf      postfix/compat_conversion_warning   boolean  true
debconf      postfix/procmail     boolean    false
debconf      postfix/recipient_delim    string    +
debconf      postfix/mailname    string    devops.lab
debconf      postfix/main_cf_conversion_
warning    boolean    true
debconf      postfix/tlsmgr_upgrade_warning    boolean
debconf      postfix/chattr     boolean    false
debconf      postfix/dynamicmaps_conversion_warning    boolean
debconf      postfix/root_address    string
debconf      postfix/mailbox_limit    string    0
debconf      postfix/protocols    select    ipv4
debconf      postfix/main_mailer_
type    select    Internet Site
debconf      postfix/mydomain_warning    boolean
debconf      postfix/relay_restrictions_warning    boolean    #
```

The highlighted terms, HOSTNAME and TRUSTED_NETWORK, will be automatically replaced when the Docker image is built with the environment values you defined in the *Dockerfile*. This is a handy way to update variables without needing to edit multiple files to do it.

This takes care of the Postfix container. You've added all the necessary components to build and configure the service. Be sure to edit the MYUSER, MYPASS, and other ENV variables to suit your needs if you're not using the default values shown in my *Dockerfile* example.

This is just half of your mail server, so it's time to create the Dovecot service container. It will also set a username and password—matching the ones you set in the Postfix Dockerfile—so it will install ***openssl*** as part of that process before creating the appropriate email directories and installing the Dovecot packages.

Create a new *Dockerfile* in a new *dovecot* subfolder and add the following:

```
FROM ubuntu:20.04

# Create a system user
ENV MYUSER jadams
ENV MYPASS mypassword
ENV DOCKER_HOST 10.128.1.6
ENV DEBIAN_FRONTEND noninteractive

# Install openssl
RUN apt update && apt install -y openssl

RUN useradd -rm -d /home/${MYUSER} -s /bin/bash \
     -p "$(openssl passwd -1 ${MYPASS})" ${MYUSER}

RUN mkdir -p /home/${MYUSER}/mail/INBOX && \    ❶
     touch /home/${MYUSER}/mail/Sent && \
     chown ${MYUSER}:${MYUSER} /home/${MYUSER}/mail -R
```

```
# Install Dovecot
RUN apt install -y dovecot-core dovecot-imapd dovecot-pop3d ❷

EXPOSE 143

CMD [ "/usr/sbin/dovecot","-F"] ❸
```

This second *Dockerfile* begins much like the Postfix one, but then goes on to create folders inside the container that Dovecot needs to store email and sets the proper permissions ❶. This should look familiar from the VM version you installed. The *Dockerfile* then tells **docker-compose** to install the necessary Dovecot packages ❷ and start the service in the foreground ❸.

Note   Services can't be *daemonized* in a Docker container. If they are, the container will just keep restarting. That's why these containers run the applications in the foreground. This isn't true for LXCs, which behave much more like VMs and can start and run without any explicit daemon in the foreground.

To recap what's happening here, you're first defining services in a *docker-compose.yml* file and then creating *Dockerfiles* to set the base OS for the two containers, installing the necessary applications to run Postfix and Dovecot, configuring environment variables, and executing commands inside the running containers to start the mail server services via the final CMD ❿.

As you can see, you've had to define everything you want (and nothing you don't). The resulting containers will be small compared to your earlier VM, and though they're separate, they will communicate and share everything they need to provide your email services.

You're now ready to build the Docker images you've defined and run the containers. Navigate to the *mailserver* directory if you're not already there (running the pwd command in the terminal shows you your present working directory) and run

```
$ docker-compose up -d
```

That's it! This will first build the Docker images and then launch containers based on those images. You'll see output from the shell showing **docker-compose** going through the build steps, including downloading the Ubuntu image used in each container, running **apt** updates, and the rest of your commands. When it completes, it will release the console (the **-d** flag tells **docker-compose** to start the containers in the background and leave them running).

Issue the **docker ps** command to confirm your containers are running:

```
$ docker ps
CONTAINER ID    IMAGE                COMMAND
CREATED         STATUS          PORTS                    NAMES
a71e3f2c7599    mailserver_dovecot   "/usr/sbin/dovecot -F"
5 hours ago     Up 5 seconds    0.0.0.0:143->143/tcp    postfix
2b39252097d1    mailserver_postfix   "/usr/sbin/postfix s..."
5 hours ago     Up 23 minutes   0.0.0.0:25->25/tcp      postfix
```

The headers in the preceding sample output carry over to two lines in this example, but they show that the container called *dovecot* is running from an image named *mailserver_dovecot* with port *143* open. It also created a container named *postfix* running from an image named *mailserver_postfix* with port *25* open. As you can see, **docker-compose** automatically created Docker images named after the directory root where the container files are located.

If you want to see just how small these containers are, run ***docker ps -s*** to add the size to the preceding output. In my example, the *dovecot* container is just 110MB, and the *postfix* container is 168MB. Although relatively small, they contain everything needed to run your mail services.

With the email server containers running, go back to Evolution on your workstation and add a new email account, this time using the username and password you set in the *Dockerfile* and an email address that's *<username>@devops.lab*. Accept and save the certificate credentials, and you're ready to start emailing!

Conclusion

In this chapter, you successfully deployed a local email server as a virtual machine and in Docker containers. You can now use that email system for any other server in your lab that needs email capabilities.

In the next chapter, you'll follow similar steps to set up a LAMP server using Linux, the Apache web server, the MySQL/MariaDB database server, and the PHP scripting language. With this configured, you'll be able to create any number of websites, including a MediaWiki or WordPress site for documentation or database-driven web applications. You'll also learn how to deploy the RainLoop webmail application, which uses a LAMP stack to provide a browser-based interface that takes advantage of your new email server.

CHAPTER 5

Building a LAMP Stack: Apache and PHP

A LAMP stack is the combination of Linux with Apache, MariaDB or MySQL, and PHP, that provides a robust, versatile platform for creating websites and web applications. It's a perfect addition to your Linux lab because it can become the foundation for a wide variety of freely available and custom software tools.

In this chapter, you'll begin building a LAMP stack by installing and configuring Apache to serve up two unique websites from a single server. As part of that process, you'll install PHP and deploy the PHP-based RainLoop webmail application to work with the mail server you set up in the last chapter. Finally, you'll containerize your deployment with Docker to demonstrate how individual services work together for faster, repeatable coding. In the next chapter, you'll install MariaDB (or MySQL) to complete the stack.

© John S. Tonello 2022
J. S. Tonello, *Practical Linux DevOps*, https://doi.org/10.1007/978-1-4842-8318-9_5

Why LAMP?

Apache, formally known as the Apache HTTP Server, is free, open source, cross-platform web server software that powers more than 65% of all websites. When combined with the PHP programming language, MariaDB, and Linux, it's the basis of popular content management platforms like WordPress, Drupal, and Joomla, shopping cart applications like OpenCart, as well as management tools like Webmin and Adminer. Apache is stable and well documented, and has been tested and run for decades, which means if you need help, you'll easily find useful online examples, tutorials, and tips.

PHP has evolved to become a reliable Apache companion, providing not just a versatile environment for custom applications but also a robust framework for interacting with *application programming interfaces (APIs)*. Many popular third-party applications, from the Spotify music platform to Facebook to Weather Underground, rely on it. These and many other APIs allow you to use a LAMP server to incorporate remote data and manipulate third-party services in your own custom applications.

Configure a Web Server VM and Install the Packages

Start your web server deployment by creating a new Ubuntu virtual machine in Proxmox, either from scratch or by cloning an existing server, as explained in Chapter 2. Give the server at least 16GB of storage, 2GB of RAM, and a static IP address on your private network. Since the *docker. devops.lab* host you created in Chapter 4 has the address of 10.128.1.6, give this server the address of 10.128.1.7. You could assign any IP address in your lab subnet (10.128.1.0/24) pool, but to keep things simple, use the next unused IP address.

It's worth noting that Proxmox offers pre-built templates that will provide you with a full LAMP stack (and other stacks) in one step. Feel free to try those if you like, but for this chapter and the next, you'll deploy a server from scratch to see how all the moving parts fit together.

Update Your DNS Settings to Add Websites

As with other steps in this book, you'll start by updating your DNS server entries so you can resolve each website in the following examples with real domain names, not just IP addresses. While your new VM is deploying, log in to your DNS server and add a new *A record* entry for this server, as described in Chapter 3. Enter the hostname and IP address in both the forward and reverse zone files. Also add a CNAME entry named myserver that points to *web.devops.lab*:

```
--snip--
web             IN A         10.128.1.7
myserver      IN CNAME      web
--snip--
```

In the preceding example, the fully qualified domain names (FQDNs) are shortened to their bare minimums, web and myserver, without a trailing dot. These are valid entries when DNS is handling a single domain. The myserver CNAME entry acts as an alias for the web A record entry. Both addresses—*web.devops.lab* and *myserver.devops.lab*—will resolve to the host with the same *10.128.1.7* address.

Although both DNS names resolve to the same physical host, Apache will treat them as separate destinations, allowing you to create two distinct websites on the same server. You can use this technique to create as many websites as you want on a single physical or virtual server.

Note   Don't forget to increment the `serial` number in each DNS zone file before saving and running `rndc reload` to apply your DNS edits. If you make changes to your DNS entries but don't increment the serial number, your changes won't take effect.

With each DNS change, perform a ***ping*** or a ***dig*** from your workstation to test the DNS entry:

```
$ ping web.devops.lab
$ dig web.devops.lab
$ dig myserver.devops.lab
```

The output of the dig commands should look something like this:

```
; <<>> DiG 9.11.2 <<>> myserver.devops.lab
;; global options: +cmd
;; Got answer:
;; ->>HEADER<<- opcode: QUERY, status: NOERROR, id: 42360
;; flags: qr aa rd ra; QUERY: 1, ANSWER: 2, AUTHORITY: 1,
ADDITIONAL: 2

;; OPT PSEUDOSECTION:
; EDNS: version: 0, flags:; udp: 4096
; COOKIE:
b5755587306b17e9d136aed85e8480a10761b848f40f5f41 (good)
;; QUESTION SECTION:
;myserver.devops.lab.          IN    A

;; ANSWER SECTION:
myserver.devops.lab.    172800   IN    CNAME   web.devops.lab.
web.devops.lab.         172800   IN    A       10.128.1.7
--snip--
```

The output contains a lot of information, but the last two lines show the answer to the "question" you asked—what you entered after your *dig* command—the correct entries in your DNS zone file.

With your *web.devops.lab* host VM up and running and DNS set, you're ready to install the base packages for your web server.

Install the Core LAMP Packages

Setting up a LAMP stack requires more than just the Apache base application; you also need to install modules that enable Apache to understand PHP and communicate with MariaDB databases. These modules allow your web server to run PHP files that interpret and compile the code when a page is requested. In addition, you'll install packages that will make your web server ready to run RainLoop webmail later.

Install the following Apache and PHP packages on Ubuntu 22.04:

```
$ sudo apt update && sudo apt install apache2 \
  php8.1 libapache2-mod-php8.1 php8.1-common \
  php8.1-curl php8.1-xml php8.1-mysql php-date \
  php8.1-fpm php8.1-json php8.1-cli
```

Note   Ubuntu 22.04 uses 8.1, but older Ubuntu 20.04 uses 7.4, and Ubuntu 18.04 uses 7.2.

Two packages worth noting are *libapache2-mod-php8.1* and *php8.1-mysql*. The *libapache2-mod-php8.1* package provides the PHP module for *apache2*, which enables the server to understand and manipulate *.php* files (and files with other extensions you want to properly parse PHP). Without this module, your web server would just show *.php* files as plain text. The *php8.1-mysql* package provides the module that allows PHP and MariaDB (or MySQL) to speak to each other. This module is necessary when building PHP applications that you want to read from and write to your databases.

When the package installation is complete, Apache starts automatically and will be running with two important directories in play: */var/www/ html*, which is the default root directory for your files, and */etc/apache2/*, which contains the default web server configuration files. The main configuration file is */etc/apache2/apache2.conf*, and it defines everything from the log files it should create to how many simultaneous requests it should handle, to site-level file permissions. You can configure these settings to suit different needs, but keep the defaults for now.

Create Two Web Server Directories

As mentioned previously, a single Apache instance can serve up content from two or more distinct domain names. To see how this works, you'll create two websites and, therefore, two website directories: one at the default directory location and another in a new directory where you'll store files to run a simple application.

Before leaving the shell, create a new directory under */var/www/* called *myserver* and change its ownership to the *www-data* Apache user, preceding each command with **sudo** to provide the necessary root privileges:

```
$ sudo mkdir /var/www/myserver
$ sudo chown www-data:www-data /var/www/myserver
```

This new directory will be home to the documents for your second website.

To test your web server, open a browser and visit the domain name you provided, which in this example is http://web.devops.lab. If it works as expected, you've successfully revised your DNS entries, your network configurations are correct, port 80 is open on your web server, and Apache is properly configured. It might seem like a small thing, but it can be gratifying to see that welcome page.

Note   Ports 80 and 443 are the defaults for web servers. When you created the SMTP server in Chapter 4, it used port 25.

Now point your browser to http://myserver.devops.lab to test the CNAME you created. This is a little less exciting because it shows you the same welcome page you just saw. With a few Apache modifications, however, you can quickly define two completely independent websites on the same host.

Define Two Different Websites in Apache

To create the two separate websites, you'll edit the Apache parameters in */etc/apache2/apache2.conf* and add separate site configuration files in the */etc/apache2/sites-available* directory. In essence, the *apache2.conf* file sets server-wide configuration values for Apache. Those settings aren't the same as firewall rules that generally open or close specific ports on your server. This file is where you set your website permissions, such as which files can be served up and which other remote machines can access them. The named files in */etc/apache2/sites-available* control parameters for specific websites, including the directories where their files are stored.

Since you'll be running two sites, *web* and *myserver*, open */etc/apache2/apache2.conf* and find the default directive that looks like this:

```
--snip--
<Directory /var/www/>
        Options Indexes FollowSymLinks ❶
        AllowOverride None ❷
```

```
    Require all granted ❸
</Directory>
--snip--
```

The Indexes and FollowSymLinks directives ❶ in this configuration file tell Apache to allow your server to return a directory listing if a file like *index.html* or *index.php* isn't present and that it's okay to follow *symlinks* (also known as soft links) to other locations on the server. You can test this by renaming the file */var/www/html/index.html* to */var/www/html/index* and see what happens when you access http://web.devops.lab. You'll get a directory listing because the option Indexes is included in the preceding configuration.

The AllowOverride None ❷ directive tells Apache not to process any directives it finds in an external *.htaccess* file, which can be placed in the root of the web server directory or any of its subdirectories. Using *.htaccess* files is a handy way to change how a site performs, but doing so also makes it easy for users to break things, like setting rules that override your security. That's one of the reasons it's set to None by default. If you set that directive to AllowOverride All or provide specific entries for the site, such as requiring authorization, those *.htaccess* directives will be processed by the web server first, superseding directives in *apache2.conf*.

The Require all granted ❸ directive tells Apache to allow HTTP requests from servers on *any* domain name. You can change this directive to Require host devops.lab to limit this to only your Linux lab domain.

Acceptable names for default index files are specified in the module configuration file */etc/apache2/mods-available/dir.conf*, which includes *index.html* and *index.htm*. By default, the listing looks like this::

```
<IfModule mod_dir.c>
    DirectoryIndex index.html index.cgi \
        index.pl index.php index.xhtml index.htm
</IfModule>
```

Modify it to look like this, with index.php first:

```
<IfModule mod_dir.c>
    DirectoryIndex index.php index.html index.cgi \
    index.pl index.xhtml index.htm
</IfModule>
```

When you installed the PHP and XML modules earlier, the *index.php*, *index.cgi*, and *index.xhtml* files were added to the default index file list automatically. That means if any file matching one of those names is found in the website's root directory, it will be shown without needing to be added explicitly to the URL (like http://web.devops.lab/index.php).

Your server will follow the order of the filenames listed in the *dir. conf* file and load the first one it finds that matches, so if you have both an *index.html* file and an *index.php* file in the same directory, the server will load *index.html* and ignore *index.php* if *index.html* is listed first in DirectoryIndex. If you change the order and place *index.php* before *index. html* in *dir.conf*, the server will load the *index.php* file by default. Make sure the PHP file is listed first. Otherwise, if both an *index.html* and *index. php* file are placed in the same web directory, visiting a site like http://web. devops.lab will load the *index.html* file, not *index.php*. If you're running a PHP application, that means the default URL will serve up the plain *index. html* file, not the *index.php* file that includes all your scripting. The file listing order matters.

Finalize Settings for the First Website

By default, the */etc/apache2/apache2.conf* entries apply to all sites located in directories below */var/www*, including */var/www/html*, the default location of the website's files, and any other sites you create in that directory tree. If you want different directives for your *myserver* website, such as redirecting certain URLs, loading additional server modules, or denying access to specific files, this is the file where you should add those entries. See *https://httpd.apache.org/docs/2.4/sections.html* for more information on Apache's options.

Note   The <Directory> entries in *apache2.conf* apply their enclosed directives server-wide, with the directory path identifying the system path to the location of the web server's root, which is */var/www/* by default. Since this *apache2.conf* file is responsible for the permissions that apply to all of your websites, it can contain separate entries for each of them.

Adding an additional site-specific directive for *myserver.devops.lab* in */etc/apache2/apache2.conf* might look like this:

```
--snip--
<Directory /var/www/> ❶
        Options Indexes FollowSymLinks
        AllowOverride None
        Require all granted
</Directory>

<Directory /var/www/myserver> ❷
        AllowOverride All
</Directory>
--snip--
```

The first entry ❶ remains unchanged and applies to all websites located under */var/www*, which now includes *html* and *myserver*. The second entry ❷ contains a single directive, `AllowOverride All`, which allows that site to read server settings from *.htaccess* files, which can override entries in */etc/apache2/apache2.conf*. Even though the `Options` and `Require` directives from the first entry aren't explicitly defined in the second entry, they still apply to the *myserver.devops.lab* site because its document root directory is under */var/www/*. The only difference is that the `<Directory /var/www/myserver>` entry overrides the `AllowOverride` directive in the `<Directory /var/www/>` entry, which enables the *myserver* site to parse *.htaccess* files.

Configure Apache to Serve Up the Website Properly

The next step maps your server settings (the website name and file locations), so when the web server receives a request for a certain domain name, Apache recognizes it and serves up the files located in the `DocumentRoot` you set up earlier.

Save your *apache2.conf* file, and then find the default website configuration file, *000-default.conf*, in the */etc/apache2/sites-available* folder, which you should edit to look like the example below, changing (or uncommenting) `ServerName www.example.com` to `ServerName web.devops.lab`. The document root is often defaulted to `/var/www/html`, but not always:

```
<VirtualHost *:80>
--snip--
        ServerName web.devops.lab
        ServerAdmin webmaster@localhost
        DocumentRoot /var/www/html
```

```
    ErrorLog ${APACHE_LOG_DIR}/error.log
    CustomLog ${APACHE_LOG_DIR}/access.log combined
--snip--
</VirtualHost>
```

This file sets the ServerName for your primary website, */var/www/ html*, as your DocumentRoot, log paths, and other parameters. The parameters you apply here set the rules for all web pages for the website you define by ServerName. Since the ServerName variable isn't initially defined by default in *000-default.conf*, uncomment that line and insert your default server's hostname, which is *web.devops.lab* in this example.

The *000-default.conf* file begins and ends with <VirtualHost> tags. Each Apache website, even the default, is set up as a virtual host using those tags. This setting provides versatility and allows you to create as many virtual hosts (different websites) as you want on the same server. You could create one to listen on port 80 and another to listen on port 8080, one to have a document root at */var/www/html,* and one at */var/www/ myserver* or customize each directive as you see fit.

Leave the rest of this file as is and save it. In the next step, this file will become a template for your second site. Each website you create on a single Apache web server has its own *.conf* file, often given a name to match the website itself, such as *myserver.conf* or even *myserver.devops. lab.conf.*

Create and Enable the Second Website

When you configured Apache for the first website, *web.devops.lab* is enabled by default, and if you look in the */etc/apache2/sites-enabled* directory with *ls -l*, you'll see a linked file named *000-default.conf* that points back to the */etc/apache2/sites-available* file:

```
# ls -l /etc/apache2/sites-enabled
```

```
total
lrwxrwxrwx 1 root root 35 Apr  1 00:33 000-default.conf -> ../
sites-available/000-default.conf
```

Its presence in the *sites-enabled* directory means that site is both available and activated.

To create the second site's configuration file, **cd** to */etc/apache2/sites-available* and copy *000-default.conf* to a new file called *myserver.conf* in that same directory. Edit the new myserver.conf file to look like this:

```
<VirtualHost *:80> ❶
        ServerName myserver.devops.lab ❷
        ServerAdmin webmaster@localhost
        DocumentRoot /var/www/myserver ❸
        ErrorLog ${APACHE_LOG_DIR}/error.log
        CustomLog ${APACHE_LOG_DIR}/access.log combined
</VirtualHost>
```

This example sets the server name to *myserver.devops.lab* ❷ and locates the DocumentRoot at */var/www/myserver* ❸. This site also uses the default port 80 ❶, which means Apache will serve up files from */var/www/myserver* when it receives a request for http://myserver.devops.lab. Apache listens for requests, and when it receives a ServerName request (the URL for your website), it checks the enabled site configuration files for a match and returns pages found in the DocumentRoot directory for the VirtualHost you define. Requests for http://web.devops.lab will be served separately, from */var/www/html*.

To give your second website something to present to visitors, enter the following to output a simple line of text to a new *index.html* file:

```
$ echo "This is myserver.devops.lab." | sudo tee /var/www/
myserver/index.html
```

```
$ sudo chown www-data:www-data /var/www/myserver -R
```

This places an *index.html* file in the */var/www/myserver* directory and changes the ownership (***chown***) of that file's user and group to *www-data*, providing the server a page to load for testing purposes and giving the default Apache user and group permission to access it.

Before you can see this simple *index.html* file from your browser, you need to enable the *myserver* site. Apache includes tools that make it easy to enable sites (and modules). Run **a2ensite <config-filename>** and then reload the Apache configuration to apply the changes:

```
$ sudo a2ensite myserver
$ sudo systemctl reload apache2
```

If you don't see any errors, you're ready to test your two websites. Open a browser and point it to http://web.devops.lab. You'll see the Apache2 Ubuntu default page telling you the site is up and running, just as before. Now point your browser to http://myserver.devops.lab. It should show the contents of your simple i*ndex.html* file: "This is myserver.devops.lab."

Note   The different domain names are important, which is why you set them up in DNS. They provide information Apache can use to direct web requests. Both websites are listening for requests on the web server's HTTP port 80, but the domain names tell Apache to use a different directory for each site's content. If you point your browser to your web server's IP address, you'll see the default site *only* and would have no way to access the *myserver* site. Give it a try at *http://10.128.1.7.*

You now know how to create any number of distinct websites on a single web server, which is much simpler (and more efficient) than needing different physical or virtual hosts for each site you want to build.

On your own, do some experimenting with your *myserver.conf* file; try changing the default port from 80 to 8080 and add `Listen 8080` to */etc/apache2/ports.conf*. With those edits, you could use the IP address (`http://10.128.1.7:8080`) to view your *myserver* site (and from the domain name at `http://myserver.devops.lab:8080`). Using different ports is a common way of routing traffic to a web server. For example, your Proxmox server uses port 8006 instead of 80, which is why you access the dashboard at `http://<server-name-or-ip>:8006`.

Take a Snapshot to Preserve Your Configuration

With your web server up and running and properly configured with two unique websites, take a Proxmox snapshot of the host before proceeding. Snapshots make a copy of the system as-is and allow you to roll back to that state at any time. If you mess something up later, you can always roll back to this pristine state of your *web.devops.lab* server.

To take a snapshot, go to the Proxmox dashboard, click the server in the VM list, and, in the right-hand panel, click **Snapshots ➤ Take Snapshot**. Give it a name and description—I like to add a date to my snapshot names and enough information to remind me what exactly I did up to that point—and apply. Proxmox takes a little time to create the snapshot, and you can monitor the progress as it does its thing. Proxmox will say "TASK OK" when it's done, and the snapshot will remain available so you can roll back to it. Taking snapshots is a lot faster than recreating VMs from scratch.

Use PHP with Your Website

Now that you have the snapshot as a backup, let's start working with PHP to create and use scripted software applications, including RainLoop webmail. You'll first test your PHP to make sure it's installed and configured properly to serve up any number of PHP scripts.

During the initial web server installation, you added modules for PHP and MariaDB (MySQL), so you don't need to install anything else to make your server handle *.php* files properly. The PHP module was enabled automatically when you installed it, so if you list the contents of */etc/apache2/mods-enabled*, you'll see *php8.1.conf* and *php8.1.load* in the output.

Test the PHP Installation

The next step is to test that PHP is working and configured correctly. Create a *test.php* file in */var/www/html* that contains the phpinfo() command:

```
$ sudo vi /var/www/html/test.php
<?php
     phpinfo();
?>
```

This simple phpinfo() command is interpreted and compiled at load time, and it shows your web server's details (including system information and installed modules) when you visit it at http://web.devops.lab/ test.php.

When you access that page, you'll see the lilac and gray tables that phpinfo() generates. Scroll through the page to review the various settings. You'll find configuration information, system variables, and a wide range of data about the server and the PHP module itself. This is a good place to start troubleshooting if you run into any problems.

If for some reason *test.php* doesn't load properly, use the ***a2enmod***
command (short for *Apache2 enable module*) to ensure that the PHP
module is enabled:

```
$ sudo a2enmod php8.1
Enabling module php8.1.
To activate the new configuration, you also need to run:
  systemctl restart apache2
```

The ***a2enmod*** command is similar to the ***a2ensite*** command you used
earlier to enable your *myserver* website. Apache site configurations that
aren't enabled won't work, and those sites and site capabilities (like PHP)
won't be available until you run the ***a2enmod*** command and reload (or
restart) Apache.

When the ***a2enmod*** command finishes, it reminds you to reload
apache2 by entering the following:

```
$ sudo systemctl restart apache2
```

If this command is successful, it won't provide any output, but you can
confirm Apache is running with the `status` command:

```
$ systemctl status apache2
● apache2.service - The Apache HTTP Server
   Loaded: loaded (/lib/systemd/system/apache2.service;
enabled; vendor preset:
  Drop-In: /lib/systemd/system/apache2.service.d
           └─apache2-systemd.conf
   Active: active (running) since Wed 2022-04-20 16:00:07 UTC;
   3min 27s ago
  Process: 25672 ExecStop=/usr/sbin/apachectl stop
(code=exited, status=0/SUCCES
  Process: 12611 ExecReload=/usr/sbin/apachectl graceful
(code=exited, status=0/
```

```
 Process: 25677 ExecStart=/usr/sbin/apachectl start
 (code=exited, status=0/SUCC
Main PID: 25705 (apache2)
   Tasks: 10 (limit: 4659)
-- snip --
```

Here you can see that the service is running, that it was stopped, gracefully reloaded, and started.

Note   Be sure to reload or restart ***apache2*** whenever you make changes to your web server configuration.

With PHP enabled, you can start creating and deploying web-based applications, such as RainLoop. Apache now can interpret PHP code, compile it when a *.php* file is requested, and return content appropriately. This is the heart of creating dynamic web pages that can return database content, execute functions that trigger actions based on user input, and much more. Of course, PHP isn't your only choice. You can enable Apache to recognize many programming languages, including Perl, Python, and Ruby, and, as you'll see in the next chapter, many external tools and databases like MariaDB.

Note   It's considered good form to not leave a file like test.php hanging around in the website directory of a production server. The phpinfo() command gives detailed insight into your web server, making it easy for hackers to exploit it.

Install RainLoop Webmail

With your web server set up with Apache and PHP, you're ready to install a web-based application to demonstrate its advanced capabilities. Specifically, you'll install the community edition of RainLoop, a browser-based email client you can use to connect to the Postfix and Dovecot mail server you created in Chapter 4.

The RainLoop Email Client   RainLoop is one of several available webmail programs, and it's a good tool for your Linux lab because it has an array of features and capabilities that are easy to understand and use, particularly if you're familiar with tools like Gmail. It provides all typical email functions from a web browser, such as sending and receiving email and creating folders for storing messages. The RainLoop community edition is freely available at www. rainloop.net/repository/webmail/rainloop-community-latest.zip.

Set Up RainLoop

To install RainLoop, log in to *web.devops.lab* via the terminal shell and use *wget* to download the RainLoop *.zip* file, but first install *unzip* so you can uncompress it:

```
$ sudo apt install unzip
$ wget https://www.rainloop.net/repository/webmail/rainloop-
community-latest.zip
$ sudo unzip rainloop-community-latest.zip -d /var/www/html/
```

Running the *unzip* command with the *-d* flag lets you tell unzip to uncompress RainLoop to a target directory (saving you some steps), in this case extracting into the document root of your default website directory located at */var/www/html/*. Unlike installing a binary (such as a *.exe* or *.rpm* or *.deb* package), the RainLoop application is really just a folder full of *.php* and configuration files. By unzipping it, you're moving the files to a specific directory in the root of your website.

Set RainLoop Permissions

For RainLoop to work properly, set the permissions for the directories and files it needs. Its directories must be publicly executable, and its files must be publicly readable.

Run the following commands inside the */var/www/html* directory to look for directories and files and change their permissions:

```
$ cd /var/www/html
$ sudo find . -type d -exec chmod 755 {} \;
$ sudo find . -type f -exec chmod 644 {} \;
$ sudo chown -R www-data:www-data .
```

The *find* command is used with the *-type* flag, applying different read, write, and execute properties to directories (-*d*) and files (-*f*) appropriately. The *chown* command changes the ownership of the files and directories to the *www-data* system user, the default for Apache on Ubuntu. This may be different on other Linux distros. For example, on Red Hat-based systems, the user is *apache*.

Configure RainLoop via the Admin Panel

With the basics in place, you can finish the mail server configuration with the RainLoop web-based admin panel. When it installs, RainLoop automatically creates the folders and files it needs, using Apache and PHP to serve up the application. If you installed it according to the previous instructions, open a browser and go to http://web.devops.lab/?admin. Use the default credentials *admin/12345* to log in.

Change the default *admin* password via the Security menu. Next, click **Domains** to set up RainLoop to work with your mail server, as shown in Figure 5-1. You'll need two settings (see Chapter 4 for an email refresher): one for sending email (Postfix) and one for receiving email (Dovecot). For the mail server target, use either your *mail.devops.lab* VM or *docker. devops.lab* containerized setup. Be sure your DNS records are configured correctly for whichever you plan to use.

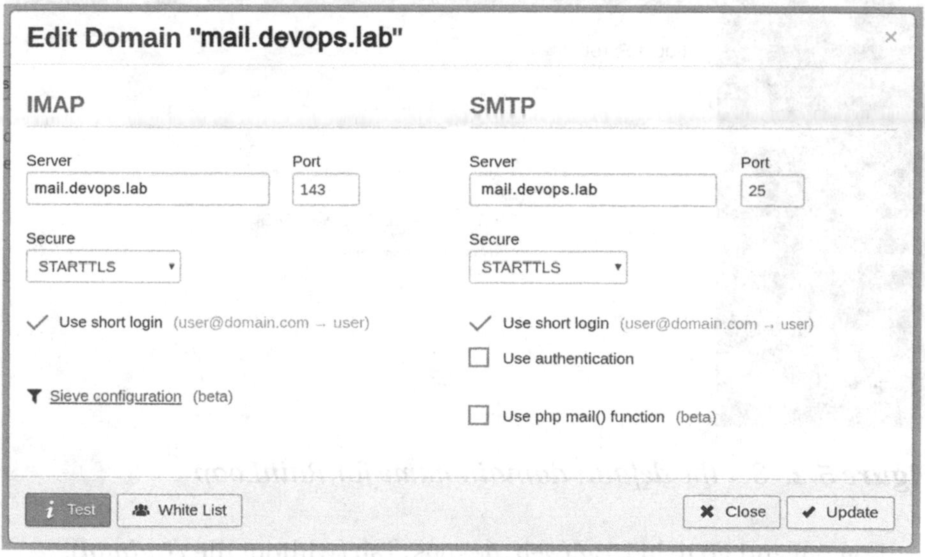

Figure 5-1. *The RainLoop domain configuration, with STARTTLS and short login enabled*

Both the IMAP and SMTP server addresses are *mail.devops.lab* with the same port numbers (143 and 25, respectively) you used when setting up Evolution in Chapter 4. Be sure to select **STARTTLS** from the **Secure** drop-down menu for each service and leave **Use authentication** unchecked under **SMTP**. If you want to log in with just the email username, such as *jadams* and not jadams@devops.lab, check the **Use short login** boxes. Once you've entered all the settings, click **Test**. If everything is green and works properly, click **Add** (or **Update**) to save the configuration.

Before leaving the admin panel, click the **Login** menu to set the Default Domain to *devops.lab*, as shown in Figure 5-2. Leave the **Try to determine user domain** box unchecked. These are the minimum settings you need to start using RainLoop; you can explore the rest of RainLoop's menus later on your own.

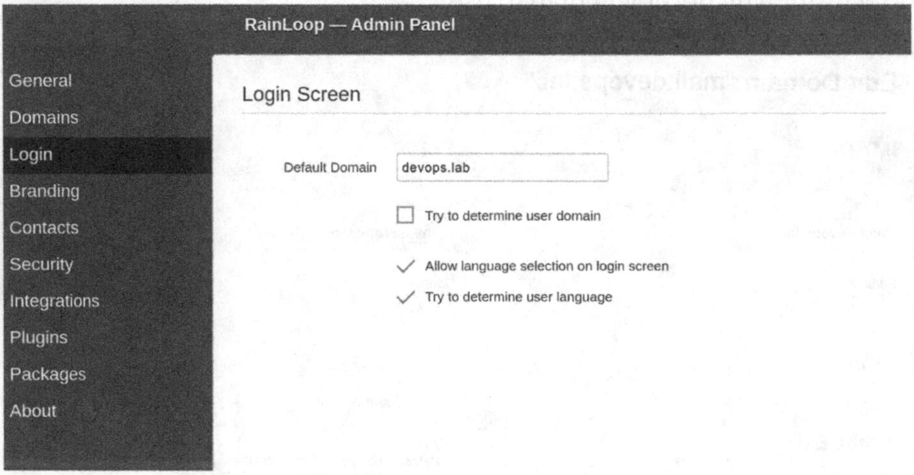

Figure 5-2. *Set the default domain name for RainLoop*

Log out and go to http://web.devops.lab (without the */?admin*). You'll notice that the login form is different from the admin one, namely, showing Email in the first box. Enter the email username (such as *jadams*, without the @*devops.lab*) and your password. You should see the main *Inbox* view. If you previously sent and received email using Evolution, those emails will appear in RainLoop too.

> **Note**   This email works without the *mail* subdomain because you configured *mail.devops.lab* in your DNS MX record.

Deploy Apache, PHP, and RainLoop as Docker Containers

Now that you've seen how all the pieces of your web server work, try the same deployment using a webmail server and interoperable Docker containers, also known as *microservices*. Unlike the virtual machine deployment, the container version splits each component into its own separate service, namely, *httpd* (Apache and PHP), *rainloop*, *postfix*, and *dovecot*, but all are running on the same physical host so they can interact and easily share a network and storage volumes. In the previous VM example, Apache, PHP, and RainLoop were running on one server, and Postfix and Dovecot on another. That's perfectly fine, but it also means lots of separate moving parts that can make maintenance and troubleshooting more difficult and time-consuming. Containers allow you to make changes or update individual aspects of your application without having to touch the others.

How the Containers Interact

Each distinct Docker service, including *httpd* and *rainloop*, will run independently but on the same physical host, where they can communicate and share storage. You'll also create persistent volumes, which you can think of as shared drives that each service can see and use. By creating Apache and RainLoop as separate services, you can modify one without modifying the other. When you build applications this way, you can make small service changes and updates without needing to redeploy everything.

Prepare the Docker Host

As with the containerized version of your mail server in Chapter 4, you'll deploy these containers on your Docker host, *docker.devops.lab*. To avoid conflicts, ensure that your DNS MX record points to your Docker host and that the containers and images you deployed for the Docker mail server are stopped by issuing a simple ***ping*** command:

```
$ ping docker.devops.lab
```

To stop all running containers on your Docker host, execute the following command:

```
$ docker container stop $(docker ps -aq)
```

This returns the container ID for all running containers and stops them. To remove them (so you can reuse the container names later), you can run the prune command to purge them:

```
$ docker container prune
```

Create a Docker Context for RainLoop

In the Docker mail server example from Chapter 4, you created a directory named *myserver* on *docker.devops.lab* to provide a home for all your Dockerfiles. You can reuse that directory and add subfolders for the new services or create a new directory called *rainloop*. Let's do the latter to keep things separate for now.

In the new *rainloop* directory, create four subdirectories, one for each container service:

```
$ mkdir -p rainloop/{httpd,rainloop,postfix,dovecot}
```

In the root of the *rainloop* directory, create a *docker-compose.yml* file with the following contents:

```
version: '2.1'
services:
  httpd:
    build: ./httpd
    restart: always
    ports:
      - "80:80"
    container_name: httpd
    volumes:
    - 'rainloop:/var/www/html/rainloop'

  rainloop:
    build: ./rainloop
    restart: always
    container_name: rainloop
    volumes:
    - 'rainloop:/var/www/html/rainloop'

  postfix:
    restart: always
    hostname: docker.devops.lab
    build: ./postfix
    container_name: postfix
    ports:
      - "25:25"
    volumes:
      - 'mail:/var/mail'
      - 'home:/home'
      - 'postfix-certs:/etc/ssl'
```

```
dovecot:
  restart: always
  hostname: docker.devops.lab
  depends_on:
    - postfix
  build: ./dovecot
  container_name: dovecot
  ports:
    - "143:143"
  volumes:
    - "mail:/var/mail"
    - "home:/home"
    - "dovecot-certs:/etc/dovecot/private"
volumes:
  mail:
  home:
  postfix-certs:
  dovecot-certs:
  rainloop:
```

This is similar to the email server version you created in Chapter 4, but it adds two more services (`httpd` and `rainloop`) and an additional persistent volume the two containers share (one that keeps its data when a container restarts), which means the *httpd* and *rainloop* containers can both access the data stored there. The *httpd* container, which builds Apache with PHP, has port 80 open to allow web requests. When it serves up files from */var/www/html/rainloop*, thanks to the shared volume, it actually accesses files you deploy in the separate *rainloop* container.

As before, the `postfix` and `dovecot` services defined in your *docker-compose.yml* file point to subdirectories containing Dockerfiles, and again, they have ports 25 and 143 exposed, respectively.

In the *rainloop/dovecot* directory, reuse the same *dovecot* Dockerfile you used in the previous chapter. Similarly, in the *rainloop/postfix* directory, reuse the *postfix* Dockerfile and the *postfix-debconf* file you created. Being able to reuse Dockerfiles is one of the advantages of containerized environments; there's no need to start from scratch, and each service is deployed the same way every time.

Add Additional Docker Containers to the RainLoop Application

The first all-new container service you'll add to your existing RainLoop services is *httpd*, which includes both a *Dockerfile* and an *entry.sh* script that's executed when the container starts. Bash scripts like *entry.sh* are often added to container projects to execute commands inside a running container. By contrast, *Dockerfiles* build images pre-populated with packages and configurations, but some actions need to be performed when the container is actually running, such as grabbing the live IP address.

In *rainloop/httpd*, create a *Dockerfile* with the following contents:

```
FROM ubuntu:22.04
ENV DOCKER_HOST 10.128.1.6
ENV MAIL_HOST docker.devops.lab
ENV DEBIAN_FRONTEND noninteractive

RUN apt update && apt install -y apache2 \
    php8.1 \
    libapache2-mod-php8.1 \
    php8.1-common \
    php8.1-curl \
    php8.1-xml \
    php8.1-mysql \
```

```
    php-date \
    php8.1-fpm \
    php8.1-json \
    php8.1-cli
ENV APACHE_RUN_USER www-data   ❶
ENV APACHE_RUN_GROUP www-data
ENV APACHE_LOG_DIR /var/log/apache2
ENV APACHE_RUN_DIR /var/www/html ❷

WORKDIR /usr/src/app
COPY entry.sh .

CMD ["bash", "entry.sh"] ❸
```

This Dockerfile includes the same commands you previously ran to install Apache and PHP on your *web.devops.lab* virtual machine. It also includes some environment variables that configure Apache to run as www-data ❶ and use /var/www/html ❷ as the default document root for the website. That directory will be shared with the rainloop service container through the persistent volume. These default settings were automatically applied when you installed Apache on your virtual machine, but here you're explicitly defining them.

In order to add variables to a running container, and not during the Docker build process, you'll run a Bash script as the final step of your Dockerfile to enter the correct values and then start Apache.

The *entry.sh* ❸ file writes entries into */etc/hosts* and */etc/hostname* that set the IP and hostname for name resolution and a fully qualified domain name to prevent Apache warnings. It then runs the apache2 service in the foreground to start the container.

For this to work, create a new file in *rainloop/httpd* named *entry.sh* and add the following contents:

```
#!/bin/bash
```

```
echo "${DOCKER_HOST}   ${MAIL_HOST}" >> /etc/hosts ❶
echo "${MAIL_HOST}" > /etc/hostname ❷
exec /usr/sbin/apache2 -D FOREGROUND ❸
```

The edits this Bash script *entry.sh* makes to */etc/hosts* ❶ and */etc/hostname* ❷ echo the contents of ENV variables set in the *Dockerfile* to files in the running container.

Note   These hostname entries aren't strictly necessary because Docker containers can resolve each other by name, thanks to the way Docker handles its own networking and name resolution. That is, each container in this application can automatically resolve any other container listed in the *docker-compose.yml* file by its name, like *postfix*, not just its IP address. Later, when configuring RainLoop SMTP and IMAP settings, you can use the container names *postfix* and *dovecot* as the server targets instead of *docker.devops.lab*, and RainLoop will work just fine.

The last command in *entry.sh* starts Apache in the foreground. The -D FOREGROUND ❸ is critical to ensuring the container starts and remains running. If you try to start Apache without this flag, the container will continue to restart over and over.

Finally, create the second new service by adding a *Dockerfile* in the new *rainloop/rainloop* directory that defines the RainLoop service:

```
FROM ubuntu:22.04

RUN apt update && apt install -y wget unzip ❶

RUN wget https://www.rainloop.net/repository/webmail/
rainloop-community-latest.zip ❷
```

```
RUN mkdir -p /var/www/html/rainloop

RUN unzip rainloop-community-latest.zip -d /var/www/html/
rainloop && \ ❸
    chown -R www-data:www-data /var/www/html/rainloop/ && \  ❹
    find /var/www/html/rainloop/ -type d -exec chmod 750
{} \; && \
    find /var/www/html/rainloop/ -type f -exec chmod 640 {} \;

CMD tail -f /dev/null ❺
```

As you can see, this Dockerfile contains all the instructions you passed on the command line when you built RainLoop in a virtual machine. Both *wget* and *unzip* ❶ are installed, the community edition of RainLoop is downloaded ❷ and unzipped to */var/www/html/rainloop* ❸, and the file and directory permissions are changed appropriately ❹. This is slightly different from the VM version. Namely, the URL to reach RainLoop will be http://docker.devops.lab/rainloop. The final line in the Dockerfile ❺ does nothing by itself except to create a foreground service inside the *rainloop* container. RainLoop doesn't have its own service, since it's just a folder with *.php* and related files, so this *tail* command prevents the container from constantly restarting.

Start the Multicontainer RainLoop Docker Application

With everything in place, run *docker-compose up -d* to build the images, deploy your containers, and release the terminal when it's done. This simple command builds the container images and then starts all your containers:

```
$ cd ~/myserver/rainloop
$ docker-compose up -d
```

After a few moments, you'll see output showing that your containers are building and starting. You'll now have four containers—*postfix*, *dovecot*, *httpd*, and *rainloop*—that can communicate and work together. Since they all contain only the packages they need, they're much smaller than separate VMs. They also use less system resources, enabling them to start and restart quickly.

When *docker-compose* finishes, access the RainLoop admin and email login pages the same way you did earlier from http://docker.devops. lab/rainloop/?admin and http://docker.devops.lab/rainloop/. When creating a new domain, remember you can use either *docker.devops.lab* for the SMTP and IMAP server addresses or just postfix and dovecot. If you use the latter, you'll notice in the RainLoop dashboard that those hostnames are resolved properly, highlighting the fact that the containers share a network and have functioning name resolution. The *httpd* container will use those container names to correctly resolve the two mail services.

Troubleshoot the Docker Deployment

If you run into trouble with the Docker container deployment, it could be that you're having conflicts with previously generated Docker images, containers, and volumes. You can use the *docker system prune* command to purge everything, but be careful. It will delete anything you've built and deployed so far. It won't remove your *Dockerfiles* or any files you created in the main *rainloop* directory, but it will remove containers, images, and volumes created when you ran the *docker-compose up* command previously.

The following commands stop and delete Docker items and essentially give you a clean slate. Running all of them will remove your images, containers, and volumes. When you do any future Docker builds, new images, containers, and fresh volumes will be created:

```
$ docker container stop $(docker ps -aq)
$ docker container rm $(docker ps -aq)
$ docker ps -a
$ docker image prune -a
$ docker volume prune
```

Recreating your web server in containers will give you a clear idea of how your stack works and how Docker enables you to group separate services together to make a powerful application.

Conclusion

In this chapter, you successfully installed an Apache web server with PHP capabilities and put it to work with the ready-made webmail program RainLoop, which can send and receive email from your own lab mail server. These core capabilities—including setting up multiple virtual hosts on a single server and adding PHP—allow you to deploy any number of home-grown or off-the-shelf web applications. This is just the beginning of what you can do.

The Docker version deploys the same setup using containers, providing a taste of how you can use microservices to deploy applications that require a number of separate components. This exercise also demonstrates how services interact and how you can turn other services into containerized applications to expand their capabilities.

In the next chapter, you'll finish building your LAMP stack by installing MariaDB, the open-source database server. Adding MariaDB will enable you to develop and use an even wider variety of web applications, including simple scripts and powerful web content tools like WordPress.

CHAPTER 6

Installing MariaDB and Creating a Simple Web Application

In Chapter 5, you deployed three of the four pieces necessary for your LAMP stack, and you learned how Apache and PHP can work together on a Linux host to serve up dynamic content. In this chapter, you'll add the database component: *MariaDB*. The simple application you'll create will read some information from a database table and show it in a browser.

In this chapter, you'll first learn some MariaDB and Structured Query Language (SQL) basics to see how data is stored in a database and retrieved, providing the basis for the PHP commands you'll execute and run later. Since the syntax is identical for SQL commands executed on the command line and in your small PHP application, everything you learn about MariaDB will transfer to the programming side of things.

MariaDB is a popular open-source relational database that provides backing for a vast array of use cases, from small scripts to large cloud-based applications. It's an enhanced version of (and drop-in replacement for) MySQL, which bloomed after Oracle acquired MySQL in 2008.

MariaDB is easy to learn and use, works well on its own or in conjunction with multiple programming languages, and is ideal for anyone who needs a relational database—that is, data stored in tables made of

© John S. Tonello 2022
J. S. Tonello, *Practical Linux DevOps*, https://doi.org/10.1007/978-1-4842-8318-9_6

rows and columns that can stand alone or reference data from other tables. Once defined, the tables are structured and uniform, providing an internal integrity that allows you to join related tables and perform complex queries that return data consistently. Relational databases are best in cases where you know ahead of time the shape of the data you want to store, such as names, addresses, dollar amounts, dates, and so on.

Note   Non-relational databases, also known as NoSQL databases, provide flexibility when you're not sure what shape your data may take. This is called unstructured data. Such databases are useful when you're trying to store lots of data that has variable elements and sizes you don't know ahead of time, such as Twitter tweets. With NoSQL databases, you can define your data structures as you go.

For the purposes of the examples in this chapter, you'll create structured data, predetermining the size and type of each field, or column, in your database.

Set Up and Log In to MariaDB

Installing MariaDB on Linux is straightforward and provides everything you need to access the database from the command line and interact with it via PHP scripts.

Log in to your web server and enter the following commands:

```
$ sudo apt update && sudo apt upgrade -y
$ sudo apt install mariadb-server
```

This will update your system and install *mysql* and *mysqladmin* along with a number of scripts and default configurations. A soft link from /usr/bin/mariadb will point to /usr/bin/mysql, the main database binary.

Even though you're using MariaDB, under the covers, it often uses MySQL naming conventions. For that reason, executing either `mariadb` or `mysql` from the command line does the same thing.

Note   As you use MariaDB, you'll notice that many of the commands are similar to those in MySQL, as MariaDB mostly adheres to SQL naming conventions. For example, you can launch the database from the command line with either *mariadb* or *mysql*. Some of the SQL commands do differ, however, so for the purposes of this book, you'll use MariaDB SQL statements.

To use MariaDB, you'll need to set an initial password for the database's *root* user. If you don't do this, the database won't be accessible, and there's not much you can do with it. After creating the root user, you can create other non-root users, databases, and tables, and you'll be able to run any number of SQL queries to create and assign privileges to users and insert, select, update, and modify data. Though you'll initially run commands as root, you'll create a user with fewer privileges later in order to avoid making routine database queries with root, a security no-no that can wreak havoc with your database.

Log in to your web.devops.lab server (where you previously installed the MariaDB server), and enter the following to set the root password:

```
$ sudo mysql_secure_installation
```

This command prompts you to enter a password and asks some follow-up questions intended to secure your database installation, such as removing anonymous users, disallowing remote root logins, and removing the test database. Reply **Y** to those and to the final question that asks whether you want to reload privilege tables, which will apply and save your configurations.

Note   Be sure to jot down the password you use. Resetting the root password is possible, but it can be a real hassle if you forget it.

If you now run **systemctl status mariadb** from the command line, you should see the database server is up and running. It'll also start automatically when your server boots and be running in the background every time you start or restart your web.devops.lab server.

Log in to MariaDB from the command line as root with the password you just created:

```
$ sudo mysql -u root -p
Enter password:
```

The **-p** flag allows you to enter the password privately, not in clear text. This is more secure than entering the password where it can be read by other logged-in users interested in viewing your commands using history.

After logging in, the command-line prompt changes, showing you're no longer in the Bash shell, but in MariaDB itself:

```
Welcome to the MariaDB monitor.  Commands end with ; or \g.
Your MariaDB connection id is 48
--snip--
Type 'help;' or '\h' for help. Type '\c' to clear the current
input statement.
MariaDB [(none)]>
```

The MariaDB prompt includes brackets around (none) to indicate you have yet to connect to a specific database, also known as a *schema*.

Basic SQL Commands

From this point on, you'll interact directly with different MariaDB databases and execute commands in SQL as the root user. Don't worry if you don't know the language well. You'll need only a handful of commands, and you can always run **help** from the MariaDB command line for assistance.

Character case doesn't matter when entering SQL commands, but it's good form to enter SQL commands in uppercase and arguments in lowercase. Be sure to end all commands with a semicolon (;) to tell MariaDB you're done entering your query. Leaving that off before pressing Enter brings you to a new line, which means MariaDB is waiting for additional input before executing your query.

To show the available databases that MariaDB installs automatically, enter the SHOW command followed by the databases argument:

```
MariaDB [(none)]> SHOW databases;
+--------------------+
| Database           |
+--------------------+
| information_schema |
| mysql              |
| performance_schema |
+--------------------+
3 rows in set (0.00 sec)
```

The three main databases installed by default (*information_schema*, *mysql*, and *performance_schema*) contain data about MariaDB's base configuration. They set your database system's default parameters and don't need to be altered, but you can query them like any other database you create later.

Let's do a simple query of the built-in *mysql* database's user table, which stores data about all existing MariaDB users. The SELECT command

175

is one you'll use often (along with FROM) to show data stored in one or
more tables:

```
MariaDB [(none)]> SELECT host, user FROM mysql.user;
+-----------+------+
| host      | user |
+-----------+------+
| localhost | root |
+-----------+------+
1 row in set (0.00 sec)
```

In a SQL SELECT statement, the FROM identifies the database and table
you want to query, which follows the *database.table* format. This example
tells MariaDB to select the column values *host* and *user* from the *user* table
in the *mysql* database. The SELECT statement output shows the headers for
the two columns and the values localhost and root, which indicate that
the 'root'@'localhost' user has been created with permissions set to
accept requests only from *localhost*. That makes sense, since you disabled
remote root logins earlier during the installation.

To connect to a specific database, use the USE mysql; command,
which places you in the *mysql* database context. From there, you can run
the SELECT command without the mysql. prefix in the FROM argument.
Connecting to a specific database shortens your commands and lets you
keep track of where you are.

Run the USE command and notice how the context shown in the
MariaDB prompt changes:

```
MariaDB [(none)]> USE mysql;
MariaDB [mysql]> SELECT host, user FROM user;
```

The SELECT query's output will be the same as the previous, slightly
longer query.

Create MariaDB Users and Set Permissions

Creating non-root MariaDB users for your databases is just as important as creating non-root users on your Linux systems. These users are allowed to run routine SQL commands without all the privileges available to root, which is safer and more secure.

Like usernames for a Linux system, the name you give to a regular MariaDB user can be pretty much anything you want. I like to create usernames that describe a little about their purpose. In this case, you'll create the user **webuser** to use later for your web-based application.

The syntax includes both the *username* and the *hostname*, which, in this example, will grant the user privileges on connections made to MariaDB from the *localhost* only and not from any external hosts. Log back in to MariaDB as the root user and then execute the following command:

```
$ sudo mysql -u root -p

MariaDB [(none)]> CREATE USER 'webuser'@'localhost' IDENTIFIED
BY 'mypassword';
Query OK, 0 rows affected (0.00 sec)
```

This creates the *webuser* user, sets *mypassword* as the password, and limits connections to *localhost* only. If you want to execute database queries from a different virtual machine or server that has a different IP address, you could replace localhost with a single IP address, an entire IP range like 10.128.1.0/24, or the % wildcard to allow connections from anywhere. That last option, as well as setting password as the *mypassword*, is not secure and should not be used in production.

You can create the same user with different hosts like 'webuser'@'localhost' and 'webuser'@'10.128.1.10' to grant permissions to the database from two specific hosts. This combination is a good way to secure access to your data.

To create a user with access to your entire lab network, shown as *jadams* in this example, enter the following:

```
MariaDB [(none)]> CREATE USER 'jadams'@'10.128.1.0/24'
IDENTIFIED BY 'mypassword';
Query OK, 0 rows affected (0.00 sec)
```

If you rerun the SQL query you executed earlier, you'll see the new user (or users) you created:

```
MariaDB [(none)]> SELECT host, user FROM mysql.user;
+----------------+----------+
| host           | user     |
+----------------+----------+
| 10.128.1.0/24  | jadams   |
| localhost      | root     |
| localhost      | webuser  |
+----------------+----------+
3 rows in set (0.00 sec)
```

The output shows I now have the *root*, *webuser*, and *jadams* users. Notice that *jadams* has permission to connect from any machine on the lab subnet, `10.128.1.0/24`. The rows and columns in this query result show how MariaDB presents table data.

The next step is to run `FLUSH PRIVILEGES;` to commit your changes and log out as the *root* user and back in as the *webuser* user:

```
MariaDB [(none)]> FLUSH PRIVILEGES;
Query OK, 0 rows affected (0.000 sec)
MariaDB [(none)]> EXIT;
Bye

$ sudo mysql -u webuser -p
Enter password:
```

When you're back in MariaDB, rerun the SHOW databases; query. You'll see only the *information_schema* database. That's because *webuser* doesn't yet have permission to see or access anything else. Let's change that by creating a new database and granting *webuser* permissions to use it.

Create a Test MariaDB Database

You're now going to create a custom database, grant permissions for *webuser*, and build your first database table. You can perform these steps again and again to create any number of databases to suit your needs. Since the *webuser* doesn't have any privileges to do anything yet, you'll need to EXIT; MariaDB and perform these steps by logging in again as the root user.

As the *root* MariaDB user, execute a CREATE query to create a new database. The name of the database doesn't matter, but if you don't follow my example, remember what you set. After creating the new database, run the SHOW query again to see that your new database has been created:

```
MariaDB [(none)]> CREATE DATABASE mydatabase;
MariaDB [(none)]> SHOW databases;
+--------------------+
| Database           |
+--------------------+
| information_schema |
| mydatabase         |
| mysql              |
| performance_schema |
+--------------------+
4 rows in set (0.00 sec)
```

The output confirms that you've created the new database called *mydatabase*.

That's good, but remember, you created this database as the MariaDB *root* user; *webuser* doesn't have permissions to use it. You need to grant privileges explicitly in order for *webuser* to write to, read from, and otherwise interact with the new database.

Connect to *mydatabase* with a USE query and then run a GRANT query to assign permissions:

```
MariaDB [(none)]> USE mydatabase;
MariaDB [mydatabase]> GRANT CREATE, SELECT, INSERT, UPDATE,
DELETE ON mydatabase.* TO 'webuser'@'localhost';
```

The GRANT CREATE, SELECT, INSERT, UPDATE, DELETE portion of the SQL statement gives *webuser* permission to create tables and also to see, add, change, and delete data in *mydatabase*. This means *webuser* can manipulate the database in every way you'll need for your web application, including creating tables and inserting data into them.

This is just one example of the privileges you can assign a user. You also can use GRANT ALL to assign all MariaDB privileges to the user, or you can replace a specific database name with a wildcard like *.* to apply privileges to all existing databases, for example:

```
MariaDB [mydatabase]> GRANT ALL ON *.* TO
'webuser'@'localhost';

MariaDB [mydatabase]> FLUSH PRIVILEGES
```

Log out of MariaDB and log back in as *webuser* and execute the SHOW databases; command to confirm the user has the correct permissions:

```
MariaDB [(none)]> SHOW databases;
+--------------------+
| Database           |
```

```
+--------------------+
| information_schema |
| mydatabase         |
+--------------------+
2 rows in set (0.01 sec)
```

If you see results like the preceding, you've created the database successfully, and *webuser* has the correct permissions to use it.

Create and Populate a Database Table

When you create a MariaDB table, you must define each column's type and length. For example, is the column an integer? Text? A date? Something else? MariaDB provides different field types so you can maintain data integrity. For example, you can't insert text into an integer field or a float value (a decimal number) into an integer field. Behind the scenes, MariaDB uses these field definitions to keep track of things and maintain the speed and accuracy of your queries and data.

By defining the length of a field, you're telling MariaDB the maximum number of characters it can hold. For example, if you have a table column for US states, you know the length of that field should be no less than 13 characters long so it can accommodate all the letters in Massachusetts (the state with the most letters). If you have a column for US cities, you'd assign it a length of 17 to accommodate Mooselookmeguntic, Maine. Field sizes should match your intent. Too small and your data will be truncated. Too long and MariaDB will reserve unnecessary space, which can slow down queries and make the database work harder than it needs to.

With that in mind, log in to MariaDB as *webuser* and execute the command USE mydatabase so you can create a simple table called *my_users* in *mydatabase* to store first and last names. If you don't first switch into the mydatabase, you'll get an error. Remember, tables are inside databases, and MariaDB needs to know where to create the table. In this example, the table will contain *user_id*, *user_first*, and *user_last* columns. Enter the following SQL command:

```
$ sudo mysql -u webuser -p

MariaDB [(none)]> USE mydatabase;
MariaDB [(mydatabase)]> CREATE TABLE my_users (
    user_id INT(3) NOT NULL AUTO_INCREMENT, ❶
    user_first VARCHAR(30) NOT NULL, ❷
    user_last VARCHAR(30) NOT NULL, ❸
    PRIMARY KEY ( user_id ) ❹
);
Query OK, 0 rows affected (0.08 sec)
```

For the *my_users* table, the *user_id* field ❶ identifies each row of data, so you'll define an auto-incrementing integer to store a unique value to reference that row. Auto-incrementing means the field will be populated with a new integer value automatically each time you insert a new row of data. In a way, it's a counter, so this field should be long enough to accommodate the total number of rows you ultimately expect to store in your table. For example, if you're planning to enter 200 names into your table, define an INT(3) field to make sure the *user_id* field is at least three characters long (one for each digit in 200), which can accommodate an integer up to 999. If you set it to INT(2), the highest number the field can hold is 99.

The next two fields in the *my_users* table will hold text for first and last names: *user_first* ❷; and *user_last* ❸. The VARCHAR type for the column and a length of 30 tell MariaDB to ensure that names entered in those columns are variable-length strings up to 30 characters long. The database won't reserve the space needed for all 30 characters; it'll use only what it needs up to that number. That means it uses fewer resources and is more flexible (and more common) than using the fixed-length CHAR string type.

The SQL command for creating the *my_users* table should also define a PRIMARY KEY ❹, which is a unique identifier for that row of data to ensure no two rows can share the same primary key value. No duplicates are allowed, and this guarantees you won't have two rows with the same user_id value. Primary keys can be created from one field, such as the *user_id* integer in this example, or multiple column values, such as *user_id*, *user_first*, and *user_last*.

The NOT NULL phrase added to each field definition in the example tells MariaDB that whenever it inserts a new row of data, those fields can't be empty. A SQL query with missing values for those fields will fail, which helps MariaDB ensure data integrity.

This example *my_users* table is very basic, but it contains the same structure you'd use to create any other database table. MariaDB offers many more options than shown here. Visit www.mariadb.org for more information.

Note   The field names I used in the example are standardized. Underscores or CaMeL caps are common because they're easy to read and remember. Being consistent from the beginning will help you avoid headaches later.

To confirm that your table was created the way you intended, log in as webuser and enter the following:

```
$ sudo mysql -u webuser -p

MariaDB [(none)]> USE mydatabase;
MariaDB [mydatabase]> SHOW tables;
+----------------------+
| Tables_in_mydatabase |
+----------------------+
```

```
| my_users              |
+-----------------------+
MariaDB [mydatabase]> DESCRIBE my_users;
+------------+-------------+------+-----+---------+----------------+
| Field      | Type        | Null | Key | Default | Extra          |
+------------+-------------+------+-----+---------+----------------+
| user_id    | int(3)      | NO   | PRI | NULL    | auto_increment |
| user_first | varchar(30) | NO   |     | NULL    |                |
| user_last  | varchar(30) | NO   |     | NULL    |                |
+------------+-------------+------+-----+---------+----------------+
3 rows in set (0.00 sec)
```

The SHOW tables; command shows all the tables in your database, similar to how the SHOW databases; command shows all the databases. The DESCRIBE my_users; command outputs the structure of the table itself so you can check that all is as expected. Be sure to confirm as you go to make sure everything in your lab works.

Add Data to a Table

Database tables are flexible and powerful, but they're not worth much if they don't have any rows of data. As mentioned previously, MariaDB tables are rows and columns of data. Creating the table defined the columns; INSERT statements add the rows.

Each INSERT statement identifies the table, columns, and column data to add and takes the following form:

```
INSERT INTO <tablename> (<column1>, <column2>) VALUES
('<value1>', '<value2>');
```

The column names and column values have a distinct relationship. MariaDB inserts *value1* into *column1* and so on. Each column is set to specific field types, such as *text*, *integer*, or *date*, and type mismatches can prevent a SQL query from executing. String and date values are enclosed in single quotation marks. Integers are not. Keep things orderly to ensure you're inserting all your data properly.

Log in to MariaDB as *webuser* and connect to *mydatabase* to add your first row of data:

```
MariaDB [none]> USE mydatabase;
MariaDB [mydatabase]> INSERT INTO my_users (user_first, user_
last) VALUES ('John', 'Adams');
```

Notice that *user_id* is not included in the field or value lists. That's because it's set to auto-increment—the integer will increase by one each time a new row is added—and will be inserted automatically by MariaDB.

You can use the up arrow to see your last command and rerun this query a few more times, changing the VALUES items as follows:

```
INSERT INTO my_users (user_first, user_last) VALUES ('Betsy',
'Ross');
INSERT INTO my_users (user_first, user_last) VALUES ('George',
'Washington');
INSERT INTO my_users (user_first, user_last) VALUES ('Ben',
'Franklin');
INSERT INTO my_users (user_first, user_last) VALUES ('Thomas',
'Jefferson');
```

Now that you have rows of data, use the SELECT statement to show the values. This takes the form of SELECT <fields> FROM <table> WHERE <fields> and can be a list of column names separated by commas or an asterisk to show all fields:

```
MariaDB [mydatabase]> SELECT * FROM my_users;
```

```
+----------+------------+-------------+
| user_id  | user_first | user_last   |
+----------+------------+-------------+
|        1 | John       | Adams       |
|        2 | Betsy      | Ross        |
|        3 | George     | Washington  |
|        4 | Ben        | Franklin    |
|        5 | Thomas     | Jefferson   |
+----------+------------+-------------+
```

The *user_id* has auto-incremented with each new row, providing a unique value. Since that table field value was set to INT(3), it can auto-increment up to 999.

Update Table Entries

To change values in any row of data in a MariaDB table, use a SQL WHERE clause to reference specific rows by the *user_id* (primary key) value to update and delete entries. Updating takes the following form:

```
UPDATE <table-name> SET <column-name>='<newvalue1>' WHERE
<primary-key> = <value>;
```

In this example, the WHERE clause tells MariaDB to update only the column value in the row with the designated primary key value. If you leave off the WHERE clause, every record will be updated, which usually isn't what you want.

Change the *user_first* value from *Thomas* to *Tom* to test updating a table entry:

```
MariaDB [mydatabase]> UPDATE my_users SET user_first='Tom'
WHERE user_id=5;
```

```
Query OK, 1 row affected (0.00 sec)
Rows matched: 1  Changed: 1  Warnings: 0
```

The primary key value for that row is 5, so it's used in the SQL statement. Since the *user_first* field is a string, the value is enclosed by single quotation marks.

Now, when you run the SELECT statement, you'll see the change:

```
MariaDB [mydatabase]> SELECT * FROM my_users WHERE user_id=5;
+---------+------------+------------+
| user_id | user_first | user_last  |
+---------+------------+------------+
|       5 | Tom        | Jefferson  |
+---------+------------+------------+
1 row in set (0.00 sec)
```

The WHERE clause limits the output to a single row of data, but you can use any field to limit your query, for example:

```
MariaDB [mydatabase]> SELECT * FROM my_users WHERE user_first
LIKE 'T%';
+---------+------------+-----------+
| user_id | user_first | user_last |
+---------+------------+-----------+
|       5 | Tom        | Jefferson |
+---------+------------+-----------+
1 row in set (0.00 sec)
```

This limits the search to the *user_first* column by using the LIKE command and the MariaDB wildcard (%) to indicate the first name value must begin with **T** followed by any other character. Think of a WHERE clause as a filter you can use to narrow your query results to just the values or table entries you want.

Delete Table Entries

Deleting rows is similar to updating them, but be careful. It's easy to delete everything in your database table if you don't limit the SQL query with a WHERE clause. The syntax looks like this:

```
DELETE FROM <table-name> WHERE <column-name> = <value>;
```

Use the *user_id* column again as the reference to delete the Tom Jefferson entry:

```
MariaDB [mydatabase]> DELETE FROM my_users WHERE user_id=5;
Query OK, 1 row affected (0.01 sec)
```

Now, when you rerun a SELECT query to show all values in the table, Tom Jefferson is gone:

```
MariaDB [mydatabase]> SELECT * FROM my_users;
+---------+------------+------------+
| user_id | user_first | user_last  |
+---------+------------+------------+
|       1 | John       | Adams      |
|       2 | Betsy      | Ross       |
|       3 | George     | Washington |
|       4 | Ben        | Franklin   |
+---------+------------+------------+
4 rows in set (0.00 sec)
```

If you execute a new INSERT statement to add Thomas Jefferson back to your table and rerun the SELECT query, you'll see the entry is back, but it has a new *user_id* value. MariaDB picks up where it left off with the auto-incrementing and will never reuse a previous value, even if that record has since been deleted. Try it!

Read MariaDB Data with PHP

With a little SQL under your belt, it's time to create a simple PHP script that can query the MariaDB database and show the results on a web page. This basic capability is the heart of your LAMP stack.

Rather than creating static HTML files in the following examples, you'll create PHP pages that read content directly from the database, allowing for real-time browser-based interactions.

The dynamic content generation works by having PHP connect to and read from MariaDB, execute database queries, and present data on a web page. PHP provides the programming logic, and Structured Query Language (SQL) commands select the appropriate MariaDB data to return. A single PHP file can present different content based on parameters you or your application's users define.

So far, you've used MariaDB to manipulate data from the command line. Now you'll hand off those commands to PHP, which you installed and configured in Chapter 5, to communicate with the database. Your PHP script will initiate a connection to MariaDB, define a SQL query, execute it, and show the results in a web browser.

Open a shell and log in to your web.devops.lab virtual machine, where you'll create a .php file named *index.php* in the document root of your myserver.devops.lab (the second website you created in Chapter 5), that is, /var/www/myserver/index.php. Your entire application will consist of this single file, leveraging the power of your LAMP stack.

Add the following typical HTML to the index.php file:

```
<html>
<head> ❶
    <title>My Users</title>
    <style type="text/css">
        table, th, td {
            border: solid 1px #eee;
```

```
                border-collapse: collapse;
                padding: 5px;
        }
        th {
                width: 200px;
                background-color: #eee;
        }
    </style>
</head>
<body>
<?php ❷

$host = "localhost";
$user = "webuser";
$password = "mypassword";
$database = "mydatabase";
$link = mysqli_connect($host, $user, $password, $database); ❸

$SQL = "SELECT user_id, user_first, user_last FROM my_
users"; ❹
$result = $link->query($SQL); ❺

echo "<table>\n";
echo "<thead><tr><th>First name</th><th>Last name</th></tr></
thead>\n"; ❻

while ($row = mysqli_fetch_assoc($result)) { ❼
        $user_id = $row['user_id'];
        $user_first = $row['user_first'];
        $user_last = $row['user_last'];
        echo "<tr><td>$user_first</td><td>$user_last</td></
        tr>\n"; ❽
};
```

```
echo "</table>\n";
?>
</body>
</html>
```

The header is the same as in a usual .html page ❶. I've added some optional Cascading Style Sheets (CSS) in the header to make the output pretty. In the main body, the <?php ❷ indicates the start of the PHP code. Everything between that and the ending ?> is in PHP, including the *$host*, *$user*, *$password*, and *$database* variables used to connect to the database with mysqli_connect() and assign that connection to a variable named *$link* ❸. The credential values match the credentials and database you created in the previous step. The built-in PHP mysqli_connect() command negotiates the connection to MariaDB.

The next element assigns a simple SQL statement you executed in the previous exercise to a *$SQL* variable ❹, which is then used with the *$link* variable to query the database and create a result set stored in a variable called *$rs* ❺. This means the PHP script will connect to *mydatabase* as *webuser* and execute the query. The query output is stored as an array in the *$rs* variable, and the next step will format the content to be viewable in a browser.

I've added a standard HTML table header ❻ before the step that iterates and presents the data stored in *$rs* to make the table look nicer. The iteration is done with a PHP *while* loop ❼ and assigns each value stored in the *$rs* array to variables that PHP can use. This *while* statement is like telling the script, "While there are rows of data in *$rs* to show, keep showing them until you're done." Each time the loop proceeds to a new element in the array, it assigns its value to a new variable specific to the columns in the *my_users* database table.

Finally, the PHP script wraps some HTML around the variables to present the output in neat rows and columns ❽. The HTML table element is closed with `</table>`, and the PHP section is closed with `?>`, and the file ends with standard HTML `</body>` and `</html>` tags.

I've left out some error-checking to simplify this file, but it contains all the necessary elements to view the contents of your database table. Open a browser and go to `http://myserver.devops.lab` to see the results.

Containerize It

Making a MariaDB container can be straightforward if all you want is the standalone database, but for this example you want both MariaDB and an Apache server with PHP. This can be accomplished by creating two Docker containers that can communicate with each other and share persistent volumes. Though each container will be distinct, the outcome—a full LAMP stack—will be the final result.

As in the Chapter 5 example, you'll be able to deploy these containers on your docker.devops.lab host. Unlike the previous example, though, you'll use raw Docker images (downloaded directly from Docker Hub) alongside a customized container.

Create the PHP Container

It's possible to create separate containers for PHP and Apache, but there's a Docker image available that combines the two. You'll use that in a Dockerfile. For MariaDB, you'll use the public image, which means you won't need to create a separate Dockerfile for it. You'll also create a companion container running Adminer, a graphical tool you can use to interact with the MariaDB database.

In your work directory, create a new folder in your home directory called `lamp` and create a subdirectory inside it called `php`:

```
$ cd ~
$ mkdir -p lamp/php
```

In the lamp/php folder, create a new Dockerfile with the following contents:

```
FROM php:8.0-apache
RUN docker-php-ext-install mysqli
WORKDIR /var/www/html
COPY index.php index.php
EXPOSE 80
```

This will use the PHP 8.0 image with Apache built in, as indicated in the FROM statement. The RUN command installs and enables the mysqli module, which you should recall as one of the Apache modules you installed when manually setting up your server in a virtual machine. Without this RUN statement, the index.php script will fail because it requires the module to work.

The rest of the Dockerfile should be self-explanatory. It sets /var/www/html as the working directory, which is where you'll copy in the index.php file from you workstation directory. Exposing port 80 ensures your small web app is reachable.

Create MariaDB and Adminer

Save your *php* Dockerfile and create a new index.php file by copying the index.php you used in the previous example. It will be identical except for a single edit. Change the line that reads

```
$host = "localhost";
```

to

```
$host = "db";
```

193

This is necessary because the container will have "db" as its hostname (not localhost). Save this index.php file in the lamp/php/ directory.

With these two files complete, create a new docker-compose.yml file in the root of your /lamp folder. This will define the rest of your containerized LAMP stack. The file should look like this:

```
version: '3.3'

volumes:
  wwwroot:
  database:

services:
  php:
    build: ./php
    container_name: php-apache
    privileged: true
    volumes:
      - wwwroot:/var/www/html
    networks:
      - frontend
      - backend
    ports:
      - 80:80

  db:
    image: mariadb
    container_name: db
    environment:
      - MYSQL_ROOT_PASSWORD: "mypassword"
      - MYSQL_DATABASE: "mydatabase"
    volumes:
      - database:/var/lib/mysql
```

```
  networks:
    - backend

adminer:
  image: adminer
  container_name: adminer
  ports:
    - 8080:8080
  networks:
    - frontend
    - backend

networks:
  frontend:
  backend:
```

Notice that the file begins with a *volumes:* entry, which defines two persistent volumes you'll want for this example. The wwwroot volume is for the php-apache container content you want to preserve; the database volume will be used to preserve the MariaDB data files. Persistent volumes retain their contents even when a container is stopped and restarted. Without these, your database and /var/www/html directory will be wiped clean each time. That may not be what you want if you're planning to keep this content available—even after shutting it down.

In the services: section, you're defining three containers: php-apache, db, and adminer. The first creates the image based on the contents of the Dockerfile you created in the last step. It's given a name (php-apache), set as a privileged container, and assigned two networks: frontend and backend. Docker will create these networks when you build the images later, and it will enable the containers to communicate with each other. The frontend network is intended for external traffic (like someone visiting your app), and the backend network is intended for local container-to-container communication only. This is a good security measure that means the MariaDB server is never available directly outside your Docker host, but containers that use it—php-apache and adminer— can reach it.

The db service is a little different. Instead of using the build: directive to reference a local Dockerfile, it uses the image: directive to fetch and use the latest version of MariaDB. In a production setting, you'd also set the version you want with a tag like mariadb:10.7.1. I've left that out for clarity. The container is given a name, and then some environment variables are identified. These will be passed to MariaDB to set passwords and the mydatabase values for you. These entries, in this format, are not considered secure. In a production environment, you'd use Docker secrets or a secrets file to obfuscate your sensitive data.

The container's volumes: directive uses the volume created earlier that points to the /var/lib/mysql directory inside the container. That's where MariaDB stores the files that hold data. By adding this line, you're telling Docker to create a volume that will remain known to the container, even after the container is shut down and restarted. Note that the networks: for this container is set to just backend.

The third container builds and deploys Adminer. Like the MariaDB container, it's built directly from the Docker Hub image. There's no local Dockerfile needed to configure it. The container is given a name; and, since Adminer runs on port 8080, that port is opened. Note that this container has both the frontend and backend networks defined, which allows users to access the web-based dashboard, and Adminer to communicate internally with the db containerized database.

The final entry in the docker-compose.yml defines the networks. The format is very similar to how you define volumes. These networks will be created during the docker-compose steps that come next.

Launch Your Containerized Stack

With everything complete, you're now ready to launch your containerized stack and your small PHP application. Remember, the first time you do this, Docker will need to download any images that aren't yet available on your local machine, so the initial launch will take some time. Once those images are local, all future launches will be considerably faster.

On the docker.devlops.lab host, enter the following:

```
$ cd ~/lamp
$ docker-compose up -d
```

This will download the images the containers need, configure them, copy in your index.php file, and launch the containers. If you point your browser to your Docker VM, you should see a basic page with some PHP errors. That's because no database, table, or content has been created in your MariaDB container. You can do that now by using the Adminer interface or by issuing the following command on your Docker host, which will import all the SQL statements necessary to create and populate your database in a file named *mydatabase.sql*.

The mydatabase.sql contains all the commands you used in your virtual machine example, as shown in Listing 6-1.

Listing 6-1. The contents of the mydatabase.sql file

```
SET NAMES utf8;
SET time_zone = '+00:00';
SET foreign_key_checks = 0;
SET sql_mode = 'NO_AUTO_VALUE_ON_ZERO';

SET NAMES utf8mb4;

DROP DATABASE IF EXISTS `mydatabase`;
```

197

```
CREATE DATABASE `mydatabase` /*!40100 DEFAULT CHARACTER SET
utf8mb4 */;
USE `mydatabase`;

DROP TABLE IF EXISTS `my_users`;
CREATE TABLE `my_users` (
        `user_id` int(3) NOT NULL AUTO_INCREMENT,
        `user_first` varchar(30) NOT NULL,
        `user_last` varchar(30) NOT NULL,
        PRIMARY KEY (`user_id`)
) ENGINE=InnoDB DEFAULT CHARSET=utf8mb4;

INSERT INTO `my_users` (`user_id`, `user_first`, `user_last`)
VALUES
(1,     'Betsy',     'Ross'),
(2,     'George',    'Washington'),
(3,     'Ben',       'Franklin'),
(4,     'Thomas',    'Jefferson');

CREATE USER 'webuser'@'%' IDENTIFIED BY 'mypassword';

GRANT CREATE, SELECT, INSERT, UPDATE, DELETE ON mydatabase.* TO
'webuser'@'%';

FLUSH PRIVILEGES;
```

Docker has a way to interact with a running container without actually initiating a shell for you. The following command logs in to the container and runs a MySQL command, namely, importing the local mydatabase. sql contents:

```
$ docker exec -i db mysql -uroot -ppassword mydatabase <
mydatabase.sql
```

Try Out Adminer

Since Adminer was set to listen at port 8080, point your browser to `http://docker.devops.lab:8080`. You'll see the login page, as in Figure 6-1.

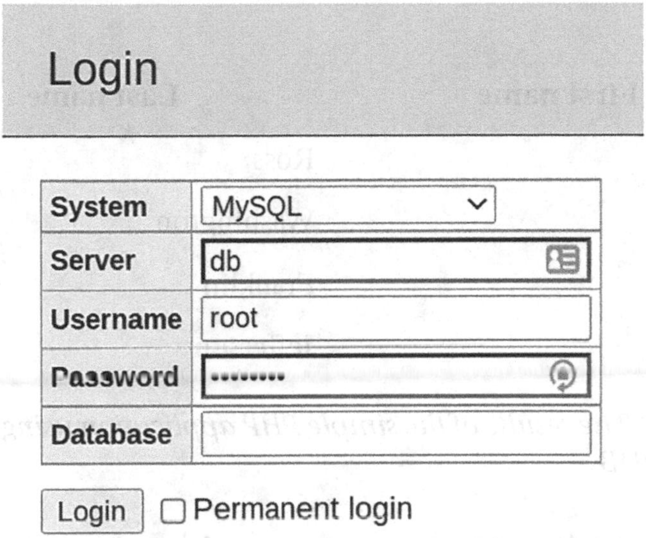

Login

System	MySQL ⌄
Server	db
Username	root
Password	••••••••
Database	

Login ☐ Permanent login

Figure 6-1. *The Adminer login screen*

As in the preceding example, enter the container name for the server (db), root as the Username, and "`password`" as the Password. These are the same as the values you set in the `docker-compose.yml` file.

After logging in, you can create a new database called `mydatabase`, create a table called `my_users`, and insert rows of data. You can use the SQL commands provided earlier in this chapter or use Adminer's graphical interface to do that. I won't go into specific detail about Adminer here, but feel free to explore its capabilities. It's a nice, easy-to-use tool for manipulating MariaDB and other databases.

Once you've created your database and table, and granted your webuser permission to access them, return to your browser and point to `http://docker.devops.lab`. The result should appear like that in Figure 6-2 below, showing you the same content you saw in the virtual machine example.

First name	Last name
Betsy	Ross
George	Washington
Ben	Franklin
Thomas	Jefferson

Figure 6-2. *The results of the simple PHP application using data from MariaDB*

When you're done, you can destroy the stack by using docker-compose from inside your `lamp/` directory:

```
$ docker-compose down
```

That command will stop the running containers and disconnect the networks and volumes. If you want to purge your system completely, you can run `docker system prune [-a]`, adding the `-a` option to delete everything—so be careful!

Conclusion

In this chapter, you learned how to use MariaDB to store data and create a user, database, and table. You also learned how to manipulate that data on the command line and with a simple PHP script. Finally, you deployed the application using Docker containers.

These examples should provide a good understanding of how a LAMP stack can work to create dynamic applications. Understanding this basic framework will give you a feel for creating web applications of all kinds; they don't need to be limited to a LAMP stack. You can use the same concepts with other programming languages, such as Python, and other databases, such as PostgreSQL or MongoDB.

In the next chapter, you'll learn how to extend your simple PHP script so you can insert, update, and delete database fields and rows in your MariaDB tables right from your web application.

CHAPTER 7

Web Server Alternatives

In the last two chapters, you got a good Apache workout, configuring a robust LAMP stack to handle a variety of web-based applications. In this chapter, you'll take a look at a common alternative, the popular NGINX web server. You'll wrap up with trying your hand at some web server alternatives for times when you only need something quick and lightweight.

Before diving into NGINX, try your hand at deploying a WordPress server. WordPress is a PHP application that uses MariaDB (MySQL) as the back end to store all the content for a website. It's a free, flexible, and powerful way to deploy websites that have a professional look and, perhaps more importantly, a good WYSIWYG interface that one or more contributors can use to build site content.

Armed with what you know about creating a LAMP stack, installing WordPress is a breeze. It takes full advantage of your existing LAMP environment; and, like other PHP-based applications, it can be installed by simply downloading a `.zip` or `.tar` file and unpacking it to a new or existing web directory, such as `/var/www/html/`.

© John S. Tonello 2022
J. S. Tonello, *Practical Linux DevOps*, https://doi.org/10.1007/978-1-4842-8318-9_7

Deploy WordPress

The easiest way to install WordPress is to fire up your existing LAMP VM (or LXC) on Proxmox, shell into it with SSH, and download the latest version. Use wget to download the file and the -O flag to output it directly to your website directory. The -nc flag added at the end of the command tells wget to *not clobber* (don't overwrite) a file of the same name:

```
$ ssh user@lamp.develops.lab
$ sudo wget https://wordpress.org/latest.tar.gz -O /var/www/
  html/latest.tar.gz -nc
```

The file is in a compressed format, so you can use gunzip to unpack the .gz file, which leaves yet another compressed file called latest.tar. Instead, you can just use tar with the -z flag to un-tar and unzip the file in one step:

```
$ sudo tar -xzvf /var/www/html/latest.tar.gz
```

The result will be a new directory, /var/www/html/wordpress, initially owned by root, which can create permission problems. Use *chown* to change the ownership to the web-data user with the following command:

```
$ sudo chown www-data:www-data /var/www/html/wordpress -R
```

With permissions set, point your browser to your server, such as https://web.devops.lab/wordpress, for the graphical setup, as shown in Figure 7-1. With WordPress, there's no need to manually edit any of the files you just downloaded.

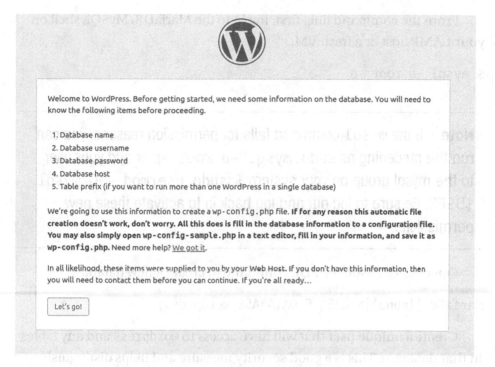

Figure 7-1. *The browser view of the WordPress initial setup screen (after selecting a language)*

WordPress tells you it will do its best to set up everything for you and lets you know how to do some basic fiddling if necessary. To complete the graphical install, you'll need

- The name of your WordPress database

- The database's username and password

- The MariaDB hostname

To create the database (and give it a user), refresh your memory with a look back at Chapter 6. You can log in to MariaDB from the command line or use Adminer for these tasks.

From the command line, first, log in to the MariaDB/MySQL shell on your LAMP host or a fresh VM:

```
$ mysql -u root -p
```

Note   If the `mysql` command fails for permission reasons, you can run the preceding as `sudo mysql -u root -p` or add your user to the mysql group on your system:`$ sudo usermod -aG mysql $USER`. Be sure to log out and log back in to activate these new permissions.

Once inside, issue the SQL command to create a new database:

```
MariaDB [(none)]> CREATE DATABASE wordpress;
```

Create a unique user that will have access to `wordpress` and any tables in that database. This is a good security measure and helps distinguish between various users and roles you assign to MariaDB:

```
MariaDB [(none)]> CREATE USER 'wordpress'@'localhost'
IDENTIFIED BY 'mypassword';
```

With the user created, grant it permissions to access your `wordpress` database and all its tables, identified as `wordpress.*` in the following example:

```
MariaDB [(none)]> USE wordpress;
MariaDB [mydatabase]> GRANT CREATE, SELECT, INSERT, UPDATE,
DELETE ON wordpress.* TO 'wordpress'@'localhost';
```

Before exiting, run the command to update user privileges:

```
$ FLUSH PRIVILEGES;
```

Create a WordPress System User

Your new WordPress site is really just a folder, but it may not have the correct permissions to allow the graphical installer to continue. That is, WordPress needs to be able to *write* to some files in the website directory, not just read them.

To make that work, first change the permission on the /var/www/html/ wordpress directory to www-data:

```
$ sudo chown www-data:www-data /var/www/html/wordpress -R
```

The trailing -R flag makes the change recursive, meaning the folder and all its subfolders and files are now owned by www-data.

One final step before you continue is to create a new system user called wordpress and add that user to the www-data group. This enables that user to read from and write to the WordPress application folder (to which you gave wordpress ownership):

```
$ sudo adduser wordpress
$ sudo usermod -aG www-data wordpress
```

Finish the WordPress Installation

Armed with your database name, username, and password, continue the graphical WordPress installation. In the setup screen, enter the values you created in MariaDB, noting that the *Username* and *Password* WordPress wants in this view are the values you just set when creating the database user, which are **wordpress** and **mypassword** in the example shown in Figure 7-2.

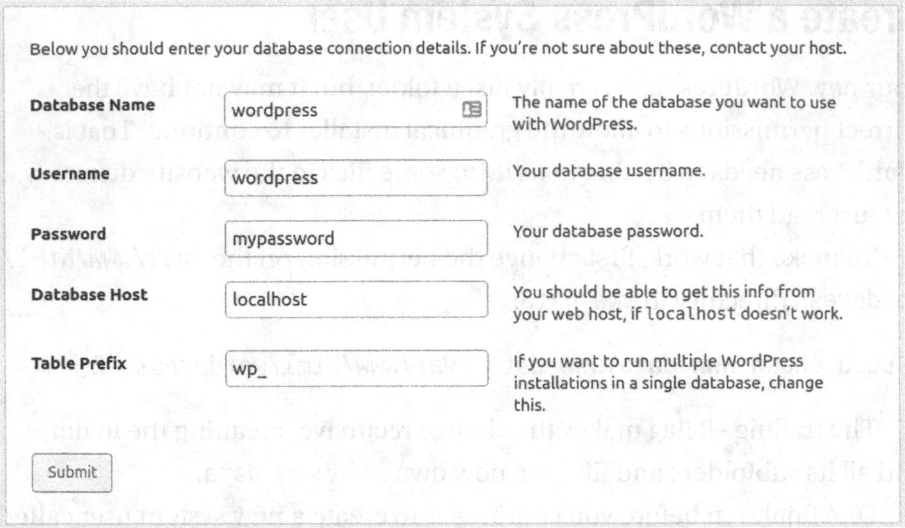

Below you should enter your database connection details. If you're not sure about these, contact your host.

Database Name	wordpress	The name of the database you want to use with WordPress.
Username	wordpress	Your database username.
Password	mypassword	Your database password.
Database Host	localhost	You should be able to get this info from your web host, if localhost doesn't work.
Table Prefix	wp_	If you want to run multiple WordPress installations in a single database, change this.

Submit

Figure 7-2. *Enter the same values in the WordPress setup that you just created in MariaDB*

If all goes well, WordPress will tell you you're ready to run the installation. During this step, it automatically creates a number of tables in your MariaDB database and populates them with some dummy data to get you started. If you get a *write* error, double-check the permissions on your /var/www/html/wordpress directory. The folder should be owned by www-data and be readable and writeable (mode 755).

While WordPress is doing its configuration, it will prompt you for a website title, a username, a password, your email, and search engine visibility. These can be whatever you want, but make sure to make note of what you enter. For the email, you can use your new mail server address, such as jadams@devops.lab.

It only takes a moment for WordPress to finish the installation. When it does, it'll take you to the login screen, and you're off and running!

I won't go into detail about using WordPress here (there are a lot of good resources on the Web), but feel free to play around with the site's appearance, adding plugins and creating content.

Before you move on to installing and using the NGINX web server, it's important to note that you can use WordPress there too. The NGINX version you install will include PHP and MariaDB, all set for WordPress and other web applications.

Install and Configure NGINX

Like Apache, NGINX is a common open source web server. It's grown in popularity because it's lightweight, easy to configure, and especially capable when serving static web pages, such as HTML or PHP files. In fact, some research shows it to be up to 2.5 times faster than Apache at serving up static pages.

As you proceed in this section, you'll notice that many of the NGINX configurations will seem familiar. For example, setting up two distinct websites with two distinct domains on a single server is possible with NGINX just as it is with Apache. NGINX also has configuration directories for `sites-available` and `sites-enabled`, so your familiarity with how an Apache web server works will be valuable here.

Manually Install NGINX

When it comes to installing NGINX, you have a lot of options, including using a Proxmox template (complete with *FastCGI* and MariaDB to run your PHP application), deploying a container on your Docker host, or manually with some basic command-line work. To get you familiar with NGINX, we'll start with the latter.

For this example, deploy a basic Ubuntu or Debian LXC in Proxmox. It doesn't need more than one core and 512MB of RAM, but give the instance a static IP address, such as 10.128.1.61/24 or the next available address in your DevOps lab subnet.

While the machine is launching, step over to your DNS server and add two entries to the zone files. In the examples you've used so far, these are

- /etc/bind/zones/devops.lab.zone

- /etc/bind/zones/10.128.zone

In the first, increment the Serial entry and then add an A record and a CNAME. The idea here is to create two distinct domain names that point to the same server, just as you did in the Apache examples. These new entries in your devops.lab.zone file will look something like this:

```
...
nginx.devops.lab.   IN     A        10.128.1.61
nginx2.devops.lab.  IN     CNAME    nginx
```

The single entry in your 10.128.zone file will look like this:

```
...
61.1  IN    PTR     nginx.devops.lab.
```

Save these files and update DNS by running rndc reload. You can test your DNS by pinging your two new domains from your workstation.

Configure NGINX

Over on your new base Ubuntu or Debian instance, install the nginx package with sudo apt install nginx. This will create the /etc/nginx directory where all the configuration files are stored.

Like Apache, NGINX has a base nginx.conf file that holds all the core settings for your web server. The virtual host websites you create on the server will all draw from the base configurations listed in this file. It's even possible to define your virtual hosts in nginx.conf, but it's not recommended. Doing so would make your configuration file bloated and unwieldy. It's better to create different sites in the /etc/nginx/sites-available/ directory, recognizing that they inherit certain capabilities from the main nginx.conf file.

For most cases, the default settings in nginx.conf are fine to keep as is. Two lines in this file are particularly important. On line 4 is the following:

```
...
include /etc/nginx/modules-enabled/*.conf;
...
```

This tells NGINX to look in that directory for any server modules you want to work with your websites.

On line 60 in Ubuntu 22.04 (line 62 in Ubuntu 20.04) is a similar directive that tells NGINX where to look for sites that should be enabled. In this case, you'll have the default, served up when you visit http://nginx.devops.lab, and nginx2, served up when you visit http://nginx2.devops.lab:

```
...
include /etc/nginx/sites-enabled/*;
...
```

For this example, you'll leave the default website (virtual host) as-is and create a second site for *nginx2*. Like Apache, NGINX has a lot of options when it comes to configurations, including directives that enable SSL (port 443) and adding FastCGI to enable PHP and other capabilities. For now, start with the basics.

Create a new folder under your /var/www directory called nginx2 to hold your HTML files:

```
$ sudo mkdir /var/www/nginx2
$ sudo chown www-data:www-data /var/www/nginx2
```

Go ahead and add a simple index.html file to that directory, for example:

```
$ echo "NGINX 2 website" | sudo tee /var/www/nginx2/index.html
```

With this file, you'll be able to quickly see that the site is different from the default website.

With your index.html file in place, go ahead and create a configuration file in /etc/nginx/sites-available/ called nginx2.devops.conf. It will tell NGINX to listen on port 80, serve up content from /var/www/nginx2/, and look for an index.html file by default. It will also set a default action to load the index.html file if no file is explicitly indicated in the URL path (http://nginx2.devops.lab/ vs. http://nginx2.devops.lab/index.html).

This content looks like this:

```
server {
  listen 80;
  server_name nginx2.devops.lab;
  root /var/www/nginx2;
  index index.html;
  location / {
    try_files $uri $uri/ =404;
  }
}
```

To enable this site, you need to make a symbolic link to it to the /etc/nginx/sites-enabled directory:

```
$ sudo ln -s /etc/nginx/sites-available/nginx2.devops.conf /
etc/nginx/sites-enabled/nginx2.devops.conf
```

Reload NGINX to run a test to confirm the server process is running:

```
$ sudo nginx -s reload
$ sudo nginx -t
```

Note   You can also run `sudo nginx -s restart`, but if there is a failure due to a misconfiguration, the server will be dead. The `reload` action instead attempts to apply the configurations, but won't kill the server if there's an error.

That's it! Now visit the two distinct URLS—`nginx.devops.lab` and `nginx2.devops.lab`—to see the results.

Install NGINX Using a Proxmox Template

Getting NGINX up and running from scratch is pretty straightforward, but Proxmox has a ready-made template you can use to do the same thing. The Turnkey version includes NGINX along with Webmin, a graphical tool for managing the entire system; PHP (FastCGI); MariaDB/MySQL; and Adminer, the browser-based tool for interacting with the database. This option is a good choice if you're looking to quickly spin up a site and perhaps install WordPress or some other application without much fuss.

To install the template, go to your main Proxmox dashboard, click the *local* storage icon under your Proxmox host, and click the **CT Templates** menu item. In that view, click the **Templates** button. This will give you a pop-up window from which you can select the template called *turnkey-nginx-php-fastcgi*, as shown in Figure 7-3.

Type	Package ↑	Version	Description
lxc	turnkey-mediawiki	16.1-1	TurnKey MediaWiki
lxc	turnkey-mibew	16.2-1	TurnKey Mibew
lxc	turnkey-moinmoin	16.1-1	TurnKey MoinMoin
lxc	turnkey-mongodb	16.1-1	TurnKey MongoDB
lxc	turnkey-moodle	16.1-1	TurnKey Moodle
lxc	turnkey-mumble	16.1-1	TurnKey Mumble
lxc	turnkey-mysql	16.1-1	TurnKey MySQL
lxc	turnkey-nextcloud	16.1-1	TurnKey Nextcloud
lxc	turnkey-nginx-php-fastcgi	16.1-1	TurnKey Nginx PHP FastCGI Server
lxc	turnkey-nodejs	16.1-1	TurnKey Node.js
lxc	turnkey-observium	16.1-1	TurnKey Observium
lxc	turnkey-odoo	16.1-1	TurnKey Odoo
lxc	turnkey-omeka	16.1-1	TurnKey Omeka
lxc	turnkey-opencart	16.1-1	TurnKey OpenCart
lxc	turnkey-openldap	16.1-1	TurnKey OpenLDAP
lxc	turnkey-openvpn	16.1-1	TurnKey OpenVPN
lxc	turnkey-orangehrm	16.1-1	TurnKey OrangeHRM
lxc	turnkey-oscommerce	16.1-1	TurnKey OSCommerce

Figure 7-3. *Select and download the turnkey-nginx-php-fastcgi template in Proxmox*

As with other LXCs you've created, give this system a name, static IP address, one core, and 1024MB of RAM. You can adjust these if you plan to run a web application that requires more horsepower, but these basics will get you started.

Note   If you plan to reuse the same IP address you used earlier (10.128.1.61/24), destroy that container and create a new one. Otherwise, use a new IP address and set up DNS accordingly. Otherwise, you'll have an IP conflict and have some real problems.

With Proxmox templates like this one, some of the configuration is done after you first log in. With that in mind, deploy the template and then switch to the **Console** view in Proxmox and log in with root and the password you set.

As soon as you log in, you'll get a series of screens prompting you to set a root password for your database, an admin email for reporting (you can use your "jadams@devops.lab" example), and some confirmation screens. Feel free to skip the *Backup and Migration* option. Once that's done, quit out of the configuration console. If you make a mistake, you can always rerun this configuration by logging in as root and running the turnkey-init command.

If you used the same IP address you set up with your previous example (10.128.1.61/24), you can just point your browser to https://nginx. devops.lab. You'll get warnings for the self-signed certificate (it's okay to proceed) and then notice the built-in control panel with access to a graphical shell, Webmin, and Adminer, as shown in Figure 7-4.

Figure 7-4. *The turnkey template-based NGINX dashboard with access to a shell, Webmin, and Adminer*

These are all handy tools you can use to administer your NGINX server. The login for **Webmin** is *root* and the password you set when you first created the Proxmox instance. If you click the **Adminer** button and enter your credentials—***adminer*** and the password you set during the post-configuration step—you can log in and start creating databases, tables, and content.

215

As an exercise, try creating a separate website using the previous instructions. You can also deploy WordPress on this server; just be sure to create the necessary database and user settings explained previously.

When a Little HTTP Is All You Need

While there are certainly occasions when you need a full-up web server like Apache or NGINX, sometimes all you need is a little HTTP server to test some functionality, either on your workstation, in a container, or on a server that only needs web services temporarily. For those occasions, there are some readily available options using Python and PHP CLI.

Python 3 http.server

Most modern Linux systems come installed with Python 3, a powerful programming language that comes with a number of built-in features, including an HTTP service. If Python 3 isn't installed on your system, install it using your package manager, such as

```
$ sudo apt install python3
```

Python includes a wide variety of capabilities, but for now you'll just be experimenting with the http.server, which will start a very small web server in the directory where the command is run (the default) or in a directory you define. This makes a useful way to test network access, a simple HTML page, or a directory listing. I've actually used this as a sort of quicky and dirty file server to access and download files from another machine to my workstation.

Try this first on your Linux workstation by moving into your Downloads directory and starting the http.server:

```
$ cd ~/Downloads
$ python3 -m http.server
```

This is the most basic option of the command, using the defaults. It will immediately start serving up content in the current directory on port 8000. When you open a web browser and navigate to *http://localhost:8000,* you'll see the contents of the Downloads directory.

You can use other ports by just adding the port to the end of the command, such as

```
$ python3 -m http.server 8088
```

You can also designate a directory other than the current working directory by adding the -d flag:

```
$ python3 -m http.server -d /var/www/html 8088
```

Notice that these examples don't use port 80, the common HTTP port. It's reserved (along with all ports under 1024) and can only be used if you run the preceding command as root (e.g., using sudo):

```
$ sudo python3 -m http.server -d /var/www/html 80
```

Go ahead and experiment with this useful service and consider using it in a small container when you want to test simple web services or network connectivity.

Use the PHP CLI Built-In Server

In Chapter 6, you installed a complete LAMP stack using Apache, PHP, and MariaDB, but there may be times when all you want or need is a simple test environment to test your PHP code. For that, you can use PHP CLI, a command-line interpreter for the language that allows you to run PHP commands from the shell or serve up PHP files as web pages.

To make this work on your Linux workstation or in a virtual machine, you'll need php-cli installed. It's a widely available package that doesn't add much overhead to your machine. Install it with your Linux package manager, such as

```
$ sudo apt install php-cli
```

As with the Python 3 server, the `php-cli` integrated server exposes the content in the directory from which the command is run. That behavior can be changed by adding the target directory flag, `-t`. Running with that flag might look like the following:

```
$ php -S localhost:8080 -t ~/Documents
```

Unlike the Python server, the `php-cli` server understands and parses PHP files much like your LAMP stack (minus the database bit). This can be incredibly useful for testing and can be readily observed using the `phpinfo()` command in a simple file. Place an `index.php` file with the following content in the folder you want to serve:

```
<?php
    phpinfo();
?>
```

When you start your server in that directory and open a browser to view it, you'll see the PHP configuration page just like you did on your LAMP server. If you compare this side by side with the same file accessed from a full LAMP stack, you'll notice some differences, but for basic testing, the `php-cli` integrated server is hard to beat.

Run php-cli in a Container

The next chapter will take a deep dive into containerizing and automating the deployment of your web servers, but it's worth taking a moment to show how the `php-cli` server can be run on a Docker host with a couple simple commands. If your needs are limited, this is a quick way to create a PHP-enabled web server without installing anything permanently on your workstation.

Fortunately, the good folks who develop PHP make available a number of container images, including one with `php-cli` installed, such as `php:8.1-cli`. That means you can just run the image on your Docker host (or workstation with Docker installed) and use it with the integrated web server in moments.

The important things to remember when using this pre-built Docker image to run your container are that it doesn't designate your web server port exposed by default or attach itself to your DevOps lab network. If you just run the default image, it'll run for a second and stop, which isn't very useful. You can solve all these issues by defining a port, setting the network to your Docker host's network, and using a command like `tail -f /dev/null` to keep the container running after it starts.

This would look like the following command run on your Docker workstation or host:

```
$ docker run --rm --expose 8080 --network host --name
php-server -d php:8.1-cli tail -f /dev/null
```

On first run, Docker will download the `php:8.1-cli` image to your local machine. Subsequent runs will be much faster because they'll reuse that downloaded image.

The preceding example names the container *php-server*, exposes port 8080, sets the network, and runs the `tail` command to keep the container running. The `--rm` flag removes any previous container of the same name, and the `-d` flag tells Docker to run the container and then free up the terminal. Having a running container is necessary so you can execute a `docker exec` command and run the PHP server inside the container.

With the container running, execute the following command to start the server on port 8080:

```
$ docker exec -it php-server php -S localhost:8080
```

This example tells Docker to access the running container called *php-server* and execute the PHP server command. You could add a *volume* to your container that maps a folder on your workstation to a folder inside the container, a step that would enable you to save your .php files locally and have them served from the container. You'll see examples of that capability in Chapter 8.

Conclusion

In this chapter, you've learned how to deploy NGINX manually or using a Proxmox template, and how to use simple web servers for testing. These principles can be used across your DevOps lab environment and give you a sense of how some basic Linux knowledge is a great help when you look to adopt a wide variety of DevOps tools and practices.

In the next chapter, you'll take a deeper dive into how to containerize your web servers and use automation to deploy them quickly and consistently.

CHAPTER 8

Containerizing and Automating Your Deployments

Modern software engineering embraces the DevOps workflow, which highlights some key principles for rapidly developing, testing, and deploying software in a wide variety of environments. Even companies that aren't outright "software" companies are driven by technology, and they've adopted DevOps to consistently manage systems running in on-premise data centers and public clouds like Amazon and Azure and on edge devices, which are often ARM-based computing devices like the Raspberry Pi.

In this chapter, you'll take a closer look at the mechanisms that make DevOps possible, specifically containers and automation. Table 8-1 explains some core DevOps principles, which you can refer back to as you explore these technologies.

© John S. Tonello 2022
J. S. Tonello, *Practical Linux DevOps*, https://doi.org/10.1007/978-1-4842-8318-9_8

Table 8-1. *Some core DevOps principles*

Practice	Why Is It Important?
Automation	Automate routine and advanced server and application configuration, security, deployment, and testing to avoid human error and free staff to work smarter.
Common tools	Development, security, and operations (DevSecOps) teams should use and understand the same tools and languages so they can improve cooperation, speed their work, and avoid app sprawl.
Communication	Share a common language between developers and architects that encourages on- and off-line collaboration and trust.
Agile development	Use and integrate continuous integration/continuous delivery (CI/CD) practices to ensure reliable and rapid application builds, tests, and deployments.
Security aforethought	Company policies and rules and third-party regulations should be built in to system environments and applications from the start, not as an afterthought.
Shift Left	Collaborate and test sooner, not later.
Observability and continuous feedback	Real-time views of outages, problems, breaches, misconfigurations, and fixes are critical—collaboration and transparency into remediation workflows, too.

(continued)

Table 8-1. *(continued)*

Practice	Why Is It Important?
Continuous testing	Test code, environments, and policies in build, test, and deployment phases.
Cultural practices (autonomy, trust, and learning)	Developers should have the confidence to autonomously create approved environments and code. Code sharing and other practices build trust, and the work culture should support learning and boldness, not caution.
Broad use of open source software	Accelerate development by leaning in to developer communities and their expertise, not by creating everything from scratch. Draw on large communities of developers to dolivor bottor appo.
Faster time to value and outcomes	DevOps practitioners deploy code 45 times more frequently, commit to deploy 2,500 times faster, recover from incidents 2,600 times faster, and have change failure rates that are 7 times lower.

Thinking in terms of Containers and Microservices

Having DevOps principles in mind makes it easier to understand the value of containerizing applications. They make developing applications consistent and repeatable and, just as importantly, make it possible to deploy them successfully to any platform. In this section, you'll take a look at the process by deploying NGINX with Docker.

As you learned in the last chapter, deploying NGINX is fairly straightforward. Armed with that knowledge, you can better understand how to do the same thing with Docker. In a production setting, NGINX containers may act as the front end for a wide range of applications, all running in their own separate, but linked, containers. This is especially useful when it comes to scaling applications based on demand. For example, a company like Walmart can quickly add capacity to its retail website during times of high demand (such as the Christmas season) and then scale it back when the holidays are over.

Deploy an NGINX Container

Getting basic NGINX up and running in a container is quite straightforward, and it's something you can try from either the command line or by creating a full-blown `docker-compose.yml` file and an associated `Dockerfile`. The good folks at NGINX (and others) have made available a number of different versions of the application, including a base Docker image with just NGINX on it and other versions with PHP, Perl, and useful preinstalled modules. Check out `https://hub.docker.com` to see some options.

Let's try the base container and fire it up using the command line. Of course, you can create a more sophisticated Docker deployment using a `docker-compose.yml`, but this will get you started.

Since the Docker command-line arguments automatically reference Docker Hub, you can run an NGINX container with a simple `docker run nginx` command, but it's worth adding some configurations to make it more useful.

Shell into your `docker.devops.lab` host (or use your workstation if you're running Docker there) and create a directory called `nginx` with a subdirectory called `files`:

```
$ mkdir -p ~/nginx/files
```

Place an `index.html` file in the `files/` directory with whatever content you want. It can be full HTML or just some simple text. This file will be copied into the NGINX image (and the container) in this example by passing the -v (volume) flag and placing the file or files it finds into the running container's /usr/share/nginx/html/ directory. The following command also gives the container a name and forwards the default port 80 traffic to port 8088 so it won't conflict with other web servers you may be running on your Docker host. The -d flag tells Docker to build and run the container and then release the terminal:

```
$ docker run --name mynginx -v /home/$USER/nginx/files:/usr/
share/nginx/html:ro -p 8088:80 -d nginx
```

This default image uses /usr/share/nginx/html/ as the root of the NGINX server (not, say, /var/www/html/). The ro sets the folder and files contained in it to read-only, meaning you won't be able to edit it as any user other than root. The first time you run this command, Docker will download the nginx image from Docker Hub and build the container from that file. On subsequent runs, Docker will use that local nginx image, and your deployments will be much faster.

When the build completes, confirm your container is running:

```
$ docker ps
```

Point your browser to your Docker host, being sure to add the port number to the URL: http://docker.devops.lab:8088. You'll see the content of your index.html file.

The way this container was created, with the -v flag, mapped your ~/nginx/files/ folder to the base NGINX directory in the running container. That means you can edit your index.html file on your Docker host (or workstation) and reload the browser to see the changes in real time. If you used docker exec -it mynginx /bin/bash to actually log in to the container to attempt these edits, that would work, too, but your changes would be lost the next time you start the container from the original image. By mapping the volume, you can rapidly edit your HTML code without ever having to redeploy your NGINX container.

Automate Your NGINX Deployment

Armed with what you now know about basic NGINX configurations, it's time to try automating your web server deployment. Automation—also known as infrastructure as code—is a way to define everything you need to run in an on-premise or cloud instance without ever having to manually log in or edit configuration files by hand.

In the DevOps world, automation is critical for managing hundreds, thousands, or hundreds of thousands of virtual machines or AWS, Azure, Kubernetes, or other public cloud instances. It allows engineers to define what they want in simple code and just reapply it wherever they want to run that kind of server or application.

Note   It's important to add the caveat that the infrastructure automation described in the next section is generally not a system *provisioning* tool. That is, you have to first create some type of VM, LXC, or cloud instance to configure. Tools like HashiCorp Vagrant and Terraform, and AWS AMI templates can handle the provisioning, and tools like Ansible and Chef can configure the raw instances.

Automating the deployment of NGINX—and setting all your custom configurations—is a good starting place because much of what DevOps engineers work on these days contains some sort of web component. Plus, you now already know how NGINX should look and behave, so the automation steps will look and feel familiar.

Automate with Ansible

Many DevOps engineers start their automation journeys with Ansible, a free open-source tool that can target Linux, Windows, and macOS systems. It's agentless, which means you don't need to install anything on the target machines for it to work. It uses SSH to connect to Linux and macOS hosts and WinRM to connect to Windows hosts.

If you want to see how automation can take you from raw to configured, go ahead and spin up a new Ubuntu or Debian LXC in Proxmox. Add a local SSH key during that step to enable passwordless login or do it afterward using the ssh-copy-id command on your workstation, such as

```
$ ssh-copy-id root@ansible.devops.lab
```

If you haven't created a local SSH key on your Linux workstation, go ahead and do that with the following command. Don't add a password when prompted:

```
$ ssh-keygen
```

By default, this places id_rsa and id_rsa.pub files in a /home/*user*/.ssh/ directory on your system. When you run the preceding ssh-copy-id command, it copies the public half of the key pair to the remote host so all future logins won't require you to enter a password when using SSH to log in.

Note   If you have a Raspberry Pi device lying around, you can use that as one of your targets, too. You'll first need to put an operating system on it, such as Raspberry Pi OS or Ubuntu, but you can automate the NGINX configuration in the same way as for any other physical or virtual system.

To work with Ansible, you need to install the ansible package on your workstation, which is available in the standard Ubuntu (and other Linux) repositories:

```
$ sudo apt update && sudo apt install ansible -y
```

Ansible uses a concept of an *inventory* to identify one or more systems you want to target with your configurations. You can add single machines by their domain names or IP addresses or even create groups of machines. These are then referenced in a configuration file called an Ansible playbook. By previously sharing your SSH key, you'll be able to run Ansible commands without having to enter a password each time.

By default, the inventory file (in Ubuntu 20.04 LTS) is located at /etc/ansible/hosts, and it contains a number of base examples to get you started. If the folder doesn't exist on your version of Ubuntu (including 21.10 and 22.04 LTS), create it with the following command:

```
$ sudo mkdir -p /etc/ansible
```

Listing 8-1 is an example Ansible host file that has individual entries, a group called mynginx that includes only the IP address of a single server, and a group called webservers that identifies multiple servers:

Listing 8-1. An Ansible inventory file

```
# This is my default ansible 'hosts' file.
nginx.devops.lab
rpi4.devops.lab
server22 ansible_host=10.128.1.99

[mynginx]
10.128.1.62
[webservers]
nginx.devops.lab
```

```
rpi4.devops.lab
10.128.1.62
```

With this Ansible host file, you can use either of the first three entries as the hosts value in your playbook to target those specific nodes one at a time, or you can use the myngnix group to target the host at 10.128.1.62 or use the webservers group to target those three servers at the same time. You can add many servers to a group, which should give you an idea of why DevOps engineers like to use automation to configure a whole lot of servers at once. The only hitch is that your workstation is doing all the work, so there's a limit to how many nodes it can manage.

Instead of setting inventories system-wide, you can alternatively create inventory files in your project directories. For example, in the following example, you could create an ./ansible/inventory file with the preceding contents instead of editing or creating /etc/ansible/hosts. This is invoked with the -i <inventory-file-name> flag when running your playbook, as shown later.

Ansible Playbook Example

Ansible playbooks are written in YAML, a text-only language that can be composed in just about any plain-text editor, such as *Visual Studio Code (VS Code)* or *vi* or *Notepad*. To keep things orderly, it's best to create a directory on your workstation and initiate it with *Git* so you can push your code to GitHub or GitLab. This is a common DevOps practice in environments where version control is critical for creating and sharing code and is explained in more detail in Chapter 10. You can install Git with the following command:

```
$ sudo apt install git
```

Setting up Git on your workstation is a common DevOps practice in environments where code version control is critical:

```
$ mkdir -p ~/ansible/files
$ mkdir -p ~/ansible/html
$ cd ~/ansible
$ git init .
```

Open VS Code or your favorite text editor for the next steps and create a file called my-nginx-website.yml inside the ~/ansible/ directory. This will be your Ansible *playbook*. Add the following content, shown in Listing 8-2.

Note The spacing in this YAML document is important. YAML doesn't recognize tabs, so you need to enter spaces (or ensure your code editor uses spaces). Each sub-element begins with two spaces, and content like the *tasks and vars entries* all have the same indentation.

Listing 8-2. Contents of an Ansible playbook for configuring NGINX on a node

```
---
- hosts: webservers ❶
  remote_user: root
  become: true
  vars: ❷

    document_root: /var/www/html
    app_root: html
  tasks: ❸
    - name: Update apt cache and install Nginx
      apt:
```

```
    name: nginx
    state: latest
    update_cache: true
- name: Copy website files to the server's document root
  copy:
    src: "{{ app_root }}" ❹
    dest: "{{ document_root }}"
    mode: preserve

- name: Apply Nginx template ❺
  template:
    src: files/nginx.devops.conf
    dest: /etc/nginx/sites-available/default
  notify: Restart Nginx

- name: Enable new site ❻
  file:
    src: /etc/nginx/sites-available/default
    dest: /etc/nginx/sites-enabled/default
    state: link
  notify: Restart Nginx

- name: Allow all access to tcp port 80 ❼
  ufw:
    rule: allow
    port: '80'
    proto: tcp

handlers: ❽
  - name: Restart Nginx
    service:
      name: nginx
      state: restarted
```

If you take a close look at the YAML playbook file, a lot of it should appear familiar. These few lines are very powerful, however, and provide quite a bit of capability. Let's look at the various elements.

All Ansible playbooks begin with the hosts: element ❶, which references an individual host or, as in this example, an inventory group called *webservers* in my /etc/ansible/hosts or a project-specific inventory file. When this file is applied, it will target the servers listed in that inventory group, shown as nginx.devops.lab, rpi4.devops.lab, and 10.128.1.62 in the preceding example. This section also tells Ansible to connect to those remote systems as the root user and to run with elevated privileges. If you have other privileged users on a system (which is better than logging in as root!), you could use that instead.

The vars: section ❷ defines some variables to use later in the playbook file. This is a handy way to add configurations in one place and use them elsewhere. It makes editing and debugging easier. The document_ root (/var/www/html) sets where web content will be served from, and the app_root value tells Ansible to look for a folder on your workstation relative to the playbook file called html from which to copy content. In this example, I have an index.html file in the ~/ansible/html folder on my workstation. I also have a file called nginx.devops.conf in the ~/ansible/ files folder with the content shown in Listing 8-3, which is very nearly the same as the example in Chapter 7.

Listing 8-3. A static website configuration file that will be copied into the target node

```
server {
  listen 80;
  server_name nginx.devops.lab;
  root /var/www/html;
  index index.html;
  location / {
```

```
    try_files $uri $uri/ =404;
  }
}
```

The Ansible playbook `tasks:` section ❸ defines the actual steps to be performed on your web hosts, including installing `nginx`, copying my `nginx.devops.conf` file and HTML content ❹ and ❺, making a symbolic link from the `sites-available` configuration file to `sites-enabled` ❻, ensuring port 80 is open in the firewall ❼, and restarting the `nginx` server ❽. The `handlers:` section ❽ is referenced by tasks above it to tell the server to restart `nginx` if any of those settings change.

Apply the NGINX Playbook

With the `my-nginx-website.yml` complete, you're now ready to automate the configuration of your nodes. Since all the instructions—including the target hosts—are configured in the file, it's a simple matter of executing the following command from inside your `~/ansible` directory:

```
$ ansible-playbook my-nginx-website.yml
```

If you're using an inventory file in your project directory (`~/ansible/inventory`), you can invoke it with the `-i` flag, as in the following example:

```
$ ansible-playbook -i inventory my-nginx-website.yml
```

In the terminal, you'll see Ansible running through the various steps and applying your configurations. When it's done, you can point your browser at the target server(s) IP or hostname addresses to see the results! With this little bit of code, you can configure any Linux-based system in exactly the same way without ever having to manually log in.

Automate NGINX with Chef

As you saw, Ansible can make configuring a node fast and consistent. However, it doesn't have any built-in way to test your code before it is deployed or after it's been deployed. With Chef, you can automate node configurations, test them in local environments using tools like Docker and Vagrant (with VirtualBox), and run real-time scans to verify everything.

To get started, download Chef Workstation, a free bundle of tools that provides everything you need to start creating Chef cookbooks (code for configuring nodes) and profiles (code for scanning nodes). It also has a number of other tools and capabilities that allow you to scale to true enterprise-level deployments.

Download Chef Workstation at
`www.chef.io/downloads/tools/workstation`

After installing the package on your Linux system (Ubuntu in this example), edit your `~/.bashrc` file to initialize the shell environment to use the embedded Chef resources, such as Ruby. This ensures you don't need to install anything else to make it work. Place the following "eval" statement at the end of the file:

```
$ vi ~/.bashrc
...
eval "$(chef shell-init bash)"
...
```

Of course, you can run `chef shell-init bash` each time you open a shell terminal on your workstation, but this statement ensures it's set up every time you open a new terminal.

Note   Don't worry if you don't know how to code using Ruby. The Chef language is intuitive and easy to get the hang of, even if you've never worked with the Ruby language.

Create a Chef Cookbook and Recipes

As mentioned earlier, Chef Workstation comes with the tools you need to work with the Chef language, which is based on Ruby. Don't worry if you don't know the Ruby language. Chef's Domain-Specific Language (DSL) is easy to read and understand. If you're using VS Code as your code editor, you can add the official Chef extension to your environment with a few clicks. The plugin offers code completion and error-checking built right in.

To create an NGINX cookbook, make a new folder on your workstation to hold your code. Chef has generators that do most of the work for you, including generating a Chef repository (a directory to hold all your automation content), cookbooks, recipes, profiles, templates, and more.

Start by generating a repo:

```
$ cd ~
```

```
$ chef generate repo chef-repo
```

This command will create the ~/chef-repo folder in your home directory and auto-create a number of subfolders and files. Move into the ~/chef-repo/cookbooks/ folder and use a similar chef generate command to create your NGINX cookbook, adding the -k dokken flag to have Chef automatically create a Test Kitchen kitchen.yml file that works with Docker. Test Kitchen allows you to fully test and verify your Chef code locally before trying it out on a separate target node:

```
$ cd ~/chef-repo/cookbooks
$ chef generate cookbook nginx -k dokken
```

Again, Chef will create the ~/chef-repo/cookbooks/nginx folder along with several subfolders and files. Among these is a compliance folder, which holds Chef *profiles*. These are separate files that you use to test and verify everything set up by the cookbook is working as expected. The ~/chef-repo/cookbooks/nginx/compliance/profiles folder is where you create one or more Chef profiles that can be used to scan your nodes.

Don't be put off by all the files the chef cookbook generate command creates. You won't use everything in this example. The important elements are the following in the ~/chef-repo/cookbooks/nginx/ directory:

```
├── compliance/
├── kitchen.yml
├── metadata.rb
├── recipes/
└── templates/
```

It's always a good habit to edit the metadata.rb file before doing anything else, adding your name, email, and application version number, such as 0.1.0. As your needs and application change, you can increment the version number as you make updated versions of your cookbook. Before leaving this file, make sure the chef_version is set to at least '>= 17.5' to take advantage of the features described in the next steps.

Creating a cookbook can be done with some manual Linux shell commands, but it's best to use the built-in Chef generator. The same is true when creating profiles to work with Chef InSpec, one of the Workstation tools. To do that, use the inspec init profile <profile-name> command from within the compliance/profiles/ folder:

```
$ cd ~/chef-repo/cookbooks/nginx/compliance/profiles
$ inspec init profile nginx
```

Again, Chef creates an nginx folder with a controls subdirectory with an example.rb inside it and an inspec.yml file. Rename the example.rb file default.rb. You'll edit it later.

If you open the `inspec.yml` file, you'll notice that the Chef generator completed much of it for you, including a version 0.1.0. It's a good practice to increment the version as you make future iterations of your InSpec profile. Note that Chef considers your cookbook and your InSpec profile as two different things that can be versioned separately. For example, you can have version 0.1.0 in your `metadata.rb` file for your cookbook version and version 0.3.0 for your `inspec.yml` profile. They don't need to be in sync.

Create a Chef Recipe

In Chef, recipes are the files that contain your infrastructure configuration code. As in the YAML example with Ansible, Chef recipes include a wide variety of tasks using built-in resources to automate the things you want. Because recipes are Ruby files, you can add logic that allows you to set recipes to do different things based on your target nodes' platforms, specific OS, and many other system values.

You may notice that the `recipes` folder contains a `default.rb` file already. You can add as many recipes as you want, but for this example, you'll create just one in addition to the `default.rb` that will hold your web server configurations. Use the built-in Chef generator to create this second recipe:

```
$ cd ~/chef-repo/cookbooks/nginx
$ chef generate recipe webserver
```

After this command runs, a new file named `webserver.rb` will appear in your cookbook's `recipes` folder. Chef adds the `.rb` extension automatically.

Open the `./recipes/default.rb` file and add the following lines. These tell Chef to use both your `webserver.rb` file and the NGINX profile you'll create in the next step. The paths use Chef notation:

```
# Cookbook:: nginx
```

```
# Recipe:: default
#
include_recipe 'nginx::webserver'
include_profile 'nginx::nginx'
```

The include_recipe path points to ./recipes/webserver.rb;
the include_profile path points to ./compliance/profiles/nginx/
controls/default.rb. This shorthand is used throughout Chef code to
reference local files relative to the cookbook folder.

Save the default.rb recipe and edit the webserver.rb, adding the
content shown in Listing 8-4. You'll notice many similarities with the
Ansible version, but this example will import some template files and pass
them to the node. Templates provide a way to standardize your code while
also inserting dynamic content from each node itself.

Listing 8-4. The content for your webserver.rb recipe

```
# Cookbook:: nginx
# Recipe:: webserver
package 'nginx'  ❶
package 'curl'

directory '/etc/nginx/ssl' do  ❷
  owner 'root'
  group 'root'
  mode '0755'
  action :create
end

openssl_x509_certificate '/etc/nginx/ssl/mycert.pem' do
  common_name 'node[:fqdn]'
  org 'Chef'
```

```
  org_unit 'Lab'
  country 'US'
  mode '0600'
end

template '/etc/nginx/nginx.conf' do  ❸
  source 'nginx.conf.erb'
  owner 'root'
  group 'root'
  mode '0644'
  notifies :restart, 'service[nginx]', :delayed
  action :create
end

template '/etc/nginx/sites-available/default' do
  source 'server.erb'
  owner 'root'
  group 'root'
  mode '0644'
  notifies :restart, 'service[nginx]', :delayed
  action :create
end

template '/var/www/html/index.html' do
  source 'index.erb'
  owner 'root'
  group 'root'
  mode '0644'
  action :create
end

service 'nginx' do  ❹
  action [:enable, :start]
```

```
end

service 'nginx' do
  subscribes :reload, 'file[/etc/nginx/ssl/mycert.pem]',
:immediately
end
```

Chef automates the installation of the latest versions of the nginx and curl packages with the package resource ❶. You could also set specific versions of each (a good DevOps practice). This recipe creates a location for SSL certs and uses built-in resources to generate them ❷.

The next group of resources uses the *template* resource to copy configuration and .html files to the target node ❸. Templates are nice because you can embed elements that Chef reads from the target system, such as the FQDN of the host, shown in the previous example as node[:fqdn]. In that way, you can use the same template on all your target hosts without editing anything. Chef has a file resource to copy files as-is from your workstation to your node, and that's a good option for static content.

The recipe ends with service resources that enable and start nginx and tell the target node to reload nginx if the SSL certificate changes. The subscribes element is similar to Ansible's notify directive.

After you've created and saved your recipes, run *Cookstyle*, the built-in Chef code-checker (linter), on the directory. The -a flag autocorrects any errors it finds:

```
$ cookstyle -a
```

Cookstyle is a great way to verify your code as you go, and it's particularly handy if your new to Chef. The VS Code plugin also shows you errors as you write, helping ensure your code is solid before moving on.

Create Templates

As mentioned previously, Chef template files can be used to define content with some variables populated from the target system itself. Your template files become static files on each target node, but will contain content defined when the cookbook is applied.

This NGINX example has three templates: `nginx.conf.erb`, `server.erb,` and `index.erb`. The `.erb` extension indicates a template, but these also use Ruby as the base language. As with earlier examples, you can use a Chef generator to create the template files:

```
$ cd ~/chef-repo/cookbooks/nginx
$ chef generate template nginx.conf
```

The preceding command will create `nginx.conf.erb` in a new `./templates` directory inside your `nginx` cookbook folder. Add the content from Listing 8-5 (which is the same as the content you used to configure NGINX with Ansible) to the new .erb file.

Listing 8-5. The nginx.conf template file, a generic NGINX configuration

```
user root;
worker_processes auto;
pid /run/nginx.pid;

events {
        worker_connections 768;
}

http {
        sendfile on;
        tcp_nopush on;
        tcp_nodelay on;
```

```
    keepalive_timeout 65;
    types_hash_max_size 2048;

    include /etc/nginx/mime.types;
    default_type application/octet-stream;

    ssl_protocols TLSv1.2 TLSv1.3;

    access_log /var/log/nginx/access.log;
    error_log /var/log/nginx/error.log;

    include /etc/nginx/sites-enabled/*;
}
```

Next, create the server configuration file:

```
$ chef generate template server
```

This template contains server configuration content, as shown in Listing 8-6, including the dynamically supplied server name, which Chef will populate from information it collects from the target node itself. This is shown in the <%= ... %> content. In the configuration file on the target node, this variable will be written based on that system's unique domain name.

Listing 8-6. The virtual host NGINX server configuration template server.erb with dynamic content

```
server {
  listen 443 ssl;
  server_name <%= node[:fqdn] %>;
  ssl_certificate /etc/nginx/ssl/mycert.pem;
  ssl_certificate_key /etc/nginx/ssl/mycert.key;
  ssl_protocols TLSv1.2 TLSv1.3;
  ssl on;
  root /var/www/html;
}
```

The final template is the HTML page for your NGINX server. It contains several dynamic elements that will be written to the static `index.html` file on your server:

```
$ chef generate template index
```

Add the following content to it, as shown in Listing 8-7. Notice the elements in the `<%= ... %>` tags. This information will be grabbed by Chef during configuration and written to the static `index.html` file.

Listing 8-7. The index.erb file with dynamic content

```
<html>
<head>
    <title>Nginx Site Created by Chef</title>
</head>
<body>
    <h3>This is Nginx by Chef</h3>
    <p><b>Hostname:</b> <%= node[:hostname] %></p>
    <p><b>FQDN:</b> <%= node[:fqdn] %></p>
    <p><b>IP Address:</b> <%= node[:ipaddress] %></p>
    <p><b>Platform:</b> <%= node[:platform] %></p>
</body>
</html>
```

With these templates configured, take another look at the `webserver.rb` recipe you created previously. You can see that the *template* resources define the path on the node where the resulting file should be placed, using templates it finds in the `./cookbooks/nginx/templates` directory, such as the snippet in Listing 8-8.

Listing 8-8. A Chef template resource showing the node path and local source path

```
...
template '/etc/nginx/nginx.conf' do ❶
  source 'nginx.conf.erb' ❷
  owner 'root'
  group 'root'
  mode '0644'
  notifies :restart, 'service[nginx]', :delayed
  action :create
end
...
```

In the preceding example, ❶ is the file that will be created on the node, /etc/nginx/nginx.conf. The source directive points to ./cookbooks/nginx/templates/nginx.conf.erb ❷.

In the next step, you'll create a compliance profile you can use to verify all the configurations defined in your Chef recipes are correct.

Create a Chef InSpec Profile

Chef *profiles* contain *controls* that allow you to separate various actions into logical groups. In the following example, you'll create two controls. One will contain *configuration* tests; the other will contain *security* tests. Sophisticated profiles can contain hundreds of controls.

Note In a production environment, you would use Chef Infra Server to store your cookbooks, profiles, and other content and Chef Automate to graphically interact with data about all your nodes. You won't be using those in this example, but the approach outlined here sets you up to use them.

Profiles have many things in common with recipes, but instead of applying configurations, profiles describe *resources* that define the system states you want. The following profile, located in `./compliance/profiles/nginx/controls/default.rb`, includes only a few of the tests that could be run to verify NGINX is installed and configured as you want.

Edit the preceding `default.rb` file (renamed from the original `example.rb` created by the `inspec init` command earlier) and add the content shown in Listing 8-9.

Listing 8-9. Contents of the default.rb profile file with tests to verify your NGINX node

```
control 'nginx-config' do  ❶
  impact 0.7
  title 'Nginx configuration'
  desc 'Nginx configuration'
  describe port(80) do
    it { should_not be_listening }
  end
  describe port(443) do
    it { should be_listening }
  end
  describe package('nginx') do
    it { should be_installed }
  end
  describe http('https://localhost:443/', ssl_verify:
  false) do  ❷
    its('status') { should cmp 200 }
    its('body') { should match /Nginx Site Created by Chef/ }
  end
end
```

```
control 'nginx-security' do ❸
  impact 1.0
  title 'Nginx TLS security'
  desc 'Do not support TLSv1.1'
  describe ssl(port: 443).protocols('tls1.1') do
    it { should_not be_enabled }
  end
  describe ssl(port: 443).protocols('tls1.2') do
    it { should be_enabled }
  end
end
```

The first control, `nginx-config` ❶, contains information about the profile (severity level rated on a scale of 0.0 (minor) to 1.0 (critical)), a *title,* and a *description.* The four *describe* resources in this control check to ensure port 80 is not listening, port 443 is, NGINX is installed, and the website itself returns a correct portion of the content ❷. The second control, `nginx-security`, uses two *describe* resources to check that the server is not using TLS 1.1, but is using TLS 1.2 ❸.

You might think, "Gee, can I use this profile for the node I configured with Ansible?" The answer is yes! Even though the Ansible node didn't use Chef for its initial configuration, Chef InSpec profiles like this one can be used on any target node, regardless of how they were originally configured.

Apply and Test Your Chef Configuration

In the following steps, you'll run what Chef calls *ad hoc* commands, one-offs that are useful for configuring one or two nodes at a time. It has more production-friendly alternatives, but the next steps are valid for your small lab environment.

Before running these commands, run `cookstyle -a` again in the root of your `nginx` cookbook directory:

```
$ cd ~/chef-repo/cookbooks/nginx
$ cookstyle -a
```

The following example targets an Ubuntu node running in an LXC in Proxmox called `ubuntu05`. I've pre-shared an SSH key, so I can add the `-i` flag to point to my key file and the `--user` flag for clarity. The *chef-run* command defaults to using the root user, and if an SSH key has been set up and added already, Chef knows about the credentials and uses them.

On your workstation, run the following from inside your `nginx` directory:

```
$ chef run ubuntu05.dcvops.lab recipes/default.rb -i ~/.ssh/
id_rsa --user root
```

In the shell, you'll see Chef doing its thing, starting by installing the `chef-client` agent and then installing and configuring your node. The `chef-client` is small and lightweight, but very powerful. It does all the work on the node, not your workstation, and can be set to run at regular intervals without any interaction from you. This is a great DevOps principle that ensures your node is configured and stays that way over time without any human interaction.

When the `chef-run` completes, run it again. You'll see how much faster subsequent runs are. That's because Chef recognizes that everything is configured already and it doesn't need to take any actions or make any changes, a concept called *idempotency*.

When running `chef-run` in this example, you're actually doing configuration and verification in one step. The verification shows up in your terminal in green-colored (passed) or red-colored (failed) tests. To verify your configuration without running `chef-run` (which reports the state of the node because you've included the profile as part of your default.rb cookbook with the include_profile resource), you can run Chef InSpec by itself. It doesn't require the chef-client to work, so try it with both your Chef and Ansible nodes:

```
$ cd ~/chef-repo/cookbooks/nginx

$ inspec exec compliance/profiles/nginx -t ssh://root@ubuntu05

$ inspec exec compliance/profiles/nginx -t ssh://root@rpi4
```

In each case, you should see the all green results and confirmation of success!

```
Profile: Nginx profile (nginx)
Version: 0.1.0
Target:  ssh://root@ubuntu05:22

✓  nginx-config: Nginx configuration
   ✓  Port 80 is expected not to be listening
   ✓  Port 443 is expected to be listening
   ✓  System Package nginx is expected to be installed
   ✓  HTTP GET on https://localhost:443/ status is expected
      to cmp == 200
   ✓  HTTP GET on https://localhost:443/ body is expected to
      match /Nginx Site Created by Chef/
✓  nginx-security: Nginx TLS security
   ✓  SSL/TLS on ubuntu05:443 with protocol == "tls1.1" is
      expected not to be enabled
   ✓  SSL/TLS on ubuntu05:443 with protocol == "tls1.2" is
      expected to be enabled

Profile Summary: 2 successful controls, 0 control failures, 0
controls skipped
Test Summary: 7 successful, 0 failures, 0 skipped
```

Test with Test Kitchen

When you first created your cookbook with the -k dokken flag, Chef created a kitchen.yml file in the root of your ~/chef-repo/cookbooks/nginx directory that's set up to use Docker to test your configuration locally. Let's see how that works.

Test Kitchen is installed when you installed Chef Workstation, and it has plugins that enable you to do local testing with Docker, Vagrant, and even cloud accounts in AWS and Azure, among others. The Dokken (Docker) version requires that you have Docker on your workstation. The Vagrant version requires the Vagrant application and something like VirtualBox to create local virtual machines where you can test instances. For this example, you'll use Docker.

If you haven't previously installed Docker on your Linux workstation, execute the following commands:

```
$ sudo apt install docker.io docker-compose
```

When the installation is complete, add your user to the docker group on your system:

```
$ sudo usermod -aG docker $USER
```

Log out and log back in to enable that group setting and run a quick test to ensure your user has permission to run Docker:

```
$ docker ps
```

Test Kitchen with Dokken spins up containers that are more like real VMs so you can do full-blown testing. You can deploy your code to multiple flavors of Linux, too, and Test Kitchen will create everything, apply your code, and test it in one step. From a DevOps standpoint, this makes fast code iteration possible, and the resulting code can be confidently applied to live test and production servers.

Take a look at the `kitchen.yml` file in the root of your ~/chef-repo/cookbooks/nginx directory. Modify it to look like the example in Listing 8-10.

Listing 8-10. An example kitchen.yml file

```
---
driver:
  name: dokken
  privileged: true              # allows systemd services
  chef_version: latest

provisioner:
  name: dokken

transport:
  name: dokken

verifier:
  name: inspec

platforms:
  - name: ubuntu-20.04
    driver:
      image: dokken/ubuntu-20.04
      pid_one_command: /bin/systemd
      intermediate_instructions:
        - RUN /usr/bin/apt-get update
  # - name: centos-8
  #   driver:
  #     image: dokken/centos-8
  #     pid_one_command: /usr/lib/systemd/systemd

suites:
```

```
- name: default
  run_list:
    - recipe[nginx::default]
  verifier:
    inspec_tests:
      - compliance/profiles/nginx
  attributes:
    audit:
      reporter: 'cli'
```

The preceding example includes a couple edits to the default `kitchen.yml` file that was first auto-generated, namely, telling Test Kitchen to build and run the containers as *privileged,* to use the latest version of the *chef-client,* and to use the profile you created earlier. This version also shows the CentOS entry commented out because the `webserver.rb` recipe doesn't contain logic to handle the differences between Ubuntu and Red Hat Linux.

The *driver, provisioner,* and *transport* elements are all set to `dokken`, which will handle how Test Kitchen creates the containers and sets up networking. The *verifier* is set to `inspec`. Notice in the *suites* section that Test Kitchen has a *run_list* (cookbooks assigned to a node) set to `recipe[nginx::default]`, which will apply your `default.rb` and `webserver.rb` recipes. It also has an *inspec_tests* value set to the relative path of your `compliance/profiles/nginx` profile.

To make this work, you'll need Docker running on your workstation. If that's set, run the following from the root of your `./nginx` directory:

```
$ cookstyle -a
$ kitchen test
```

The first command checks your code with Cookstyle; the second command creates an Ubuntu 20.04 image, applies your two cookbook recipes, runs the InSpec profile scan, and, if everything works correctly, shuts down and destroys everything. During that process, you'll see the actions Chef is taking as Test Kitchen does its thing.

Instead of doing all these steps at once, you can *create*, *converge* (apply your Chef code), *verify,* and *destroy* the test environments in separate steps:

```
$ kitchen create
$ kitchen converge
$ kitchen verify
$ kitchen destroy
```

Doing these one at a time allows you to rerun the *converge* and *verify* commands to update and revalidate your code. This is a key principle of Test-Driven Development, a common practice with modern DevOps teams.

Try your hand at modifying your Chef recipes and InSpec profiles to see how you might expand on what you've done here. You can draw on hundreds of Chef resources to configure and verify thousands of system settings—all without ever having to manually log in to your target systems.

Conclusion

In this chapter, you've learned how to deploy NGINX using both Ansible and Chef. These principles can be used across your DevOps lab environment and give you a sense of how some basic Linux knowledge is a great help when you look to adopt a wide variety of DevOps practices.

Take some time to play around with different playbooks and cookbooks and different ways to automate some of the work you've done. Check the Ansible and Chef websites for detailed documentation on how to expand on what you've learned.

In the next chapter, you'll take a look at ways to manage and maintain your servers, taking advantage of **Webmin** and the automation principles you've learned.

CHAPTER 9

Server Management and Maintenance

In the chapters so far, you've learned how to deploy a wide range of servers and tools to make your DevOps lab a truly useful environment for testing just about any modern software technology. Managing those systems over time is a critical aspect of any environment—lab or enterprise—and this chapter explains some best practices for maintaining and securing your lab, just as you would as part of a DevSecOps team.

In this chapter, you'll work with a variety of tools to graphically manage multiple systems and learn how to back up your servers and databases and use automation tools like Ansible and Chef, along with GitHub (or GitLab) to further define your infrastructure as code.

The key to system management and maintenance is visibility. Being able to know exactly what's installed, what's running, how much storage is free, and the like should be possible without you having to log in to each node to do it.

© John S. Tonello 2022
J. S. Tonello, *Practical Linux DevOps*, https://doi.org/10.1007/978-1-4842-8318-9_9

A Closer Look at Webmin

In Chapter 7, you deployed the NGINX template that included Webmin, the PHP-based dashboard for managing systems. As you saw, you can easily manage a single system with the Webmin dashboard, but you can also use a single interface to manage multiple servers that also have Webmin installed.

To be clear, Webmin is pretty lightweight in terms of resources, but it's not necessarily something you want to install everywhere. Someone with access to the dashboard can do a lot of damage. That said, when you're starting out, Webmin can provide a very useful way to analyze and configure Linux systems.

For this example, you'll use a Chef cookbook to install Webmin on an Ubuntu target node. Webmin isn't available as an apt package, so you'll need to tell Chef to download the .deb file, install some dependencies, and, for security, add a line to the configuration file to limit traffic to the server to your DevOps lab subnet. You can do a lot more, but this is a good place to start and give you a taste of the steps involved.

To create a new cookbook, again use the built-in Chef generator from the root of your workstation's cookbooks directory:

```
$ cd ~/chef-repo/cookbooks/
$ chef generate cookbook webmin -C "John Adams" -m "jadams@
devops.lab" -I apache2 -k dokken
```

This will create the directory called webmin and all the base subfolders, including recipes. I've added the -C, -m, and -I flags to automatically set my author name, email, and license in the metadata.rb file and the -k flag to create a kitchen.yml file ready to use with Test Kitchen. With that done, edit the ~/chef-repo/cookbooks/webmin/recipes/default.rb file and add the content shown in Listing 9-1.

Listing 9-1. A Chef cookbook to install and configure Webmin on an Ubuntu node

```
# Cookbook:: webmin
# Recipe:: default
#
# Copyright:: 2022, John Adams
#
if platform?('ubuntu') ❶

  %w(perl libnet-ssleay-perl openssl libauthen-pam-perl libpam-
  runtime libio-pty-perl apt-show-versions python unzip).each
  do |pkg| ❷
    package pkg do
      action :install
    end
  end

  remote_file '/root/webmin_1.994.deb' do ❸
    source 'http://prdownloads.sourceforge.net/webadmin/
    webmin_1.994_all.deb'
    owner 'root'
    group 'root'
    mode '0755'
    action :create_if_missing
  end

  dpkg_package 'webin' do ❹
    source '/root/webmin_1.994.deb'
    action :install
  end

  bash 'append-trusted-ips' do ❺
    user 'root'
```

```
  code <<-EOF
    echo "allow=10.128.1.0/24 LOCAL" >> /etc/webmin/
    miniserv.conf
  EOF
  notifies :restart, 'service[webmin]', :immediately
  not_if 'grep -q "allow=10.128.1.0/24 LOCAL" /etc/webmin/
  miniserv.conf'
end

service 'webmin' do ❻
  supports status: true
  action [:enable, :restart]
end
end
```

This cookbook example starts with a platform check ❶ that will
only apply the configurations that follow to nodes that have the Ubuntu
OS. Chef includes dozens of platform *types,* so you can include different
logic steps for different platforms. Check out https://docs.chef.io/
infra_language/checking_platforms/ to see them all.

Webmin requires a series of prerequisites to be installed for Webmin to
work ❷. This section defines the necessary Ubuntu/Debian packages (the
%w tells it to chunk each separate word into an array called pkg), and the
package resource installs the latest versions of each. To install the Webmin
package, the cookbook uses the remote_file resource ❸ to download
it and place it in the local /root/ directory. The next step uses the dpkg_
package resource to install it ❹.

Note   It's a good DevOps practice to include specific versions of the
packages you want to install, but I've left those out to simplify the
examples.

In order to better secure the Webmin server, setting up the allowed subnets prevents access from outside your DevOps lab network. This is a good security step even though your lab network isn't accessible to the outside world. In step ❺, use the bash resource to append a line to the Webmin configuration file, /etc/webmin/miniserv.conf, if the line doesn't exist already. This configuration allows both 10.128.1.0/24 and the LOCAL IP, 127.0.0.1.

The last step is to enable and start the Webmin service ❻. This section is also referenced in the append-trusted-ips section that notifies :restart, 'service[webmin]', :immediately so the server will restart the Webmin service if this configuration line is changed on the targeted server.

Deploy Webmin with Chef

With your cookbook and profile complete, it's time to apply this configuration to a node. The following example targets a node named *ubuntu04.devops.lab*. You'll again be using the ad hoc chef-run command, which will install the Chef client on the target node before applying the configuration. This command assumes you have root SSH login to the *ubuntu04* node:

```
$ chef-run ssh://root@ubuntu04.devops.lab root -i ~/.ssh/id_rsa
```

Verify Your Webmin Installation

The quickest way to see if Webmin is running on this second server is to log in using port 10000, as in https://ubuntu04.devops.lab:10000. However, you can also use Chef to verify the settings, by creating an InSpec profile that does that for you.

As you saw previously, Chef InSpec is a command-line tool you can use to remotely verify Linux, Windows, or macOS systems without having to install an agent on them. Later, you'll use it to scan systems using a Linux baseline profile that tests the hardening and security of your systems.

For this step, create an InSpec profile to test your Webmin configuration using the Chef Workstation built-in generator. Using the same system paths you used in Chapter 8, this would look like the following:

```
$ cd ~/chef-repo/cookbooks/webmin/compliance/profiles
$ inspec init profile webmin
```

Your *webmin* profile will contain a single *control* with four `describe` resources to verify your configuration. Rename the main default profile file from `example.rb` to `default.rb` and add the content shown in Listing 9-2.

Listing 9-2. A Chef InSpec profile to verify the Webmin configuration on Ubuntu

```
control 'webmin' do ❶
  impact 0.7
  title 'Webmin installed'
  desc 'Ensure Webmin is installed'
  describe package('webmin') do ❷
    it { should be_installed }
    its('version') { should cmp '1.994' }
  end
  describe port(10000) do ❸
    it { should be_listening }
  end
  describe file('/etc/webmin/miniserv.conf') do ❹
    it { should exist }
```

```
    its('content') { should match(%r{allow=10.128.1.0/24
    LOCAL}) }
  end
  describe service('webmin') do ❺
    it { should be_enabled }
    it { should be_running }
  end
end
```

This profile does everything you need in a single control❶. The included *resources* ensure Webmin is installed (with a specific version) ❷, port 10000 is open ❸, the main configuration file has the allowed subnets line ❹, and that the Webmin service is enabled and running ❺.

You can run this with the following command from your workstation:

```
$ cd ~/chef-repo/cookbooks/webmin
$ inspec exec compliance/profiles/webmin -t ssh://ubuntu04 -i
~/.ssh/id_rsa
```

If everything is successful, you'll see something like the following:

```
✓ webmin: Webmin installed
    ✓ System Package webmin is expected to be installed
    ✓ System Package webmin version is expected to cmp
      == "1.994"
    ✓ Port 10000 is expected to be listening
    ✓ File /etc/webmin/miniserv.conf is expected to exist
    ✓ File /etc/webmin/miniserv.conf content is expected to
      match /allow=10.128.1.0\/24 LOCAL/
    ✓ Service webmin is expected to be enabled
    ✓ Service webmin is expected to be running
```

You could apply this cookbook to your nginx.devops.lab server (and others) in a similar way and use them in your cluster in the next step.

Set Up Webmin for Multiple-Server Management

Adding other Webmin-enabled servers to your "main" Webmin interface using **Webmin ➤ Webmin Servers Index** in the main dashboard menu is a shortcut for reaching and interacting with your servers from a single dashboard. That's not as useful as actually managing a full cluster of servers from the same dashboard, so you need to add the *cluster-webmin* module to get everything to work that way.

To reiterate, the idea here is to use one Webmin installation as your dashboard that controls multiple systems with Webmin separately running on them. That way, you can apply configurations from one dashboard and have them take effect across your cluster. This can be quite handy for creating users and groups, executing shell commands, installing packages, and generally synchronizing base configurations across your lab. This is best for ad hoc commands in a small cluster, like your DevOps lab.

For this example, you can use your `nginx.devops.lab` machine created in Chapter 8 as your main interface. Avoid using the Turnkey template version because it sets up Webmin to use a different base port (not 10000).

Add Other Webmin Servers

The first step to setting up your cluster is to first add your other Webmin-enabled servers. In the Webmin dashboard, navigate to **Webmin ➤ Webmin Servers Index**. Clicking the **Broadcast for servers** button, as shown in Figure 9-1, will automatically search your DevOps lab network for systems running Webmin.

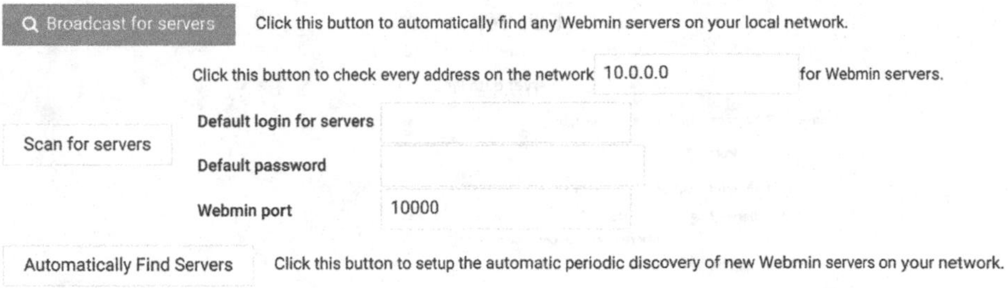

Figure 9-1. *The Webmin Servers Index view. Click Broadcast for servers to automatically find and add other Webmin servers in your DevOps lab*

After a few moments, you'll see results that look something like the output example in Listing 9-3. Notice that this example found two Webmin-enabled servers in addition to the one used to broadcast from (nginx.devops.lab in this example).

Listing 9-3. The results of using Broadcast for servers in Webmin

```
Broadcasting for servers on addresses 10.255.255.255 ,
255.255.255.255 , 00 , 10.128.1.255 ..
Found this server at https://nginx.devops.lab:10000/
Found new server at https://ubuntu04.devops.lab:10000/
Found new server at https://mail.devops.lab:10000/
```

You'll see an icon appear in the dashboard for each Webmin server found under the menu **Webmin ➤ Webmin Servers Index** (or by clicking the **Return to servers** button). If you click the icon, it'll open a new browser tab and take you to the Webmin login for that server. Instead, hover over the server icon and select the settings icon in the top-right corner to edit the entry. This will show the server settings, as in Figure 9-2. You can leave everything as is, but set **Login via Webmin with username** to an elevated user on the remote system. This example uses root and the root password.

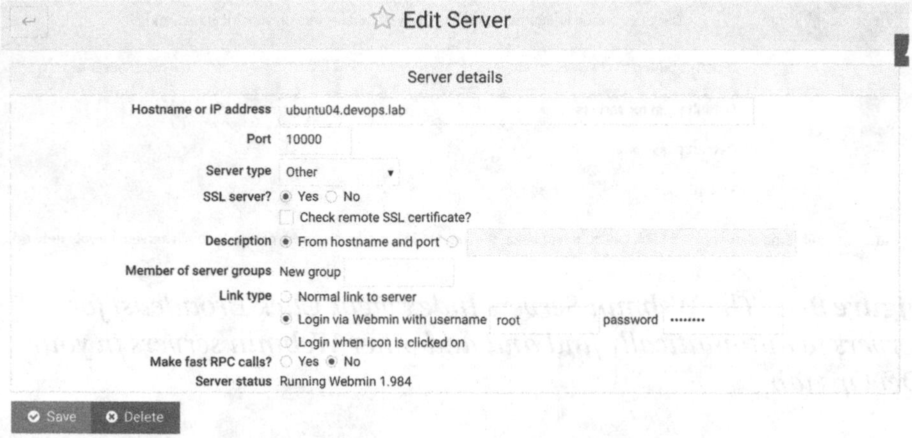

Figure 9-2. *Editing a server to set the Link type to Login via Webmin with username*

If the **Server type** doesn't match the OS (such as Ubuntu Linux), go ahead and select that from the menu before saving the settings and repeating the steps for any other Webmin servers you want to centrally manage.

Add Cluster Capabilities

In order to take advantage of the other clustering capabilities in Webmin, you need to add a module called *cluster-webmin*. In your main Webmin dashboard, navigate to **Webmin ➤ Webmin Configuration ➤ Webmin modules**. You'll install a module using a *standard module from* www.webmin.com. Type *cluster* in the search box and click the globe icon. You'll see a list of filterable options, as shown in Figure 9-3.

cluster	✕

cluster-passwd	Change passwords on multiple systems in a Webmin cluster at once.
cluster-copy	Schedule the transfer of files from this server to multiple servers in a Webmin cluster.
cluster-cron	Create scheduled Cron jobs that run on multiple servers simultaneously.
cluster-shell	Run commands on multiple servers at once.
cluster-software	Install RPMs, debian and solaris packages across multiple servers from one source.
cluster-usermin	Install and manage modules and themes across multiple Usermin servers.
cluster-useradmin	Create, update and delete users and groups across multiple servers. Unlike NIS, each server has its own passwd and group files which are remotely updated by this module.
cluster-webmin	Install and manage modules, themes, users, groups and access control settings across multiple Webmin servers.

cluster-webmin	✔ Select

Figure 9-3. *Add the cluster-webmin module from the Webmin modules dashboard*

Click the *cluster-webmin* link so it appears in the box next to the **Select** button and then click **Select**. Back on the main Webmin modules screen, set **Grant access to option** to root and click **Install Module**.

If you get errors installing this module, check that you have the latest version of Webmin running. You can update the version in your Chef recipe (before deploying) or use the built-in Webmin upgrade tool, available on the main Webmin **dashboard** page.

It only takes a moment for the module to be downloaded and installed. When it's complete, you'll see a new **Cluster** entry in the main left-hand Webmin dashboard menu. Go there next, and choose **Cluster ➤ Cluster Webmin Servers**. This is where you add the machines you found during the Broadcast step and configure the cluster. If you don't see the servers you expect, double-check that you selected the **Login via Webmin with username** option in the previous step. Those previously added systems will appear in the Add server menu, as shown in Figure 9-4.

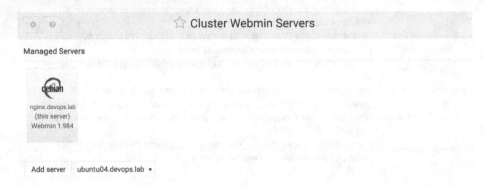

Figure 9-4. *Click the Add server button to add the selected server to your cluster*

Once added, you'll see the icon for the server in the **Cluster Webmin Servers** dashboard window. You can now add other cluster capabilities, such as installing software packages, issuing shell commands, and creating users. For most of these functions, you have to manually add cluster nodes to these capabilities, a security feature that assumes the fewest capabilities by default, not wide-open access to systems.

Test Some Cluster Actions

To try out your new cluster settings, use the **Cluster ➤ Cluster Shell Commands** tool. A simple command might be uname -a, which shows information about the running systems. Select one or more cluster nodes to see the results!

This is just one example of cluster commands you can issue from the Webmin dashboard. Some other built-in features are setting system user passwords cluster-wide, creating cron jobs, installing packages, and more.

Perhaps the most useful is the *shell commands* tool, which enables you to run pretty much any Linux command on all your nodes at once. Try a few, like df -Th to view disk space statistics on all your nodes at once.

A More DevOps Way to Analyze Systems

Webmin is a powerful tool for running ad hoc commands on a relatively small fleet of servers, but the approach is largely manual and does nothing to ensure your systems are in the state you want over time. There's also nothing to prevent someone else from making changes to a system, leading to configuration drift. In your DevOps lab, this may not be a consideration, but when you scale up or work in an engineering team, this kind of capability is a must.

To accomplish that, it's good to employ configuration management and compliance tools, define your systems with code, and verify them with coded policies. The NGINX example in Chapter 8 is a good example of this approach.

Use Chef InSpec to Scan Systems

The beauty of creating policy as code—combining configuration and compliance in one step—is that you can create your own profiles or take advantage of the open-source community to apply more sophisticated examples.

A good way to start is to make use of these publicly available InSpec profiles, such as a Linux baseline. It includes more than 100 tests to harden a system. A public GitHub repository contains a wide variety of similar hardening profiles you can use on raw systems; those managed by Ansible, Chef, or Puppet; and Docker and Kubernetes hosts.

These *DevSec Hardening Framework* files are available at `https://github.com/dev-sec`. Other publicly available profiles are available in the Chef Supermarket, a source for free cookbooks, recipes, and profiles at `https://supermarket.chef.io/tools?q=profiles`. Give these a try to get a feel for how InSpec works.

Apply a Linux Benchmark Profile

You can write simple InSpec profiles to run against any system (Linux, Windows, or macOS) as you did earlier, but if you're just starting out, it's useful to take advantage of sophisticated code that's freely available. This is the case with the following example, which uses the `https://github.com/dev-sec/linux-baseline` profile. These and other GitHub-based profiles can be downloaded and run locally, or you can apply them directly from the cloud. This is a great way to get powerful scan results with very little work.

InSpec makes this happen by grabbing a .tar.gz file from GitHub, unpacking it, and applying it to your target. For the Linux baseline, run the following on your workstation (where you've previously installed Chef Workstation and its tools), and target any one of your Linux systems. For this to work, the folder from which you run the command must be a Git-enabled directory:

```
$ cd ~/chef-repo
$ inspec exec https://github.com/dev-sec/linux-baseline -t
ssh://root@ubuntu04.devops.lab [-i ~/.ssh/id_rsa]
```

The preceding example also includes the optional `-i` flag to point to an SSH key previously shared with the target system. The results of running this will vary depending on your system and how it's currently configured (if at all). On a raw Ubuntu node, InSpec reports in the terminal that this profile has 57 controls containing 169 different tests. Of these, 27 controls pass and 30 fail.

InSpec uses the concept of *waivers* to allow you to ignore certain controls (and all the InSpec resources included in them). Waivers are compiled in a YAML file and include the name of the controls you want to ignore, how long you want to ignore them, and reasoning for your waiver. This is a great way to use public resources, but fine-tune them to your needs.

Create an InSpec Waiver File

In the following example, you'll rerun the same Linux baseline profile, but you'll add a flag to include a waiver file you create. This file will explicitly tell InSpec to ignore certain controls.

The file format is shown in Listing 9-4. Create as many blocks as you want, one for each control you want to waive.

Listing 9-4. The format of an InSpec waiver

```
control_id:
  expiration_date: YYYY-MM-DD
  run: false
  justification: "reason for waiving this control"
```

If you visit the GitHub sites for the linux-baseline, you can view all the controls listed in the files located at https://github.com/dev-sec/linux-baseline/tree/master/controls. The controls are neatly separated into *os_spec.rb*, *package_spec.rb*, and *sysctl_spec.rb* files. The waivers used in the following example reference controls found in those files.

Start by identifying some controls that are meaningful for a small test, such as the following:

- os-02

- package-02

- package-03

- sysctl-01

- sysctl-14

Before creating a waiver file, test the results of running just these controls on your target system. This is done by adding a --controls= flag followed by the names of the controls you want to run. All other controls not explicitly listed will be ignored:

```
$ inspec exec https://github.com/dev-sec/linux-baseline-t
ssh://root@ubuntu04 --controls=os-02 os-03 package-02
package-03 sysctl-01 sysctl-14
```

Notice that all of these InSpec tests pass except *sysctl-14*, which disables acceptance of all IPv4 redirected packets, as shown in Listing 9-5.

Listing 9-5. The output of an InSpec scan of specific controls

```
Profile: DevSec Linux Security Baseline (linux-baseline)
Version: 2.8.2
Target:  ssh://root@ubuntu04:22

  ✓ os-03: Check owner and permissions for /etc/passwd
  ✓   File /etc/passwd is expected to exist
  ✓   File /etc/passwd is expected to be file
  ✓   File /etc/passwd is expected to be owned by "root"
  ✓   File /etc/passwd is expected not to be executable
...
  ✓ package-02: Do not install Telnet server
  ✓   System Package telnetd is expected not to be installed
  ✓ package-03: Do not install rsh server
  ✓   System Package rsh-server is expected not to be
      installed
  ✓ sysctl-01: IPv4 Forwarding
```

✓ Kernel Parameter net.ipv4.ip_forward value is
   expected to eq 0
✓ Kernel Parameter net.ipv4.conf.all.forwarding value is
   expected to eq 0
× sysctl-14: Disable acceptance of all IPv4 redirected
   packets (2 failed)
   × Kernel Parameter net.ipv4.conf.default.accept_redirects
      value is expected to eq 0

   expected: 0
        got: 1

   (compared using ==)

   × Kernel Parameter net.ipv4.conf.all.accept_redirects
      value is expected to eq 0

   expected: 0
        got: 1

   (compared using ==)

Profile Summary: 4 successful controls, 1 control failure, 0
controls skipped
Test Summary: 15 successful, 2 failures, 0 skipped

To use an InSpec waiver to ignore the failing *sysctl-14* control, create a
waiver.yml file with the contents shown in Listing 9-6, and save it in a new
~/chef-repo/profiles/waivers/inspec-test directory:

```
$ mkdir -p ~/chef-repo/profiles/waivers/inspec-test/
```

Listing 9-6. Contents of a simple InSpec waiver.yml file

```
sysctl-14:
  expiration_date: 2024-12-31
  run: false
  justification: "Disabling redirection of IPv4 packets
  not needed"
```

Notice the *control-id* is the name of the actual control called
sysctl-14. By using this waiver file, InSpec ignores that control (run:
false) and expires this waiver at the end of 2024. It also includes a
justification that others can read and understand why this particular
waiver exists in the first place.

Note   The following example uses both the --controls
and--waiver-file flags, but you wouldn't normally do this. I've
added the --controls flag to limit the terminal output.

```
$ inspec exec https://github.com/dev-sec/linux-baseline -t
ssh://root@ubuntu04 --controls=os-03 package-02 package-03
sysctl-01 sysctl-14 --waiver-file ~/chef-repo/profiles/waivers/
inspec-test/waiver.yml
```

When you run this, you'll see the InSpec waiver did its work and didn't
run the *sysctl-14* control. It also included the justification line from the
waiver.yml file as part of the terminal output, as shown in Listing 9-7.

Listing 9-7. Results of an InSpec scan with a waiver file

```
Profile: DevSec Linux Security Baseline (linux-baseline)
Version: 2.8.2
Target:  ssh://root@ubuntu04:22
```

✓   os-03: Check owner and permissions for /etc/passwd
  ✓   File /etc/passwd is expected to exist
  ✓   File /etc/passwd is expected to be file
...
✓   package-02: Do not install Telnet server
  ✓   System Package telnetd is expected not to be installed
✓   package-03: Do not install rsh server
  ✓   System Package rsh-server is expected not to be
      installed
✓   sysctl-01: IPv4 Forwarding
  ✓   Kernel Parameter net.ipv4.ip_forward value is
      expected to eq 0
  ✓   Kernel Parameter net.ipv4.conf.all.forwarding value is
      expected to eq 0
↻   sysctl-14: Disable acceptance of all IPv4
    redirected packets
  ↻   Skipped control due to waiver condition: Disabling
      redirection of IPv4 packets not needed

By using waivers, you can take full advantage of sophisticated public InSpec profiles, but make them more meaningful for your use cases by ignoring tests you don't want or need. To actually remediate these compliance failures, you can use Ansible, Chef, or other configuration management tools to automate those settings. This is a true DevOps workflow that eliminates manual configurations and avoids the key cause of most system failures and security breaches: human error.

Other Ways to Apply InSpec Profiles

Before leaving this section, it's useful to define other ways you can run profiles to scan your nodes for compliance. The first uses a public profile available in the Chef Supermarket; the other is one you create yourself.

Apply an InSpec Profile via the Chef Supermarket

The Chef Supermarket, available at `https://supermarket.chef.io`, is a clearinghouse for a wide variety of Chef-specific content, namely, cookbooks, recipes, and profiles. You can reference them much like using the preceding Git example:

```
$ inspec supermarket exec dev-sec/linux-baseline -t ssh://root@
ubuntu04
```

In this example, InSpec uses `supermarket` as part of the command and references the `dev-sec/linux-baseline` profile. With this notation, InSpec knows where to find the supermarket.chef.io site and the profile you want. Some users deploy their own Chef Supermarkets repositories as a way to host, reference, and use their unique, verified code. This approach can add a level of trust to their DevOps workflows.

Create and Apply Your Own InSpec Profile

InSpec is flexible and fairly intuitive, making it easy to create your own compliance profiles. You saw earlier how to use a Chef generator to create a profile to include in a cookbook, but you can create simple tests in a less complex way by creating a my-inspec-test.rb file and include any InSpec resources you want to test.

> **Note**   A file like this doesn't necessarily need the same control
> structure, though it's a good idea to follow that pattern.

For this example, create a simple profile file to test if a certain user
exists on a target system, such as jadams. Your my-inspec-test.rb would
include the following:

```
describe user('jadams') do
  it { should exist }
end
```

To run this on your targets, execute the following command, which
should take a few seconds and show you output similar to that shown in
Listing 9-8:

```
$ inspec exec path/to/my-inspec-test.rb -t ssh://root@ubuntu04
```

Listing 9-8. The terminal output after running your small
InSpec scan

```
Profile: tests from my-inspec-test.rb (tests from my-
inspec-test.rb)
Version: (not specified)
Target:  ssh://root@ubuntu04:22

  User jadams
    ✓  is expected to exist
Test Summary: 1 successful, 0 failures, 0 skipped
```

Getting started with writing profiles and tests can be tricky, but a built-
in InSpec tool allows you to actually test InSpec resource commands from
the shell without having to create a file at all. This is a great way to debug
and test before committing everything to code.

273

To use the tool, use `inspec shell` to target the node you want to interact with:

```
$ inspec shell -t ssh://root@ubuntu04
```

This will drop you into a terminal session with an `inspec>` prompt on the remote node. From there, you can use InSpec resources to write your tests, one line at a time:

```
describe user('jadams') do [ENTER]
  it { should exist } [ENTER]
end [ENTER]
```

You can use any of the nearly 500 Chef InSpec resources in this way to verify your syntax and test various *matchers*, ways to reference specific values on your systems, such as package versions.

Some Useful Backup Tools

When you create systems and start building apps, it's easy to lose track of what you have or—horrors—lose your work. To minimize these risks, it's good to back up your systems, data, and code.

Since you're using a Proxmox environment, using the system snapshot feature is a good way to back up your systems in their existing state. If you mess something up, you can roll back to an earlier version and continue on your way.

Set Up Proxmox Replication

Proxmox also has *replication* capabilities that can be set to automatically back up a VM or LXC from one Proxmox node to another. To use it, you need at least two Proxmox nodes in your lab cluster. With that set up, click the Proxmox server you want to replicate and, in the right-hand menu, choose **Replicate**. When you click **Add**, you can set the parameters in the configuration window, as shown in Figure 9-5.

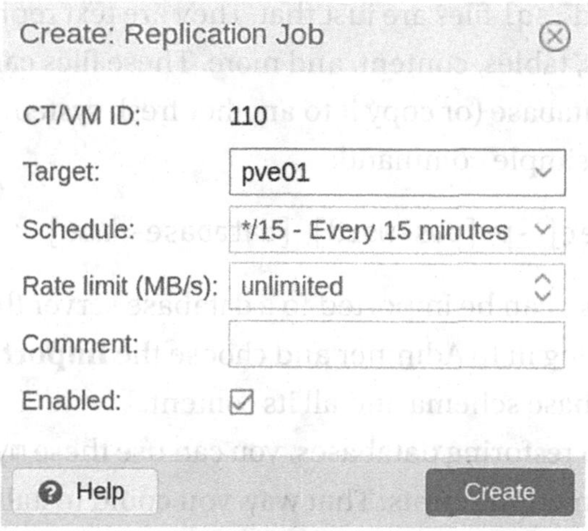

Create: Replication Job   ⊗

CT/VM ID: 110

Target: pve01   ⌄

Schedule: */15 - Every 15 minutes ⌄

Rate limit (MB/s): unlimited   ⌄

Comment:

Enabled: ☑

❷ Help   Create

Figure 9-5. *Set up replication in the Proxmox dashboard*

Replication will copy your system to an entirely different host, so if a drive fails or the underlying system dies for some reason, you can recover your system from the replica.

Back Up MariaDB Data

If you're creating databases for your own applications or for something like WordPress, it's a good idea to back up your data. For this, replication of a server works, but it's good to have the raw SQL so you can recreate and repopulate databases as necessary. This is easily done with mysqldump.

This command is available for both MariaDB and MySQL and outputs the contents of your database to a file that you define. It has a lot of arguments you can add to set the options you want (learn more with man mysqldump). Here are some examples:

```
$ mysqldump -u [user] -p [password]--all-databases >
mydatabases.sql
$ mysqldump -u [user] -p [password] --database db1 db2 > db01_
dump.sql
```

The outputted .sql files are just that. They are text representations of your databases, tables, content, and more. These files can be used to restore your database (or copy it to another fresh system running MariaDB) with a simple command:

```
$ msyql -u [user] -p [password] [database-name] < db01_dump.sql
```

These files also can be imported to a database server that has Adminer installed. Simply log in to Adminer and choose the **Import** option to recreate the database schema and all its content.

In addition to restoring databases, you can use these mysqldump output files in your automation scripts. That way, you could install MariaDB on a server and import the necessary database structure and content as part of that process using your dumped .sql file. By codifying everything—the server applications, users, content, and the like—you can recreate whole systems at will.

Use Git to Store Your Code

Though you may not think of Git as a backup solution, when used with automation and compliance code, it provides a solid way to remotely save and track your code. If using Chef or Ansible, get in the habit of creating Git repositories—GitHub and GitLab are good options—to store your content. You can deploy your own GitLab server using a built-in Proxmox Turnkey Template, and it makes a good addition to your DevOps lab.

Conclusion

In this chapter, you learned different ways to manage, maintain, and back up the systems in your DevOps lab. As the software engineering world continues to advance, you'll find infrastructure as code to be a more resilient option for not only configuring nodes but verifying those configurations and replicating them on dozens or thousands of nodes.

In the next chapter, you'll learn some ways to extend your lab by taking a closer look at GitLab.

CHAPTER 10

Extend Your DevOps Capabilities with Git

As you've proceeded through this book, you've touched on quite a few different Linux and open source technologies, and you now have some good experience under your belt. That experience has given you a grounding in the automation and containerization technologies that can help you take on more complex tasks and turn manual configurations into code. DevOps is all about repeatable actions that eliminate the need for gobs of mundane, manual work.

In this chapter, you'll look at some ways to extend that philosophy—infrastructure as code—by diving a little deeper into *Git*. Modern DevOps teams use version control systems to manage far-flung code in an organized way, and version control provides the backing for continuous integration and continuous delivery (CI/CD) of infrastructure (bare metal, VMs, and containers) and applications. Regardless of whether you classify yourself as part of dev or ops, the tools are becoming more unified, with Git right at the heart of it all.

J. S. Tonello, *Practical Linux DevOps*, https://doi.org/10.1007/978-1-4842-8318-9_10

Get Started with Git

Throughout the previous chapters, you haven't yet had a chance to dive into *Git*, the version control tool that enables you to version, remotely store, and share code. In DevOps, using Git has become automatic, particularly with well-known sites like GitHub, GitLab, and Bitbucket. In the following sections, you'll take a look at some basic Git commands, create and use a public Git repo, and deploy your own GitLab server using Proxmox.

Git is worthy of entire books; and, indeed, there are many out there for you to reference. I won't pretend to go into a deep level of detail, but there are some basics that will get you started. You'll start by creating a free GitHub account, getting a feel for using Git in your lab, and move on to setting up your own GitLab server.

Create a GitHub Account

GitHub is a good place to start with version control because it's well established, relatively easy to use and provides you with unlimited numbers of public and private repositories. A free account also gives you 2,000 minutes of GitHub Actions (used for automated software development workflows popularly known as continuous integration/continuous deployment or CI/CD), assigns shared-code owners on your public repositories, and other features. For your DevOps lab environment, a free GitHub account provides plenty of horsepower to accomplish your work.

Get started by visiting *github.com* and sign up for an account by providing a valid email address (**not** your lab email address) and setting a username. Your username will become home to your unique public GitHub space at *https://github.com/your-user-name*. For example, mine is *https://github.com/jtonello,* and the code examples in this book are all available there (as well as at the Apress GitHub repository: https://github.com/Apress/Practical-Linux-DevOps).

With your account created, return to your Linux workstation terminal to install and configure git locally. This section focuses on the command-line tool, but you can separately experiment with some of the cool graphical tools currently available. You can also integrate your remote GitHub repo with the VS Code editor to seamlessly work with your account, a handy way to keep track of changes to your work in real time.

On an Ubuntu system, installing Git is as easy as the following:

```
$ sudo apt update && apt install git
```

Though it's small and lightweight, Git is actually very powerful. It keeps track of changes to your code and allows you to create and commit different versions of your work locally and push content remotely, where it can be widely shared. To be clear, Git works fine on its own without GitHub (or GitLab, Bitbucket, or similar public storage). Getting in the habit of using it—and executing Git commands as you're working—is a great way to try new variations on your code without ever having to make bulky copies of everything. If you like a new version of your work, you can promote it (known as *merging*) and refer back to previous commits of your work.

To use Git on your workstation with GitHub, you need to set a couple local system variables, namely, your username and GitHub account email:

```
$ git config --global user.name "John Adams"
$ git config --global user.email "jadams@foobar.com"
```

By setting these variables globally, you're telling Git who owns the code and the account to use when pushing code to your remote GitHub repos. In a team setting, this allows easy tracking of who made changes where and when. The --global flag sets these configurations system-wide (for your Linux user), so no matter where on your system you create code, Git knows it's you doing the work. These global configurations are saved in your Linux home directory:

```
$ cat ~/.gitconfig
[user]
    name = John Adams
    email = jadams@foobar.com
```

These basic settings are enough to get you started, but let's set up a
secure connection between your workstation and GitHub by creating and
adding an *SSH key* to your GitHub account settings. This will enable you
to push code up to and pull code down from GitHub public and private
repos in a secure way. Private repos are just that. Other users of github.com
can't see your work unless you explicitly grant them permission. This is
how distributed teams of software developers can store and share sensitive
code among themselves, but not with the world.

Start by creating a new SSH key to use exclusively with GitHub. You
could use a previously generated *id_rsa* key, but chances are that has
access to all your systems, presenting some security concerns. Instead,
create an all-new key and give it a name that helps you remember what
it's for:

```
$ ssh-keygen -t rsa -b 4096 -C "jadams@foobar.com" \
  -N '' -f $HOME/.ssh/github_rsa
```

This command creates a new SSH key without prompting you to
answer configuration questions. In this example, you're setting the
encryption type to RSA, providing your email address, setting the password
to nothing (`-N ''`), and saving the resulting public and private keys as
`github_rsa` and `github_rsa.pub` in your `~/.ssh` directory.

To use this new SSH key with GitHub to enable secure, passwordless
access to the remote site, add the `github_rsa.pub` key to your GitHub
account. Log in to GitHub via a browser, click the account icon at the top-
right corner of the screen, and choose **Settings**. In the left-hand menu,
click **SSH and GPG keys** and then the green **New SSH key** button. You'll be
presented with a form like the example in Figure 10-1.

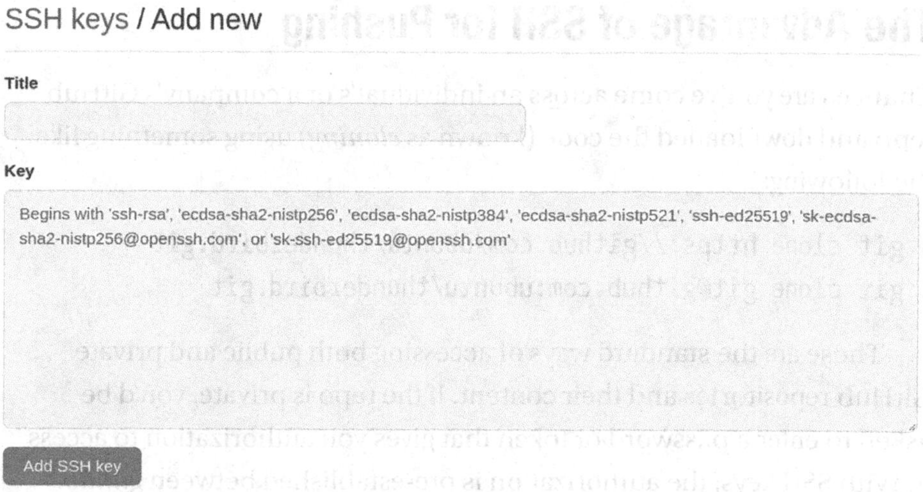

SSH keys / Add new

Title

Key

Begins with 'ssh-rsa', 'ecdsa-sha2-nistp256', 'ecdsa-sha2-nistp384', 'ecdsa-sha2-nistp521', 'ssh-ed25519', 'sk-ecdsa-sha2-nistp256@openssh.com', or 'sk-ssh-ed25519@openssh.com'

Add SSH key

Figure 10-1. *Adding a new SSH key in GitHub for secure communication*

Give this new entry a **Title** (such as your workstation's *hostname* or something like *My-Workstation*) and paste the contents of your newly created ~/.ssh/github_rsa.pub file into the **Key** box:

```
$cat ~/.ssh/github_rsa.pub
ssh-rsa AAAAB3NzaC1yc2EAAAADAQABAAACAQDUQpuzXnObas3SJJJwdp
5eQy9PGC6b/TWmeL1OnXpQYX1qqjP5hACJqcGEGu3p5q25dfXHpXseSBDl
GNjs1WRBQ3RS9c3ycOL8bInN6c5EtFmY4ZKwf8v2LASq4hzJ3YYikAjY3bxv
JyExA1LkTAh9BRcum7Epv9mxPA1VOwJgUQcxyKrsZaUWlJj5rvu9F8uOGUOQ
CawjvP9Ut8dgUYkUzwuJf1CHCsn9Qz4Ovczextd98mlY4k7wBFryCqJ9bs
GfsUsECGKSwao6LggmQ5u4W1TQls3pKk42owmqMh6ybCPf3rQ==
jadams@foobar.com
```

Shortly after clicking the **Add SSH key** button to save this entry, you'll get an email from GitHub telling you a new public key was added to your account, a nice security feature.

The Advantage of SSH for Pushing

Chances are you've come across an individual's or a company's GitHub repo and downloaded the code (known as *cloning*) using something like the following:

```
$ git clone https://github.com/ubuntu/thunderbird.git
$ git clone git@github.com:ubuntu/thunderbird.git
```

These are the standard ways of accessing both public and private GitHub repositories and their content. If the repo is private, you'd be asked to enter a password or token that gives you authorization to access it. With SSH keys, the authorization is pre-established between *github. com/your-user-name* and your workstation. This isn't such a big deal when cloning public code, but it makes life easier when you're pushing code up to GitHub (or another version control system). You won't need to enter a password or token to confirm your identity and authority, but the actions you take are secure, and the experience is seamless.

Create a New Git Repo

Today's GitHub and similar cloud services make it easy to create new project repositories from their web-based dashboards. To allow code to be shared (and essentially backed up), you can push it from your workstation to your remote GitHub repo.

Go to your *github.com/your-user-name* account, click the *Repositories* tab, and click the green **New** button to add a new repo. Enter a Repository name, choose either Public or Private, and leave the README, .gitignore, and *Choose a license boxes unchecked*, as shown in Figure 10-2.

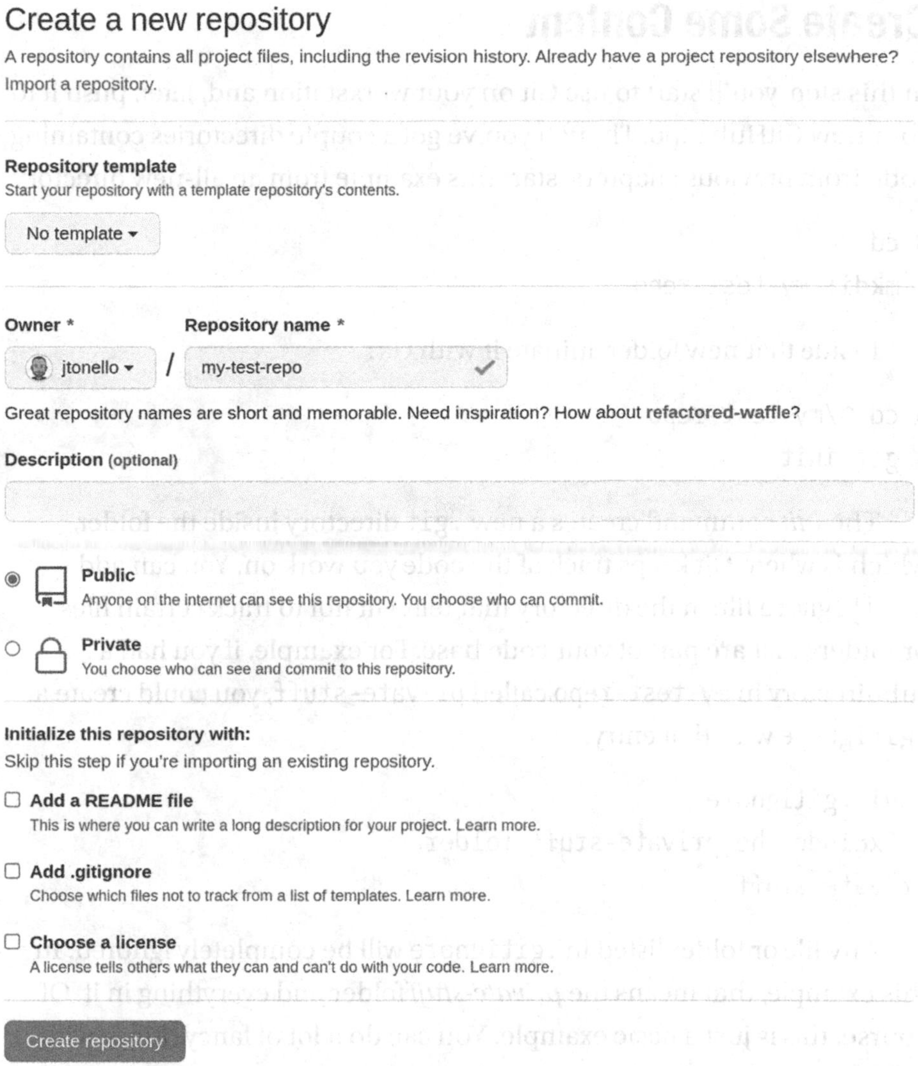

Create a new repository

A repository contains all project files, including the revision history. Already have a project repository elsewhere? Import a repository.

Repository template

Start your repository with a template repository's contents.

No template ▾

Owner *   **Repository name ***

👤 jtonello ▾   /   my-test-repo   ✓

Great repository names are short and memorable. Need inspiration? How about refactored-waffle?

Description (optional)

⬤ 📖 **Public**
      Anyone on the internet can see this repository. You choose who can commit.

○ 🔒 **Private**
      You choose who can see and commit to this repository.

Initialize this repository with:

Skip this step if you're importing an existing repository.

☐ **Add a README file**
   This is where you can write a long description for your project. Learn more.

☐ **Add .gitignore**
   Choose which files not to track from a list of templates. Learn more.

☐ **Choose a license**
   A license tells others what they can and can't do with your code. Learn more.

Create repository

Figure 10-2. *Create a new repository on GitHub*

That's it. Your GitHub repo account will now show the repo in the main dashboard *Repositories* view.

Create Some Content

In this step, you'll start to use Git on your workstation and, later, push it to your new GitHub repo. Though you've got a couple directories containing code from previous chapters, start this example from an all-new directory.

```
$ cd ~
$ mkdir my-test-repo
```

Inside that new folder, initiate it with Git:

```
$ cd ~/my-test-repo
$ git init
```

The *init* command creates a new `.git` directory inside the folder, which is where Git keeps track of the code you work on. You can add a `.gitignore` file in the directory that tells Git not to track certain files or folders that are part of your code base. For example, if you had a subdirectory in `my-test-repo` called `private-stuff`, you could create a `.gitignore` with that entry:

```
$ vi .gitignore
# Exclude the private-stuff folder
private-stuff
```

Any file or folder listed in `.gitignore` will be completely ignored. In this example, that means the *private-stuff* folder and everything in it. Of course, this is just a basic example. You can do a lot of fancy things with `.gitignore`, including having it ignore all files of a certain type (`*.pub`) and much more.

Git works by tracking files and maintaining information about them. Using `git add` and `git commit` gets this tracking started, and each commit you make is essentially a snapshot of your work in the current *branch*. Git uses *branches* to keep track of different content for the same repo, allowing you to make changes to your existing code in what are essentially all-new files while leaving the originals as is. By doing this, you don't have to make copies of files you know are "good" before changing them.

Let's see how this works with a simple text file. Add a new file to ~/my-test-repo, such as an *example.txt* file:

```
$ echo "This is my text file." > example.txt
```

If you look at the git status of this folder, your file will appear along with some other information about your current branch, which defaults to *master*:

```
$ git status
On branch master

No commits yet

Untracked files:
  (use "git add <file>..." to include in what will be
committed)
        .gitignore
        example.txt

nothing added to commit but untracked files present (use "git
add" to track)
```

This output tells you that you're in the default branch (*master*) and have files in this branch, but Git isn't doing anything with them yet. Change that by doing a git add followed by a git commit:

```
$ git add .
```

Here, the . is telling Git to add everything in the current folder my-test-repo to its tracking. You can also add your single file with git add example.txt. It's important to note that running git add will produce no output if it's successful. Use git status again to see what changed.

When you run git commit in the next example, Git will know which file or files it should include based on the git add step. Try this with the following, adding the -m flag to add a message about your commit. This is a required step that allows you to add a description about the commit itself, such as what changed:

```
$ git commit -m "First commit."
[master (root-commit) 8f9acf2] First commit.
 2 files changed, 3 insertions(+)
 create mode 100644 .gitignore
 create mode 100644 example.txt
```

Unlike git add, this command provides output, and if you run git status again, you'll see that Git has indeed begun to track your work and knows you have saved (*committed*) your work. This also sets the *head*, the most currently tracked version of your code:

```
$ git status
On branch master
nothing to commit, working tree clean
```

If you run git show, you'll see the content of your example.txt file and some information about the commit you called *First commit*.

Now, make an edit to your example.txt file, adding a new line, so it reads

```
This is my text file.

This is some more content.
```

If you now do a git add and git commit, Git is aware of both these versions of your single file and will show you the differences:

```
$ git add .
$ git commit -m "Second commit."
$ git show example.txt
```

```
commit b90729532d55b5e2e27bbfc7e0ed6d20770126b2
(HEAD -> master)
Author: John Adams <jadams@foobar.com>
Date:    Sat Mar 5 17:28:00 2022 -0500

    Second commit

diff --git a/example.txt b/example.txt
index 55e90be..302c049 100644
--- a/example.txt
+++ b/example.txt
@@ -1 +1,3 @@
 This is my text file.
+
+This is some more content.
```

The pluses (+) at the start of the last two lines of output show the changes between example.txt in your *First Commit* and *Second Commit*. If you want to roll back this commit—to tell Git you want it to undo the latest saved version—you can use git reset:

```
$ git reset --soft HEAD~1
```

Here, Git is removing the second commit, meaning it now sees your example.txt as it existed after your first commit. The --soft flag tells it not to modify your example.txt file, but just un-commit it. To actually roll back to the first version of the file and discard all changes, use the hard flag:

```
$ git reset --hard HEAD~1
HEAD is now at 8f9acf2 First commit.
```

If you look at your example.txt file, you'll see that the addition you made is now gone. Running git status at this point shows you that everything is back to being up-to-date with your first commit. In this way, you can begin to see how you can edit files and maintain an active history.

Rolling back commits is fine for small changes, but if you're refactoring some code on a whole application or making other fixes, the best approach is to use *branches*. Branches take a sort of snapshot of your work in your starting branch (usually *master* or *main*) and allow you to start making changes and commits without ever altering the original versions of your files.

You can try this by issuing a one-line command that will create a new branch and move you into it. This leaves your original content as is, and any changes you make are only viewable in the new branch:

```
$ git checkout -b newbranch
Switched to a new branch 'newbranch'
```

Issue the `git branch` command to show where you are:

```
$ git branch
  master
* newbranch
```

The asterisk in front of *newbranch* indicates you're working in that branch, which contains all the files from your my-test-repo folder, but changes you *commit* here will not overwrite the files in the *master* branch. For example, edit the example.txt file and add a new line of text to the file. Then run the *git add* and *git commit* commands:

```
$ git add .
$ git commit -m "My changes."
[newbranch fe130be] Fix commit
 1 file changed, 2 insertions(+)
```

If you *cat* the example.txt file in this branch, you'll see your latest content. Switch back to the original branch and *cat* the example.txt file, and you'll see the original:

```
$ cat example.txt
```

```
$ git checkout master
$ cat example.txt
```

From a directory view on your workstation, you'll see a single `example.txt` file, but Git is aware of the changes you've made and is now tracking two unique versions of that single file.

Typical DevOps workflows work this way. Developers clone a Git repo to their local machines, create new branches for their new content, make code changes, commit those changes, push those changes to the shared Git repo (like GitHub), and then merge the changes back into the *master* or *main* branch (usually after someone else has approved the changes). *Merging* allows the newer content to overwrite the old, and Git maintains a history of the changes, so it's easy to roll back if necessary. All this is done without having to make backup copies of code, which can get very confusing very fast.

Share Your Code

So far, all your work—edits and commits—has all been done on your local machine. Let's add in the remote capability. This is done by telling Git about your GitHub repo and setting what's known as a *remote origin*. By setting one or more *origins*, you're telling your local Git about the remote *github.com/your-user-name/my-test-repo*, so any actions you take to *push* or *clone* will use that destination. You only have to do this once in a particular local code folder:

```
$ git remote add origin git@github.com:your-user-name/my-
test-repo
```

This command uses the *git@github.com* syntax, not *https*, so it's taking advantage of your shared SSH key. You won't get prompted to enter credentials. If it works correctly, you'll see no output in the terminal, but Git has made note of the remote GitHub repo it should reference when you do a git push, using *origin* as a map to the remote *github.com/your-user-name/my-test-repo* destination. Since you've already added files and done at least one commit, you can issue a *git push* without preamble, but generally pushes are preceded by *add* and *commit*:

Note   If this is your first time connecting to GitHub using your shared SSH key, you'll get a security warning such as

The authenticity of host 'github.com (192.168.1.89)' can't be established.

ECDSA key fingerprint is SHA256:p2QAMXNIC1TJYWeIOttrVc98/R1BUFWu3/LiyKgUfQM.

Are you sure you want to continue connecting (yes/ no/[fingerprint])?

Type "yes" to continue.

```
$ git add .
$ git commit -m "Details about my commit."
$ git push origin master
Enumerating objects: 3, done.
Counting objects: 100% (3/3), done.
Delta compression using up to 8 threads
Compressing objects: 100% (2/2), done.
Writing objects: 100% (2/2), 273 bytes | 273.00 KiB/s, done.
Total 2 (delta 0), reused 0 (delta 0), pack-reused 0
To github.com:your-user-name/my-test-repo
   8f9acf2..f03d72c  master -> master
```

Check your *github.com/your-user-name/my-test-repo* on GitHub to see the results before trying your hand at using branches. So far, you've committed your example.txt and .*gitignore* files and pushed them to your *github.com/ your-user-name/my-test-repo master* branch. In the next example, you'll switch to your new branch, make some changes to the file, commit them, and push them to the same repo, but into a new matching remote branch.

Switch branches:

```
$ git checkout -c newbranch
Switched to branch 'newbranch'
Note
```

Newer versions of Git allow you to use either *git checkout* **or** *git switch* **to move between local branches.**

Make some edits to the example.txt file and then commit those changes:

```
$ git add .
$ git commit -m "Some edits"
[newbranch 7ea5afc] Some edits
 1 file changed, 2 insertions(+)
```

Push these changes to GitHub using the git push command. Instead of indicating the *master* branch, however, you'll designate your new branch called *newbranch*:

```
$ git push origin newbranch
numerating objects: 5, done.
Counting objects: 100% (5/5), done.
Delta compression using up to 8 threads
Compressing objects: 100% (3/3), done.
Writing objects: 100% (3/3), 327 bytes | 327.00 KiB/s, done.
Total 3 (delta 0), reused 0 (delta 0), pack-reused 0
To github.com:your-username/my-test-repo
   b862ab7..7ea5afc  newbranch -> newbranch
```

When you visit *github.com/your-user-name/my-test-repo*, you can view the content of both the *master* and *newbranch* by selecting the *Branches* menu, as shown in Figure 10-3. View the contents of your example.txt file in each branch and notice that your original file is unchanged and intact.

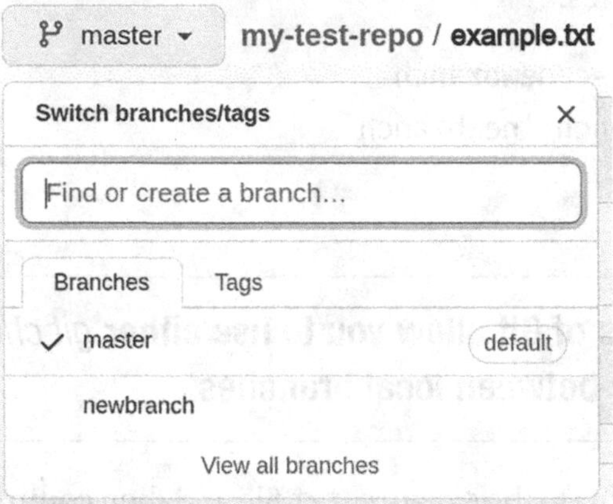

Figure 10-3. *The Branches view in GitHub*

The final step in a typical workflow would be to *merge* the two branches. This tells Git to overwrite the content of one branch with the content of another. To make your *master* branch version of example. txt match the edits you made to the *newbranch* version of example.txt, execute a git merge:

```
$ git checkout master
Switched to branch 'master'

$ git merge newbranch
Updating 72ed737..cf772ca
Fast-forward
 example.txt | 2 ++
 1 file changed, 2 insertions(+)
```

If you do a git push origin master, your *master* branch example.txt content on GitHub will be the same as the *newbranch* version, and GitHub will show you the history. So, even though you've overwritten the original, you can still look back in time to see the edits. After merging code to a master or main branch, it's considered good form to delete the new branch when you're done with it:

```
$ git branch -d newbranch
```

These examples are just the tip of the Git iceberg, but you can begin to see the value of Git when working with code, particularly when you're developing *Dockerfiles* and infrastructure as code. In the next section, you'll deploy GitLab in your DevOps lab so you can get a taste for on-premise version control.

Create a GitLab Host

Many companies have security policies and rules that don't allow them the option of using public version control cloud offerings like GitHub, so they turn to hosting it themselves. Self-hosting a Git server means you can set up secure connections to other software development tools, such as Jenkins, which is used to automate software building, testing, and deployment. In the following example, you'll use GitLab, which offers plenty of features and capabilities.

GitLab can be installed on most modern Linux distributions by adding a package repository and using your system's package manager. GitLab uses email for notifications, so you'll be able to take advantage of your *mail.devops.lab* server during the setup instead of installing another Postfix server alongside GitLab itself.

Since you're running Proxmox, you could take advantage of the Turnkey GitLab template, but I've found this implementation to have a few issues. Instead, start by creating a fresh VM or LXC host on your Proxmox server using Ubuntu 20.04 or later. Give the node a 32GB disk, two CPU cores, 4096MB of RAM, and assign an IP address on your DevOps lab subnet, such as `10.128.1.40/24`. You'll want to be sure your new GitLab host is reachable by its hostname, such as *gitlab.devops.lab*, so add an entry to your DNS server.

To make accessing this server easier, be sure to add an SSH key when creating this LXC. Use the contents of ~/.ssh/id_rsa.pub in the LXC's **SSH public key** value when creating the container.

When the machine boots, SSH into it from your workstation to continue the rest of the steps. Log in using *root* and the password you set when creating the host.

First thing, update the host and make sure it has a couple required packages, including *openssh-server*, which enables you to SSH into the node:

```
# apt update && apt upgrade
# apt install -y curl openssh-server \
  ca-certificates tzdata perl
```

You don't need to add Postfix to this server because you'll be using your *mail.devops.lab* server for all communications. Run the following command to add the Ubuntu repository for the *gitlab-ee* package:

```
# curl https://packages.gitlab.com/install/repositories/gitlab/
gitlab-ee/script.deb.sh | bash
```

The updated version of GitLab automatically enables Let's Encrypt, but this will likely fail in your DevOps lab environment, which isn't reachable from the Internet. To avoid this problem, edit /etc/gitlab/gitlab.rb and change the following line from `true` to `false`:

```
$ vi /etc/gitlab/gitlab.rb
...
```

```
letsencrypt['enable'] = false
...
```

You're now ready to do the actual installation. Prefix the command with the EXTERNAL_URL environment variable, setting it to match the FQDN of your *gitlab.devops.lab* host:

```
# EXTERNAL_URL="https://gitlab.devops.lab" apt install
gitlab-ee
```

This will take a few minutes to complete. When it's done, their installation will output the *root* password in a file located at /etc/gitlab/initial_root_password. Look at that file to get the initial password:

```
# cat /etc/gitlab/initial_root_password
dokZGqHxbfIi5M2zCXp7TxVB9zxikCs6RYgyQtd7ICM=
```

Note   Save this password somewhere on your workstation for reference. GitLab will delete the initial_root_password file 24 hours after the installation.

Before leaving your GitLab host, configure it to use your *mail.devops.lab* email server by editing /etc/gitlab/gitlab.rb. Copy the original and replace the contents with the following content shown in Listing 10-1:

```
# cp /etc/gitlab/gitlab.rb /etc/gitlab/gitlab_original.rb

# vi /etc/gitlab/gitlab.rb
```

Listing 10-1. Configure GitLab to use your lab email server by editing /etc/gitlab/gitlab.rb

```
gitlab_rails['smtp_enable'] = true
gitlab_rails['smtp_address'] = "mail.devops.lab"
```

```
gitlab_rails['smtp_port'] = 25
gitlab_rails['smtp_domain'] = "devops.lab"
gitlab_rails['smtp_enable_starttls_auto'] = false
gitlab_rails['smtp_openssl_verify_mode'] = 'none'
gitlab_rails['smtp_tls'] = false
gitlab_rails['smtp_ssl'] = false
gitlab_rails['smtp_force_ssl'] = false
gitlab_rails['service_desk_email_host'] = "mail.devops.lab"
gitlab_rails['service_desk_email_port'] = 993
gitlab_rails['service_desk_email_ssl'] = false
gitlab_rails['service_desk_email_start_tls'] = true

# If your SMTP server does not like the default
# 'From: gitlab@gitlab.example.com' you can change the
# 'From' with this setting.
gitlab_rails['gitlab_email_from'] = 'gitlab@devops.lab'
gitlab_rails['gitlab_email_reply_to'] = 'noreply@devops.lab'
```

Note   If you don't recall your Postfix settings or you're having trouble getting the configurations right, you can run the `postconf -n` command on your mail server to see the details.

Generate an SSL Key

GitLab integrates a runner—a separate server where it can run CI/CD jobs—and it can be tricky to get this to work with self-signed certificates like the ones running in your Proxmox lab. To fix this, edit your GitLab server's SSL configuration file /etc/ssl/openssl.cnf to include the content shown in Listing 10-2 under the [v3_ca] heading.

Listing 10-2. Add configurations to /etc/ssl/openssl.cnf on your GitLab server to enable self-signed certificates to work properly

```
...
[ v3_ca ]
basicConstraints = CA:false
keyUsage = nonRepudiation, digitalSignature, \keyEncipherment
subjectAltName = @alt_names

[alt_names]
DNS.1 = gitlab.devops.lab
...
```

With this edited and saved, issue the following command to generate a new certificate for your *gitlab.devops.lab* server. This will include the subjectAltName (SAN) you added in the openssl.cnf file when the certificate is created:

```
# openssl req -x509 -nodes -days 3650 \
-newkey rsa:2048 \
-keyout /etc/gitlab/ssl/gitlab.devops.lab.key \
-out /etc/gitlab/ssl/gitlab.devops.lab.crt

openssl req -newkey rsa:4096 -x509 -sha512 -days 3650 -nodes
-out /etc/gitlab/ssl/gitlab.devops.lab.crt -keyout /etc/gitlab/
ssl/gitlab.devops.lab.key -subj "/C=US/ST=New_York/L=Syracuse/
O=devops-lab/CN=gitlab.devops.lab/" -addext "subjectAltName =
DNS:gitlab.devops.lab"
```

Feel free to add your own geographic information instead of "New York" and "Syracuse". Follow up with a command to generate a .pem key based on the certificate using the Diffie-Hellman (DH) key exchange. Be patient. This can take a long time to generate:

```
# openssl dhparam -out /etc/gitlab/ssl/gitlab.devops.lab.
pem 2048
```

When the edits are complete, run `gitlab-ctl reconfigure` to apply the changes. Finally, open a browser and go to *https://gitlab. devops.lab*. You'll be greeted by the certificate warning screen. Click the **Advanced** button and the *Safe to proceed/Accept the Risk and Continue* link to get to the main GitLab login screen. If you get a 502 error, it means GitLab isn't fully up and running yet. Wait a few moments and refresh the browser.

To log in to the dashboard, use *root* as the username and the password from the file created during installation. Once you've successfully logged in, it's a good idea to change the root password by clicking the icon on the top right of the dashboard, clicking **Edit profile** in the menu, and selecting **Password** to change it.

To make an everyday user account, go to the main **Menu** at the top of the dashboard and select **Admin**. Under Overview, select **Users** and create a new non-root user. Enter something like *jadams* and your lab email address. This could match the username you set up on GitHub, but it can be anything you want, and you'll be able to create multiple accounts in the future, though you can't reuse email addresses.

Alternatively, you can log out as *root* and click the Register link on the main GitLab login page, adding basic information about your user account. See the example in Figure 10-4. If you use this method, you'll need to log back in to the dashboard as *root* to approve the user, a GitLab security feature default.

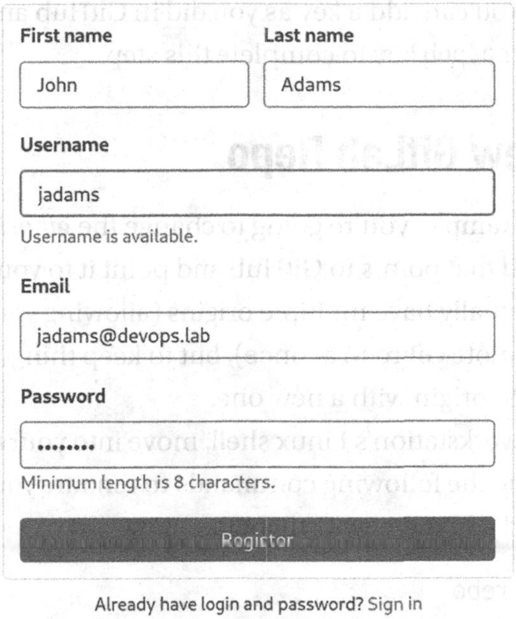

First name

John

Last name

Adams

Username

jadams

Username is available.

Email

jadams@devops.lab

Password

••••••••

Minimum length is 8 characters.

Register

Already have login and password? Sign in

Figure 10-4. Create a non-root user in the GitLab dashboard

Once the user is created, log in and select the type of user you are from the menu. You'll be taken to your main GitLab dashboard, where you can create a new repository—known here as projects—by clicking the **Create a project** button followed by **Create blank project**. As with your GitHub repo, give it the same name (*my-test-repo*), provide an optional description, and set it initially to **Public**. You can leave the "Initialize repository with a README" box checked.

In order to push content to your new GitLab server, you'll need to add an SSH key, just as you did with GitHub. When you create a new repo, you'll likely see an **Add SSH key** banner, which you can click to take you to the SSH settings. You can also start the process by navigating to your profile in the top right, clicking **Edit profile,** and choosing **SSH Keys** in the left-hand menu. You can add a key as you did in GitHub and reuse your `~/.ssh/github_rsa.pub` key to complete this step.

Use Your New GitLab Repo

In the following example, you're going to change the *git origin* you previously created that points to GitHub and point it to your new GitLab server. You can actually have multiple origins (allowing you to push to more than one remote Git repo at once), but to keep things simple, you'll just replace the old origin with a new one.

Back in your workstation's Linux shell, move into your `my-test-repo` directory and issue the following commands to rename your original GitHub origin and add the new GitLab one:

```
$ cd ~/my-test-repo
$ git remote rename origin github_origin
$ git remote add origin \ git@gitlab.devops.lab:username/
my-test-repo.git
```

You can now push your content to your GitLab server. Since the working tree is clean (your previous commits are all accounted for), edit your `example.txt` file to make a change and then commit it:

```
$ echo "some more text" >> example.txt
$ git add .
$ git commit -m "First push to GitLab."
$ git push -u origin master
```

If you look at the activity in your GitLab dashboard under *https://gitlab.devops.lab/username/my-test-repo*, you'll see your content in the *master* branch. If instead you issued the command git push -u origin --all, you would push up all your branches, namely, *master* and *newbranch (if you didn't delete it)*. When your push is successful, you'll see your content in the repo dashboard and get emails to your DevOps lab email account showing you details about the actions you just took.

Other GitLab Capabilities

GitLab offers a lot of functionality beyond just a place to store content in repositories. You can create wikis to accompany your code projects, create artifact registries, integrate with Kubernetes (for container deployments) and Terraform (for automated provisioning), and much more. One of the most valuable features is GitLab's CI/CD capability. You can use it to automate deployments of your code to actual running servers (including Docker hosts).

I won't provide a lot of detail on setting up these features, but the dashboard provides lots of help. With your own GitLab server, you can experiment to your heart's content with some of the most popular DevOps practices used today.

A Bit on CI/CD

Continuous integration/continuous delivery is the modern practice of automatically building, testing, and deploying software code. As developers push code to GitHub, GitLab, or another Git repo, those actions can serve as triggers to sophisticated steps in the software development cycle. In this section, you'll see some of the steps involved in creating what are known as *pipelines*.

In DevOps terms, pipelines are scripted automation steps that, in GitLab, are outlined in .gitlab-ci.yml files that you create and place in each of your code repositories, such as *my-test-repo*. These are straightforward YAML files that define the stages of your pipeline and specific jobs to run. Jobs can be used to test code with a linting tool (like Chef *Cookstyle* on your Chef code), package Docker images, push them to

Docker Hub, and deploy them to Docker hosts, among other things. The options are vast, and using the term "pipelines" is useful because it helps envision movement through the bends and turns of logical flows. If there are failures, you and your fellow developers can see immediately where the problems lie so you can make code edits and kick off the automated process again and again.

Create a GitLab Runner

Before you can execute a pipeline, GitLab needs somewhere to run the jobs you define. This is known as a *runner*. A runner is usually a separate virtual machine that has *gitlab-runner* installed on it along with packages needed to execute the tasks you want. For example, if you're just running simple Bash commands, the runner server needs *Bash* installed. If you're running Ansible playbooks or Chef automation actions, the runner will need those packages installed. Think of a runner as a sort of workstation that you never actually log in to and use. GitLab uses it to perform its CI/CD work for you.

To create a runner, spin up a new Ubuntu VM in Proxmox and give it the hostname *runner.devops.lab*. Configure DNS to point to the host at an address in your DevOps lab subnet, such as 10.128.1.41.

When the system boots, log in from a shell and run the following commands to install the *gitlab-runner* package. GitLab has versions for most Linux flavors, so you're not limited to Ubuntu.

First, add the repository:

Tip   To avoid getting prompted for your password each time you run sudo, you can add a file to /etc/sudoers.d/ to make that automatic:

```
$ sudo echo "jadams ALL=(ALL) NOPASSWD:ALL" > /etc/
sudoers.d/jadams
```

```
$ curl -L "https://packages.gitlab.com/install/repositories/
runner/gitlab-runner/script.deb.sh" | sudo bash
```

Install the package:

```
$ sudo gitlab-runner restart
```

Register Your Runner with Your GitLab Instance

In order for your runner and GitLab to communicate, they need to have a trusted cert shared between them. This can be a complicated process, but the following steps make this work with self-signed certificates—so long as you completed the preceding steps to update the openssl.cnf file during your initial GitLab configuration. These steps copy the necessary files from your *gitlab.devops.lab* server to your *runner.devops.lab* server.

Note   It can be helpful for your runner server to have shared SSH credentials for passwordless access to your GitLab server. Use ssh-keygen to create id_rsa credentials in ~/.ssh/ on your runner server and share them to the other using ssh-copy-id root@gitlab.devops.lab.

On your runner.devops.lab server, execute the following commands:

```
$ sudo mkdir /etc/gitlab-runner/certs
```

```
$ sudo scp -i ~/.ssh/id_rsa  root@gitlab:/etc/gitlab/ssl/
gitlab.devops.lab{.crt,.pem} /etc/gitlab-runner/certs/
```

```
# Register your runner
sudo gitlab-runner register --url https://gitlab.devops.lab/
--registration-token GR1348941s8WR5SgT8Zyr5uy3jXkA
```

The *registration-token* is available from your GitLab dashboard
(along with instructions) under your *my-test-repo* **Settings ➤ CI/CD** with
instructions) under **Runners**. Use that value for the preceding example,
not the sample value shown in **bold**.

You'll be prompted to enter some values. Just press ***Enter*** during the
gitlab-runner register step until you're asked to identify an **executor**,
which is how the runner will execute CI/CD jobs you define. Enter ***shell***
when prompted.

When the configuration is complete, restart the *gitlab-runner* service
on *runner.devops.lab*:

```
$ sudo systemctl restart gitlab-runner.service
```

Create a Pipeline

To create a pipeline in your *my-test-repo*—a series of actions that will be
run automatically each time you commit and push your code to GitLab—
you can use the basic GitLab CI/CD example.

In your GitLab dashboard, navigate to your *my-test-repo*. Click **CI/
CD** in the left-hand menu and then **Editor**. Click the **Create new CI/CD
pipeline** to start creating your `.gitlab-ci.yml` file. This will take you to
the **Edit** tab, where you can edit the YAML file right within the dashboard.
Of course, you could also create a `.gitlab-ci.yml` file in your local
workstation *my-test-repo*, edit it with a tool like VS Code, and push it to
your GitLab repository.

The example GitLab pipeline, shown in Listing 10-3, is a valid pipeline,
though it only uses some simple echo statements to output information
rather than running actual actions.

Listing 10-3. The GitLab example pipeline, complete with stages and jobs

```
stages:
  - build
  - test
  - deploy

build-job:
  stage: build
  script:
    - echo "Compiling the code..."
    - echo "Compile complete."

unit-test-job:
  stage: test
  script:
    - echo "Running unit tests... This will take about 60
      seconds."
    - sleep 60
    - echo "Code coverage is 90%"

lint-test-job:
  stage: test
  script:
    - echo "Linting code... This will take about 10 seconds."
    - sleep 10
    - echo "No lint issues found."

deploy-job:
  stage: deploy
  script:
    - echo "Deploying application..."
    - echo "Application successfully deployed."
```

In the **Edit** view, you can make changes and experiment. Note that each *job* has a name (*build-job*, *unit-test-job*, *lint-test-job*, etc.) and includes one of the three *stages* defined at the top of the file (*build*, *test*, and *deploy*). These are followed by `script:` and commands to execute tasks. These organize the jobs and make them easy to track.

If you click the **Visualize** tab, you'll see your pipeline displayed by *stage* and *job*, as shown in Figure 10-5.

Figure 10-5. *The Visualize view of a basic GitLab CI/CD pipeline*

A built-in linting tool checks the syntax of your `.gitlab-ci.yml` when you click the **Lint** tab. This checks the pipeline file *only*, not the syntax of any code you may add to your repository.

After poking around, return to the **Edit** tab, and scroll down to the bottom of the page to click the **Commit changes** button. In the dashboard, you'll see a turning status indicator while GitLab checks the file before showing you some confirmation information at the top of the screen, as shown in Figure 10-6.

Figure 10-6. *Confirmation of your saved (committed) pipeline*

When you click the **View pipeline** button, the pipeline will start and run for the first time. If all goes well, you'll see the results in the **CI/CD ➤ Pipelines** view in your *my-test-repo* GitLab dashboard.

Steps to make CI/CD work are not for the faint of heart, but getting this working has a long-term payoff: each time you make a change to your *my-test-repo* code content and commit it to your GitLab repository, the pipeline will kick off automatically. Try it by editing your example.txt file and pushing your changes:

```
$ git pull origin master
$ vi example.txt [Add or remove some content]
$ git add .
$ git commit -m "Changed text for pipeline test"
$ git push origin master
```

When the push completes, your pipeline will trigger automatically, and you'll get an email about the latest commit. You'll also see the pipeline doing its thing in your GitLab dashboard under **CI/CD ➤ Pipelines**.

Of course, this example doesn't actually do anything with your commits (like publishing them as Docker images or pushing new content to a web server), but hopefully you get a sense of the power of pipelines. Automated actions can really speed the deployment of software releases, making it a go-to capability for any DevOps team.

Conclusion

In this chapter, you learned some Git basics, set up an account on GitHub, experimented with basic Git commands on your workstation, deployed GitLab in your DevOps lab, and created your first CI/CD pipeline. These capabilities are critical to modern DevOps teams and illustrate how it's possible to successfully collaborate on rapidly evolving software development.

In the next chapter, you'll learn how to again combine capabilities you've become familiar with to automate the deployment of virtual machines using HashiCorp's Terraform. With Terraform, you'll be able to script the deployment of new systems, preconfigure them with Ansible or Chef, and get a feel for how DevOps engineers rapidly and securely create consistent environments in the cloud and in on-prem data centers.

CHAPTER 11

Automate System Deployments with Terraform

As you dive deeper into DevOps workflows, you'll find your Git skills come in handy when you really start automating your system and application deployments with infrastructure as code. Rather than manually deploying systems or making image templates (or cloning snapshots), you can describe what you want in a few code files and have fresh systems up and running in moments. The idea is to define once and deploy repeatedly anywhere.

Everything you've learned in this book so far has set you up for using Terraform, a popular tool for provisioning systems locally, in public clouds like AWS and Azure, and in your Proxmox DevOps lab. In this chapter, you'll use Terraform to create Linux instances purely with code that you can use over and over to get identical results each time.

© John S. Tonello 2022
J. S. Tonello, *Practical Linux DevOps*, https://doi.org/10.1007/978-1-4842-8318-9_11

Install Terraform

Terraform, one of the open-source tools from HashiCorp, is freely available to download and install on most modern operating systems, including popular flavors of Linux, Windows, macOS, FreeBSD, and OpenBSD. You can download binaries (.deb, .rpm, .exe, and the like), or you can add the HashiCorp repository and install it using your system's package manager. This example uses the latter.

On your Linux workstation, execute the commands shown in Listing 11-1 to add the repository key, the HashiCorp repo itself, and then Terraform. This example uses Ubuntu, but instructions are available for other Linux platforms at https://terraform.io/downloads.

Listing 11-1. Install Terraform on an Ubuntu or Debian workstation

```
$ curl -fsSL https://apt.releases.hashicorp.com/gpg | sudo
apt-key add -

$ sudo apt-add-repository "deb [arch=amd64] https://apt.
releases.hashicorp.com $(lsb_release -cs) main"

$ sudo apt update && sudo apt install terraform
```

The result of these actions places the application in /usr/bin/ terraform, which should be in your system PATH without having to take any other actions to use it. Test the installation by running the help command:

```
$ terraform -help
Usage: terraform [global options] <subcommand> [args]
...
```

A Terraform Example with Docker

The HashiCorp website has a lot of great examples on how to get started with Terraform, including how to use it to provision a Docker container that runs an NGINX web server. This is a good place to start to highlight the components of a typical Terraform project file, `main.tf`. These files define *providers* (the target platform you want to use to provision your system, such as Docker, AWS, Proxmox, VMware, and others) and *resource blocks* that describe what you want to install and configure.

Take a look at the example in Listing 11-2 to see these elements in action in a simple `main.tf` file. Create this file in a new ~/`terraform-repo/` nginx directory on your workstation:

```
$ mkdir -p ~/terraform-repo/nginx
```

Note   These examples run Docker and Terraform together on your laptop or workstation, but you could also deploy the container on your separate Docker host, *docker.devops.lab*. To use that remote Docker host, change your main.tf docker `{}` provider ❷ line to the following:

```
provider "docker" {
host     = "ssh://user@docker.devops.lab:22"
}
```

Listing 11-2. A simple Terraform main.tf file to create an NGINX container in Docker

```
terraform {
  required_providers {
    docker = {
```

```
       source  = "kreuzwerker/docker" ❶
       version = "~> 2.13.0"
    }
  }
}

provider "docker" {} ❷

resource "docker_image" "nginx" { ❸
  name          = "nginx:latest"
  keep_locally = false
}

resource "docker_container" "nginx" { ❹
  image = docker_image.nginx.latest
  name  = "tutorial"
  ports {
    internal = 80
    external = 8000
  }
}
```

Terraform main.tf files begin with the terraform {} block, which
describes required *providers*. Providers come in many, many forms,
and HashiCorp maintains a registry where you can find official and
community-contributed options. In the preceding example, the provider
❶ is defined by a specific *source* and *version*. This provider is then called in
the main body of the main.tf file with provider "docker" {} ❷. These
providers can have parameters of their own (such as adding a remote
Docker host), which you'll see later in the Proxmox example.

The main.tf file in the preceding Docker example includes two *resource*
blocks. The first one ❸ uses the native docker_image to download and use

314

the NGINX image. This is similar to running a `docker pull nginx:latest`.
The second resource ❹ creates the Docker container itself, using the `nginx.`
`latest` image defined earlier. The container is given a name ("tutorial"), and
its internal port 80 is mapped to external port 8000.

These are very basic Terraform resources, but hint at the greater
power of the tool and its ability to define infrastructure as code. You
describe what you want to configure, and Terraform does the work for
you. Regardless of the platform you're using—Linux or something else—
Terraform knows how to make it so. Later, you'll use resources to define
Proxmox LXC templates, storage and network parameters, files, and more.

Use Git to Track Your Work

Since you're now using Git, initiate the directory to start tracking
your work:

```
$ cd terraform-repo/
$ git init
$ git remote add origin git@github.com:username/
terraform-repo.git
```

To track this repo remotely, add a `terraform-repo` to your GitHub
(or GitLab) repository as described in Chapter 10. When using GitHub or
another version control system with Terraform, it's important that you not
reveal secrets and other secure keys. That would allow bad actors to access
your infrastructure. To avoid tracking (or pushing) Terraform-specific files,
create a `.gitignore` file in a new `terraform-repo/nginx` directory with the
following content. This will prevent your Terraform state files from being
uploaded to your Git repo:

```
.terraform*
```

Terraform Your First Bit of Infrastructure

To turn your `main.tf` code into a running container, execute the following commands. The *terraform init* initiates the project by downloading any plugins needed, in this case the Docker provider plugin. That's followed with *terraform plan* to confirm your code is valid, and finally *terraform apply* to build it:

```
$ cd ~/terraform-repo/nginx
$ terraform init
$ terraform plan
$ terraform apply
```

When you execute `terraform init`, you'll see output in the terminal showing you it's downloading and initializing the Docker provider. Running terraform plan and `terraform apply` will output the steps Terraform will take to deploy your NGINX container. Type "yes" when prompted.

To confirm the container is created and running, use a simple Docker command:

```
$ docker ps
```

If you're running this on your workstation, open a browser window and navigate to http://localhost:8000 to see the result. If you deployed on your docker.devops.lab host, use `http://docker.devops.lab:8000`.

When you're done, you can destroy the container (and the Terraform deployment) with a simple command:

```
$ terraform destroy
```

You'll be prompted to confirm this step, which is a nice way to avoid accidentally killing off your container. If you run `docker ps -a` afterward, you'll see the container has been removed.

You may be thinking, "Gee, this seems like a lot of work to create an NGINX container." Yes, this is slightly more involved, but in a modern

DevOps workflow, this approach enables you to confirm your container images and tags, certify different OS platforms for your applications, allow teams to share and reuse code (via Git), further automate deployments with CI/CD pipelines, and much more. This visibility allows engineers to do their work freely and collaborate at a high level.

Use Terraform with Proxmox

The simple Docker example gave you a taste of some of the capabilities and syntax of using Terraform, but let's try something a little more sophisticated using the provider for Proxmox.

For this example, you'll use a specific Terraform provider called telmate/proxmox, define a special API URL for your Proxmox host, and reference a specific Proxmox LXC template for Terraform to use. You'll also use a separate variables.tf file to store variables you'll use in your main.tf file. This is a cleaner workflow that separates out different elements of your code, making those elements easier to track and reuse in other unrelated projects.

Though the following example uses an LXC, you can also deploy a new Proxmox VM from an .iso file you've uploaded to your PVE host, clone existing Proxmox machines, and much more.

Configure Proxmox to Work with Terraform

In order for Terraform to communicate properly with Proxmox, you need to do a little setup on your DevOps lab host. These settings create a *role* and *user* with permissions to perform automated tasks. The settings can be applied via the command line on your Proxmox (PVE) host or directly from the Proxmox dashboard. The following examples use the shell commands, and if you have multiple PVE hosts in your Proxmox cluster, you only have to do this once. In the dashboard view, these actions are done at the **Datacenter** level under the *Permissions* menu.

Start by opening a terminal shell to your Proxmox host (such as ssh *root@pve01.devops.lab*) and execute the following three commands. The first creates a *role* with various privileges; the second creates a *user*; and the third attaches the role to the user. The pveum command is the Proxmox VE User Manager):

```
# pveum role add TerraformProv -privs "VM.Allocate VM.Clone
VM.Config.CDROM VM.Config.CPU VM.Config.Cloudinit VM.Config.
Disk VM.Config.HWType VM.Config.Memory VM.Config.Network
VM.Config.Options VM.Monitor VM.Audit VM.PowerMgmt Datastore.
AllocateSpace Datastore.Audit"
```

```
# pveum user add terraform-prov@pve --password <password>
```

```
# pveum aclmod / -user terraform-prov@pve -role TerraformProv
```

The username—shown as terraform-prov in the preceding examples—can be anything you want, but it's helpful to give it a name that makes it easy to identify and remember. This user also has quite a bit of authority to interact with your Proxmox cluster, so it's best to make a unique user for this purpose.

In order for Terraform to know about your new terraform-prov user, you must set some environment variables back on your Linux workstation. You can do this on the fly each time you open a new terminal, but it's easier to add these values to your ~/.bashrc file. That way, they're set each time you open a new terminal to do Terraform work.

Open ~/.bashrc with vi or your favorite text editor, scroll to the bottom of the file, and add the following lines. The *password* value in PM_PASS should match the password you provided when creating the preceding user:

```
...
export PM_USER="terraform-prov@pve"
export PM_PASS="password"
```

To activate these variables, either close and reopen the terminal on your workstation or run `source ~/.bashrc` to load them. You're now ready to move on to creating your Terraform files.

Create a variables.tf File

In your `~/terraform-repo/` directory, create a new project folder called `proxmox_lxc`. With Terraform, each project you make should be in its own folder. Create a `.gitignore` with *.terraform** in it so those files won't be tracked by Git. The following example copies the `.gitignore` from your NGINX project folder to the new project:

```
$ mkdir -p ~/terraform-repo/proxmox_lxc
$ cd ~/terraform-repo/proxmox_lxc
$ cp ~/terraform-repo/nginx/.gitignore .
```

You'll start by creating a `variables.tf` in this new project folder and adding the content shown in Listing 11-3.

Listing 11-3. Contents of a Terraform variables.tf file

```
variable "ssh_key" {  ❶
    default = "ssh-rsa AAAAB3NzaC1yc2EAAAADAQABAAABAQDDG5Rdy
V5UglPZgOOhTK7ODODTDGDwRB8Eh9oisqzPNi7He6Tc8uDOGJhufGnYIt5ksw
MptyVWjvzpO9y2wipOaC1yAkFkhlgvwd73GaHbP5syRzHkBL+TWEcPU8TOU/
YYOx8TpNI+JTy9fNt6sF3ROrbLh3AQR5C25aBY29ydTXP3AI2r9vx88oIZwkt
HHBy4H716aPFDj2YhFu4s22E6vfXjPuva8EOUU/JcgEUXN75Aw96I3WzXef
4mp/iUBVagJ8li4KN1ZdOmfcpeFqkV1SrupBMZrBbDKDoGVegO/dNE/fdHGo
8fbNB9W34f8WpyMqlP1GWcZiwC+7l1OOZH jadams@foo.bar"
}
variable "lxc_proxmox_host_name" {  ❷
    default = "ubuntu-lxc-01"
}
```

```
variable "lxc_template_name" { ❸
    default = "local:vztmpl/ubuntu-20.04-standard_20.04-1_
    amd64.tar.gz"
}

variable "root_password" { ❹
    default = "password"
}

variable "cidr" { ❺
    default = "10.128.1.51/24"
}

variable "ip" { ❻
    default = "10.128.1.51"
}
```

Each variable listed in this file will be referenced by the quoted name
you provide here. For example, ssh_key and ip will be referenced in your
main.tf file with var.ssh_key and var.ip, respectively.

The first variable, ssh_key ❶, is the contents of a public key from your
local workstation system, such as *~/.ssh/id_rsa.pub*. **Do not** use the content in
the preceding example. Use cat to view the source of your own id_rsa.pub file
and paste that content into the default value field between the quotes. Note,
too, that exposing your SSH key this way is not secure. You can use tools like
HashiCorp Vault to share secrets, but I won't go into how to do that here.

The second variable, lxc_proxmox_host_name ❷, is the name you
want to give your LXC instance on Proxmox. This can be any string you
want, but it should be in keeping with the naming convention you're using.

The third variable, lxc_template_name, ❸ defines the LXC template
you want to use to create your instance. This example references the
template *ubuntu-20.04-standard_20.04-1_amd64.tar.gz* that's available
on the **local** storage device on your Proxmox host. If you don't already
have this template on your host, go to your Proxmox dashboard, open

your main PVE instance, and click the **local** storage device and then **CT Templates**. Click the **Templates** button and choose the template you want to use. Note that the variables.tf file includes the full Proxmox path, local:vztmpl/<tempate.tar.gz>.

The root_password variable ❹ contains the default password to use when logging in to the newly created LXC host from your workstation. As you may recall, when creating an LXC by hand, you're asked to enter a root password. This is that value. Of course, this is a very insecure way to store passwords and is *not* recommended for production deployments. Terraform has other tools that allow you to obfuscate these values, including using HashiCorp Vault.

The cidr variable ❺ holds the IP address and netmask for your LXC container, as in 10.128.1.51/24. As you recall, when creating a Proxmox LXC manually, you must add the full CIDR, not just the IP address.

The final variable is ip ❻, which uses the same IP address provided in the cidr variable without the netmask (/24). This will be used by Terraform to log in to the running LXC when it needs to using *root* and root_password.

Save this file before creating a new main.tf in your project directory and adding the content from the example code in Listing 11-4.

Listing 11-4. The Terraform main.tf code for creating a Proxmox LXC

```
terraform {
  required_providers {  ❶
    proxmox = {
      source  = "telmate/proxmox"
      version = "2.9.6"
    }
  }
}
```

```
provider "proxmox" {  ❷
  pm_api_url = "https://pve01.devops.lab:8006/api2/json"
}
resource "proxmox_lxc" "advanced_features" {  ❸
  target_node     = "pve01"
  hostname        = var.lxc_proxmox_host_name
  ostemplate      = var.lxc_template_name
  password        = var.root_password
  unprivileged    = true
  ssh_public_keys = var.ssh_key
  searchdomain    = "devops.lab"
  start           = true

  rootfs {  ❹
    storage = "zfs"
    size    = "2G"
  }

  network {  ❺
    name   = "eth0"
    bridge = "vmbr0"
    ip     = var.cidr
    gw     = "10.128.1.1"
  }

  connection {  ❻
    type = "ssh"
    user = "root"
    host = var.ip
    private_key = "${file("~/.ssh/id_rsa")}"
  }
```

```
provisioner "file" { ❼
  source = "nginx.yml"
  destination = "/root/nginx.yml"
}

provisioner "remote-exec" { ❽
  inline = [
    "apt update",
    "apt install -y ansible",
    "/usr/bin/ansible-playbook /root/nginx.yml"
  ]
}
}
```

This Terraform file will replicate the manual steps you go through to create an LXC instance on Proxmox, but everything is in code. You should recognize the elements as you go.

As in the previous Docker example, this main.tf starts with the terraform {} block ❶, this time referencing the telmate/proxmox source and version. This is used to define the provider block ❷, which includes the URL of your Proxmox host.

The real work begins in the proxmox_lxc resource block ❸, which defines the target node—using the specific name of your node, which may or may not match your DevOps lab domain name. The block also references four of the variables you created in variables.tf. Notice that searchdomain is just a string value, which you could add to your variables, but I show it here to expose the inline syntax. The final element is start = true, which tells Proxmox to boot the LXC after it's created.

The rootfs section ❹ inside the proxmox_lxc resource block defines the Proxmox storage device you want to use (here, set to zfs; yours might be local-lvm). The network section ❺ defines the LXC network configuration. This uses your var.cidr to represent the IP address and *netmask*. The gw entry is the gateway IP address for your DevOps lab.

The connection block ❻ sets up an SSH connection between your workstation and the new LXC. This enables Terraform to log in to the instance and perform any tasks you want, which is why you set start = true earlier. If the instance isn't started, Terraform can't do any of the *provisioning* steps. The connection block uses the var.ip set in your variables.tf and the value of your local system's private *id_rsa* key to complete a secure login.

The connection block is followed by the first provisioner block ❽, which uses the file provisioner to copy a file from your workstation to the LXC. In this case, it's a simple Ansible playbook called nginx.yml, shown in Listing 11-5, that you should create in your current project directory. Instead of this simple example, you could reference any of your previous Ansible playbooks. This is a quick example with Ansible running on the actual node, but you could use other Terraform provisioners to apply a playbook from your local workstation to the remote node.

Listing 11-5. A very simple Ansible playbook to deploy NGINX, saved in nginx.yml

```
---
- hosts: localhost

  tasks:
    - name: Install NGINX
      apt:
        name: nginx
        state: latest
        update_cache: true
```

The final provisioner block ❾ in your project's main.tf file uses the remote-exec resource to execute commands on the running LXC. You can include multiple provision blocks to perform a wide variety of actions that occur after the system is up and running. They use the information in the connection block, and provisioners can be used to copy files, create directories, install agents and applications, and much more.

Create Your LXC with Terraform

With your variables.tf, main.tf, and nginx.yml files created and your environment variables set, you're now ready to *init, plan* and *apply* your code. Execute these commands in your project directory on your workstation:

```
$ cd ~/terraform-repo/proxmox-lxc
$ terraform init
$ terraform plan
$ terraform apply
```

As with the previous Docker example, the *init* command installs the provider plugin (this time, telmate/proxmox) and starts tracking your project. The plan and *apply* commands begin the Terraform actions to provision and configure your node.

If you get an error during the Terraform steps, make sure your environment variables are set:

```
$ echo $PM_USER
terraform-prov@pve

$ echo $PM_PASS
password
```

When the provisioning is complete, check your Proxmox dashboard to confirm the LXC has been created. Since you set up this instance to use *root* and your *id_rsa* keys, you can shell into it from your workstation by running the following:

```
$ ssh root@10.128.1.51
```

This Terraform project also deployed basic NGINX, so you can test that it's installed by opening a browser window and going to http://10.128.1.51. You should see the default NGINX welcome screen.

Make Updates or Destroy It All

As with the Docker example, you can make changes to your main. tf and variables.tf code and rerun *terraform apply* to update your target system. One caveat: Your changes to your static files—like nginx. yml—won't automatically refresh on the Terraformed system. If you make changes to that file, you'll need to destroy the current instance and run *terraform apply* again.

A key advantage of using variables is that you can pass override values at runtime with the -var flag. For example, if you want to create another instance from the same Terraform main.tf file used previously with different IP and hostname values, you can pass variables from the command line:

```
$ terraform apply -var ip="10.128.1.98" -var
cidr="10.128.1.98/24" -var lxc_proxmox_host_name="ubuntu45"
```

To destroy a deployment, which shuts down and completely removes the Terraformed instance, you can simply use the destroy command:

```
$ terraform destroy
```

You'll be prompted to confirm that you really want to delete the instance, and entering "yes" begins the process.

Conclusion

In this chapter, you learned the basics of Terraform to provision and configure Docker containers and an LXC host on Proxmox. Though these examples used your DevOps lab environment, the same principles apply to provisioning instances in cloud environments like AWS and Azure.

This Terraform example brings together many of the DevOps approaches you've learned in this book. Continue to experiment with these tools to further hone your Linux skills and embrace DevOps tools and practices.

Index

A

Access Control List (ACL), 89
Ansible playbooks, 227–233
Application programming
      interfaces (APIs), 140
ARM-based computing
      devices, 221
ARM-based processors, 4

B

Bare-bones systems, 4
Bind
    configure named.conf, 89–93
    DNS configurations, 93
    DNS server, 88
    DNS slave server, 99
    forward zone file, 94, 95
    Internet, 88
    named service, 88
    operating system, 89
    reverse zone file creation, 95–98
bind9, 88
Block devices, 26
Bridged networking
    CentOS, 56–58
    Debian, 58, 59
    Fedora, 56–58

Netplan (Ubuntu), 66–68
openSUSE, 56–58
Ubuntu desktops, 58, 59
Built-in linting tool, 308

C

CentOS, 56–58
Chef InSpec, 258
cidr variable, 321
Cloning, 46, 47, 52, 83
Clustering capabilities, 262
Cluster Shell Commands tool, 264
Cluster-webmin link, 263
Cluster-webmin module, 260
Cluster Webmin Servers, 264
Code—combining
      configuration, 265
Command-line deployments
    KVM virt-install command, 71
    Proxmox qm command, 70
Command-line interface, 120
Community-contributed
      options, 314
Consumer-grade router, 14
Continuous integration and
      continuous delivery (CI/
      CD), 279, 303

Printed in the United States
by Baker & Taylor Publisher Services